S0-AEG-035

ISLAND MARINE SUPPLY
#1 in the Caribbean

Serving the Virgin Islands marine industry for over 18 years.

St. Thomas
Sub Base
776-0753

Yacht Haven Marina
776-0088

Island Marine East
Independent Boat Yard
775-6789

Red Hook
775-6621

St. Croix
St. Croix Marina
773-0289

Tortola
Fort Burt Marina
494-2251

APPROACHES TO THE VIRGIN ISLANDS and PUERTO RICO

CAUTION: NOT FOR NAVIGATION
Tropic Isle Sketch Charts are supplements to the text of the current *Yachtsman's Guide to the Virgin Islands*. They are illustrative and not necessarily to scale.

NAUTICAL MILES
(TROPIC ISLE SKETCH CHART VI-2)
EDITION 101

0   50   100   200

FOR AN UNOBSTRUCTED OCEAN PASSAGE, BEST ROUTE FOR OFF-SHORE SAILING VESSELS IS GAINED BY SAILING EAST 400 TO 600 MILES.

PREVAILING WINDS

ATLANTIC OCEAN

VIRGIN ISLANDS

FAJARDO
SAN JUAN
PUERTO RICO
MONA PASSAGE

BAHAMA

SANTO DOMINGO
DOMINICAN REPUBLIC
HISPANIOLA
PUERTO PLATA
HAITI
CAP HAITIEN
PORT AU PRINCE

TURKS AND CAICOS ISLANDS
GRAND TURK
S. CAICOS

MAYAGUANA
ACKLINS ISLAND

SAN SALVADOR
CAT ISLAND
LONG ISLAND

ELEUTHERA

EXUMA CAYS
RAGGED ISLAND
GREAT INAGUA

WINDWARD PASSAGE

NAVASSA I.

NASSAU

GREAT ABACO

GRAND BAHAMA
BIMINI

OLD BAHAMA PASSAGE

ANDROS

CUBA

GULF STREAM

FLORIDA
FT. LAUDERDALE
MIAMI

JAMAICA PASSAGE

JAMAICA
KINGSTON

NOTE: IN STRONG NORTHERLY CONDITIONS PASSAGE UNDER THE LEE OF HISPANIOLA IS RECOMMENDED.

MAGNETIC NORTH

YACHTSMAN'S
Guide® TO THE VIRGIN ISLANDS

Meredith Helleberg Fields, Editor

Originally compiled in 1968

TROPIC ISLE PUBLISHERS, INC.

For additional books or sketch charts, contact: Tropic Isle Publishers, Mailing and Shipping Office, P.O. Box 610938, North Miami, FL 33261-0938 (telephone 305/893-4277; FAX 305/893-4278). Each additional copy $15.95 postpaid. Florida residents add applicable state sales tax. Add $4.00 for postage and handling on orders outside the United States.

Letters to the Editor: Tropic Isle Publishers, Editor's Office, P.O. Box 15397, Plantation, FL 33318.

For advertising rates and information, contact: Advertising Coordinator, Tropic Isle Publishers, P.O. Box 281, Atlantic Highlands, NJ 07716-0281 (telephone 908/291-7222; FAX 908/291-5084).

Copyright ©1992 by Tropic Isle Publishers, Inc., P.O. Box 281, Atlantic Highlands, NJ 07716-0281

CAUTION

While this book has been prepared based on the information available at the time of publication, the publisher disclaims all liability for any errors or omissions. ***The publisher further disclaims all warranties, expressed or implied, as to the quality, merchantability or fitness of this book for any particular purpose.*** *The navigator is warned not to place undue reliance on the accuracy and completeness of the sketch charts, pilotage directions, soundings, or other information contained herein, or on their continuing validity in light of constantly changing conditions.*

All sketch charts are updated from time to time; for changes consult the current edition of the Yachtsman's Guide to the Virgin Islands. Readers are urged to report any changed conditions, errors, or discrepancies to the editor, so that future editions can reflect such information. Suggestions for the improvement of the next issue must be received by March 1993.

Editor's Message

It's been 25 years now since the appearance of the original edition of this *Guide*, the first thorough cruising guide written for the Virgin Islands. The 86-page 1968 *Guide*, originally put together by John R. Van Ost, describes a quiet, simpler time. Avery's Boathouse and Yacht Haven were among the few marine facilities listed on St. Thomas while, in the BVI, Tortola Yacht Services in Road Town was about it. Foxy's was the only place for food and drink we showed on Jost Van Dyke, and at Cane Garden Bay there was Callwood's. There were two lunch counters if you wanted to eat in Cruz Bay. At North Sound, there was one restaurant/bar on Mosquito Island. Now, of course, there are at least 15 full-service, state-of-the-art marinas throughout, many more specialized marine services, excellent charter companies with a wide variety of boats available, and restaurants, bars, shops, and resorts catering to yachtsmen. In a quarter century, many enterprises have come and gone in boom-town style, and others have remained and prospered. We're proud that our *Guide* has withstood the test of time while other guides have come and gone. We like to think it's because we've been doing something right all these years.

Some of you may assume that we who publish yachting guides for a living spend our time on boats, with a notebook in one hand and a rum punch in the other. Actually, like most of you, we can usually be found in our offices, crouched before our trusty computers, talking on the telephone, and reading our mail. We get so much mail that it's impossible to respond to every letter — but every suggestion and comment we get is valuable to us. So please — write and tell us what you liked or didn't like about your cruise, what you liked or didn't like about our *Guide*, along with anything else that comes to mind. If you notice something that needs updating in next year's edition, let us know and we'll check it out. On the last page of this *Guide* is a reader survey form with room on the reverse side for comments and suggestions. If you fill it out and return it to us, we'll send you a free 11 x 17 sketch chart of your choice for your trouble.

Enjoy your cruise!

Meredith Helleberg Fields

ISBN 0-937379-11-5

CONTENTS

**What You Must Know Before Using Your
Yachtsman's Guide** **9**

Introduction to the Virgin Islands **12**
Planning Your Charter **17**
What the Skipper Should Know **21**
Diving in the Virgin Islands **38**
St. Thomas **43**
St. Thomas Harbor/Charlotte Amalie 49
Hassel Island 58
West Gregerie Channel/Water Island 59
Jersey Bay/Benner Bay 60
St. James Island/Christmas Cove 67
Cowpet Bay/St. Thomas Yacht Club 67
Current Cut 67
Red Hook/Sapphire Bay 68
North Saint Thomas 72
St. John **75**
Approaches to St. John 78
Cruz Bay 78
Caneel Bay 85
Hawksnest Bay 87
Trunk Bay/Cinnamon Bay/Maho Bay 88
Francis Bay 90
The Narrows 92
Leinster Bay 92
Haulover Bay 94
Coral Bay: Round Bay/Hurricane Hole/Coral Harbor 94
Other Anchorages on the South Coast 99
St. Croix **103**
Approaching St. Croix 107
Christiansted 107
Green Cay Marina 115
St. Croix Yacht Club/Teague Bay 116
Buck Island 117
Salt River Bay 118
Frederiksted/South Coast of St. Croix 121
Jost Van Dyke **125**

Great Harbour 127
White Bay 128
Little Harbour 130
Little Jost Van Dyke 131
Adjacent Islands 132
Northwest Tortola **134**
Smuggler's Cove 135
Long Bay 135
Cane Garden Bay 136
Brewers Bay and Eastward 138
South Tortola **140**
West End 141
Great Thatch/Little Thatch Islands 147
Frenchman's Cay 147
Nanny Cay 148
Prospect Reef Resort 151
Road Harbour 153
Wickham's Cay 156
Baugher's Bay 164
Brandywine Bay 164
Eastern Tortola **167**
Maya Cove 167
Fat Hog's Bay 169
The Camanoe Passages 169
Trellis Bay 171
Marina Cay 173
Islands to the South of the Sir Francis Drake Channel **175**
Norman Island 177
Peter Island 179
Salt Island 185
Cooper Island 186
Ginger Island 187
Round Rock to Fallen Jerusalem 187
West Coast of Virgin Gorda **189**
The Baths 191
Virgin Gorda Yacht Harbour 192
Little Dix Bay/Savanna Bay/Tetor Bay 196
Gorda Sound and Anegada **197**
The Dogs 199
Gorda Sound 199
East of Gorda Sound 205
Anegada 207
The Fish and the Fishing **211**
Stargazing for Yachtsmen **220**
Galley Guide **225**
Virgin Islands Index **229**
Advertiser Index **231**
Sketch Chart Index **232**

The Little Harbor Collection Ted Hood's quest for the perfect yacht

ensures that no two Little Harbors are quite the same. Nor should they be. Because the

nicest thing about owning one is that she can be your personal statement of what a yacht

should be. An enviable expression of your experience. A reflection of your taste. This is

precisely why we do things the way we do. Why we offer infinite custom interior lay-

outs, woods, hardware, fabrics, and styling. Why Ted, himself, as a new owner each year

and leader of the design team, enjoys lending his personal lifetime experience to your

own Little Harbor. Let us help you arrive at a luxurious yacht as personal and meaning-

ful to you as the name you give her. Call us at

LITTLE HARBOR CUSTOM YACHTS

the yard to begin the fulfillment of your dreams.

Little Harbor Custom Yachts, founded by Ted Hood in 1959, is actively
building seven designs (42', 44', 46', 51/52', 54', 58', and 63') with larger custom capabilities.
For further information, call (401) 683-5600 or Fax (401) 683-3009.
One Little Harbor Landing, Portsmouth, R.I., U.S.A. 02871

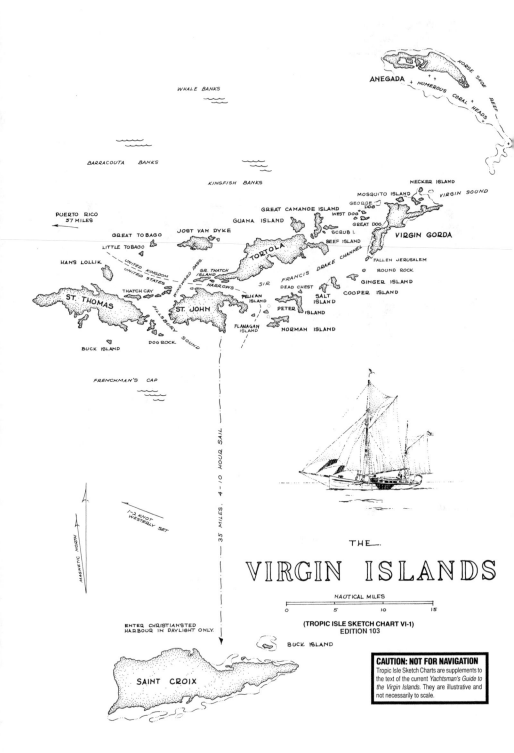

THE

VIRGIN ISLANDS

NAUTICAL MILES

0   5   10   15

(TROPIC ISLE SKETCH CHART VI-1)
EDITION 103

CAUTION: NOT FOR NAVIGATION
Tropic Isle Sketch Charts are supplements to the text of the current *Yachtsman's Guide to the Virgin Islands*. They are illustrative and not necessarily to scale.

WHAT YOU MUST KNOW BEFORE USING YOUR YACHTSMAN'S GUIDE

The *Yachtsman's Guide to the Virgin Islands* will be your invaluable cruising companion. Since we began publishing this *Guide* in 1968, it has accompanied thousands of yachtsmen as they cruised these idyllic islands. From the outset, we've been greeted year after year with enthusiastic response as the "indispensable" cruising guide to this area.

As happy as all this makes us, nobody's perfect, and we feel it's important to emphasize a few things:

• **The *Guide* alone is insufficient for navigation.** Always use it in conjunction with navigational aids such as government charts and publications. Even with the annual updating that adds to or corrects much of the text, the *Guide* can never be considered "complete." There will always be important information that we do not have and therefore cannot include.

• **The Tropic Isle charts in this book are in fact sketch charts, which means they are for illustrative purpose only.** Position on the sketch charts should be considered approximate, including land features, navigational aids and markers, depths, and landmarks. The limited scale of our sketch charts precludes the plotting of every individual rock, coral head, or obstacle. Therefore, shown routes must be used with caution. Pilotage by eye is always essential in the Virgin Islands. Sketch charts should always be used with reference to the corresponding text for clarification.

• **The *Guide* is written for the responsible skipper and**

crew. Your own experience, training, competence, and caution are essential. We provide information that will make your cruise pleasant, but we cannot give you all the information you need to make it safe.

• **Remember that in shallow or reef-strewn waters, you must proceed slowly and keep a good lookout (at the bow in a sailboat for best visibility).** The sun must be high and behind you. Above all, never attempt such tricky passages when visibility is in any way diminished.

• **Where sandbanks are a factor, it must be remembered that they shift constantly and that channels meander.** Be aware that although a sketch chart may indicate a channel existed, shifting sands may block the channel completely or change the depths at any time.

• **It must be remembered that cuts or passages exposed to the open ocean can be impassable in adverse wind or heavy swells.** A dangerous swell can exist without any wind.

• **Ground swells are a vital consideration in anchoring,** especially between November and April, when they are most prevalent. The swells originate in heavy weather thousands of miles away, and although they usually create no problem for boats under way, they can break with some violence on the coasts of islands, making otherwise calm anchorages untenable and dangerous. It's important to remember that they can build any time of night or day.

• **Be aware that all man-made markers, whether government or privately maintained, cannot be absolutely reliable.** We do our best to ascertain the position of all markers, but constantly changing and unpredictable conditions make it impossible to guarantee the continuing validity of our information.

• **The prominence of landmarks in general cannot be guaranteed.** Even over short periods of time, they can disappear, change color, and be made comparatively less conspicuous.

• **To avoid confusion and unnecessary elaboration, we do not attempt to describe every new feature that might be called a landmark.** Although we like to know about these, we feel that areas that are already recognizable will not benefit from additional and excessive detail.

• **At the risk of stating the obvious, the courses shown in this *Guide* can only approximate where boats of suitable draft have made successful passage.** Since our sketch charts are not necessarily to scale and are of too small scale to show all dangers, and since the difference between danger and safety in shallow or reefy water may be a matter of a few inches, the prudent mariner must take our courses for what they are, and realize that changed condition or a slight offset from what was for others a safe passage may be critical.

• **In general, we make no attempt at completeness in showing dangers that are significantly removed from the course lines in our text or on our sketch charts.**

• **We are a small company providing a resource network for the skipper's use and participation. We catch some of our mistakes but not all.** We do rely heavily on volunteer information, which cannot always be verified in time for inclusion in any upcoming edition. We encourage our readers to report any changes to us as soon as they become aware of them.

• **Inasmuch as new information appears in each annually updated *Guide*, all previously published editions must be considered obsolete.**

• **The prudent mariner will not rely solely on any single aid to navigation.** Always cross-check information with frequently updated sources such as your charter company's briefings, notices to mariners and other government publications, local knowledge and, of course, what your own eyes tell you.

Used judiciously with the navigational resources available to you, your *Yachtsman's Guide* will enrich your cruising experience and enjoyment immeasurably.

John, I really need to shop! All we have left is peanut butter.

Gert! Did you forget to pack my Yachtsman's Guide?

Dad, you promised we could go scuba diving today!

I wanna go home.

Plan ahead...

If that fails be sure you have the latest Yachtsman's Guide on board. The source of indispensable information for generations of yachtsmen cruising the Bahamas.
• Updated Annually
• What The Skipper Should Know
• Island Profiles
• What To Do
• Sketch Charts
• Tide Tables And More!

Call (305) 893-4277
or write to: Tropic Isle Publishers
P.O. Box 610938
North Miami, FL
33261-0938

YACHTSMAN'S
Guide
to the **Bahamas**

INTRODUCTION TO THE VIRGIN ISLANDS

The Virgin Islands are made up of six large islands and many smaller islands and cays, with American territory to the west and British crown colony to the east. St. Thomas, St. John, and St. Croix are the three largest U.S. Virgin Islands (USVI), and Tortola, Virgin Gorda, and Anegada are the three largest British Virgin Islands (BVI). Anegada is something of a loner among the Virgins, an atoll made of coral limestone and sandstone all by itself up in the northeast. The rest of the major islands are volcanic in origin and rise abrupt and roundly majestic from the sea, with the highest peak over 1,700 feet. Almost 500 years ago they apparently reminded Columbus of dozens of nubile young women stretched out between him and the horizon. The accepted story seems to be that Columbus named these islands after the 11,000 legendary companions of St. Ursula, a Christian king's daughter whose hand in marriage was demanded by a pagan prince. Before the dreaded marriage date, the devout Ursula trained her young virgins to resist barbarian advances and took them all to Rome to pledge themselves to God. The enraged prince and his army, accustomed to having their way with women, ambushed the defiant ladies as they returned from Rome and murdered every one. Thus was Columbus inspired, or so they say.

The physical beauty of the islands is stunning, but behind that first sensory impact of brilliant color and soft, scented air is a past steeped in adventure, daring, and violence. Many of the early settlers from Europe were religious pioneers or renegades from the law, seeking the freedom to live according to their morals or the lack thereof. That elusive promise of escape from routine, rules, and conventional expectations still is what lures people to the islands. Here eccentricity is the norm and the unexpected can be expected. Depending on what kind of expectations you bring, this will add to your delight or disorient and confuse you. "Island time" has little use for clocks. Electricity fails now and again, so water, a scarce commodity, often becomes unavailable for short periods of time. After the first time you've been caught in the shower in full lather, you'll learn to be prepared. That tropical punch you order will probably be a knockout because liquor here is often cheaper than mixer. At some of the best places to eat, you'll sit on old seats from dismantled cars, and the food will be cooked on a backyard grill. The customs inspector who glares at you when it's your turn to show your papers will suddenly go mellow and chuckle when you smile and wish her a good day. In other words, leave your ordinary assumptions at home and *relax*. It's the surprising detours from routine that will become your fondest memories.

It is important, though, to appreciate the inevitable problems that arise in Caribbean islands with a marked economic and racial gap between the rich and the poor. Remember that you're a visitor who represents an unattainable degree of wealth to many of the people who call these islands home. By far, most islanders are warm, honorable, and dignified, more than willing to help you if you show respect in turn. But in the more populated and tourist-infested areas especially you must take appropriate safety precautions.

History. Although there is evidence of man as early as 3000 B.C. in the islands, the first known Indians to migrate here were the Ciboneys, around 400 B.C., followed by the Arawaks around 200 A.D. Several hundred years later, the warrior Caribs arrived and conquered the peaceful Arawaks, eating the male prisoners and taking the females as slaves.

On November 13, 1493, Columbus sighted the Virgin Islands for the first time on his second voyage to the New World. He named the first island he saw Santa Cruz (now St. Croix). When he attempted to land at Salt River for fresh water, his men found Caribs waiting with bows and

arrows. After a fast getaway, he sailed north to explore Virgin Gorda, Tortola, Anegada, St. Thomas, and St. John, this time from a safe vantage point on board.

By the mid-1600s the Indians were all but extinct, killed or taken by Spanish adventurers to Hispaniola to labor in the mines. When the Spanish turned their attention to gold mining on islands further west, the Virgins were left unattended and subject to raids of privateers hired by various European nations interested in the Spanish-monopolized Caribbean trade routes. Countless skirmishes resulted in frequent changes in

Mountains of Tortola (above Nanny Cay). (Tropic Isle photo)

occupation by the Dutch, French, British, and Danes.

In the 1600s the Danish king chartered the Danish West India Company to set up a colony on St. Thomas, followed by St. John and in 1733 by St. Croix. By the late 1600s, England had taken what are now the British Virgin Islands over Dutch and French claims, and by the late 1700s had set up a governing council and justice system. Many Quakers left a life of persecution in England to settle on Tortola and Virgin Gorda.

It wasn't easy convincing Europeans to come to the new colonies. Life in paradise was brutal. Settlers in the 1600s and 1700s were discouraged if not devastated by hurricanes, droughts, starvation, fires, rampant piracy, epidemics of cholera and malaria, and inter-island plundering. Soon convicts from European jails, prostitutes, and others with an interest in lawlessness predominated in the population. People died young, and often of unnatural causes.

Attempts to cultivate the soil were most successful on St. Croix's comparatively level and fertile land, and St. Thomas quickly became the hub of the Caribbean trade routes. By the mid-1700s, by virtue of their location, the islands flourished at the center of sea-trade routes between Europe, Africa, and the Americas. Hundreds of sugar plantations thrived, and slaves outnumbered free men ten to one. Many slaves were mistreated and often severely tortured. Prosperity was at a peak, but it was short-lived.

Within 100 years, the European sugar beet had driven Caribbean sugar cane off the market. The British, followed by the Danes (in the heat of serious slave revolt) freed the slaves in the mid-1800s. In no time the economy of the islands collapsed, and the mills and greathouses fell into ruin. Plantation owners fled the islands as their dreams disappeared, and thousands of freed slaves were left with no money or property. Between 1850 and 1930 the population dwindled by half, leaving mostly the descendants of slaves.

In 1917, the United States bought the Danish islands for $25 million, with national security in mind. One week later the United States joined the First World War. Since then, American interests have invested in the development of the USVI's tourist trade, especially on St. Thomas.

Until the mid-20th century, the British islands were governed as part of the Leeward Island Group. In 1967 they established a self-governing ministerial system but they choose to remain British territory, with the Queen as head of state represented by a governor. The British islands remain economically poor in comparison to the USVI, but with their lack of development they retain a vast, uncultivated beauty appealing especially to modern sailors and others of adventurous ilk.

Recommended reading. Local bookstores in the islands carry titles that are hard to locate stateside, as well as interesting publications by local poets, writers, artists, and amateur historians.

Adventure Guide to the Caribbean, by Harry Pariser (Hunter Publishing Inc.). Off-the-beaten-track as well as offbeat guide to the islands — especially good for advice on budget lodgings and places to eat.

Cane Garden Bay, by Mary White (BVI Parks and Protected Areas Project). Locally written, charming guide to one of Tortola's prettiest shores.

Caribbean Boating (St. Thomas, USVI). Newspaper with the scoop on the local marine community. Available at most marinas.

Don't Stop the Carnival, by Herman Wouk (Doubleday). Classic fictional tale of a New Yorker who moves to his island paradise to run his own hotel. Said to be based on one of the Virgin Islands.

Guide to Coral and Fishes of Florida, the Bahamas, and the Caribbean, by Idaz and Jerry Greenberg (Seahawk Press). Illustrates over 200 species of coral and fish in full color. Available waterproof.

A History of the Virgin Islands of the United States, by Isaac Dookhan (Caribbean Universities Press/Bowker). First comprehensive history of the USVI, by an associate professor of history at the College of the Virgin Islands.

Night of the Silent Drums: A Narrative of Slave Rebellion in the Virgin Islands, by John L. Anderson (Charles Scribner's Sons). Vivid, historically detailed account of the 1733 rebellion on St. John.

Sir Francis Drake Channel. (Tropic Isle photo)

On the Trail of the Arawaks, by Fred Olsen (University of Oklahoma Press). Olsen tackles the puzzling question of the origin of the Arawaks.

The Settler's Handbook, edited by Gloria Bourne (Megnin Publishing, St. Croix, USVI).

A Short History of the West Indies, by J.H. Parry and Philip Sherlock (Macmillan). Authoritative and illuminating introduction to West Indian history.

St. John Guide Book, by Linda Smith-Palmer. Hand-lettered and drawn by one of the islands' leading artist/cartoonists, this guide to St. John is loaded with information, facts, rumors, and fun.

Tales of the Caribbean, by Fritz Seyfarth (John de Graff). An invitation to explore the modern as well as the unknown and unspoiled.

Tales of Tortola and the British Virgin Islands, by Florence Lewisohn. Entertaining accounts of the facts and legends that color Tortola's past.

Treasure Islands: A Guide to the British Virgin Islands, by Larry and Reba Shepard (Macmillan Caribbean). Includes good information on local flora and fauna and underwater life.

Virgin Islands, by George Eggelston (Krieger). Cruising the Virgins in the 1950s.

Virgin Island Sketches, by Roger Burnett (Caribbean Printing Co., Road Town). Historical points of interest and backyard scenes.

The Virgins: Magic Islands, by Jeanne Perkins Harman (Appleton-Century Crofts, Inc.) Full of interesting history, amusing anecdotes, and local lore.

PLANNING YOUR CHARTER

Bareboat or crewed? There are two types of chartering: bareboat and crewed-boat. A bareboat charter is rental of a fully equipped boat with no crew or captain. You are the skipper and the members of your group are your crew. You usually must pay a security deposit, averaging around $500, to the charter company or owner, which will be returned to you after your cruise, less any expenses for damages incurred.

Before you charter a bareboat, most companies need to know the extent of your cruising experience, and they will ask that you complete a resume detailing your boating background, your anchoring expertise, what kinds of boats you've owned, whether you've chartered before, and your knowledge of coastal navigation. They will also probably ask for personal references. For your own sake, don't try to bluff, and trust the

judgment of the charter firm. They may suggest that a member of their staff accompany you for a few days to familiarize you with the operation of their boat. Many charterers who've learned to sail at one of the sailing schools arrange for their instructor to come along. If you've never sailed these waters before, you may want to take along someone who knows the areas where local knowledge is advised.

The most popular boats are sailboats ranging from 30 feet to 50 feet in length. Prices vary from about $750 a week to over $4,000, depending on the company, the size and type of boat, and the season. Power boats accommodate more people, have more space overall, and roomier accommodations, so their prorated prices work out quite reasonably. The rates are lowest in August, September, and October, sometimes as little as half the winter rates.

A crewed charter is rental of a boat with a professional crew, including a captain and cook, as part of the package. On a crewed boat, you can determine your own destination and itinerary, within the limits of safety. Many charter captains will allow you to take the helm at times. On most boats the fee is all-inclusive, covering food, drink, and fuel. However, remember that tipping is generally expected. Crewed charters include sloops, ketches, yawls, and schooners, catamarans, motor sailors, and power boats. Some are very old, some are very new. Some are formal and some are very informal indeed. A yacht broker can help you find the right boat for your particular needs. Rates vary widely, so shop around.

Another way to charter that can make everyone happy, including those who would rather not be trapped on a boat all the time, is to make a base at one of the small resorts in the area, and daysail or overnight out of there. Then each person can choose whether to sail or stay ashore.

When to charter. Of course, everyone wants to charter in the winter, when the weather is unbearable up north. Be aware, though, that winter winds can blow hard from time to time (see section in this *Guide* on Weather, under What the Skipper Should Know).

There are advantages to sailing in the spring and summer. The trade winds settle down to a steady 15-18 knots, often blowing a little south of east (as opposed to little north of east in the winter months). The weather pattern is more dependable than in the winter months, and the temperature is generally lower in July and August than it is up north.

Booking your charter. The three busiest times, in order of popularity, are the Christmas/New Year weeks, the last two weeks of February following Washington's Birthday, and Easter vacation. You are advised to book your boat and make your airline arrangements as early as a year in advance for these periods. Some chartering firms require a minimum booking of 10 days for a charter over the Christmas and New Year holidays.

The weeks just after the rates change in the spring are usually booked well in advance, and the weeks in November around Thanksgiving are becoming more popular. In the summer, when the rates are lower, many companies will cut their rates even more for a charter of three weeks or longer. If you charter in September or October, you'll have the waters almost all to yourself.

When you book, you will probably be asked for a deposit of 50% of the charter fee (exclusive of provisions). Policies vary on refund of the deposit in case of cancellation, so be sure to inquire.

Provisions. Most charters offer full provisioning with the option of eating ashore on selected nights. You can choose instead to plan and purchase your own provisions, or there are provisioning shops that will prepare your supplies in advance and deliver them to your boat.

If your supplies need major replenishing, plan your stop in Charlotte Amalie, Red Hook, Christiansted, Cruz Bay, Road Town, or Virgin Gorda Yacht Harbour. There are small stores in other locations, but you may not find everything you need. Water and ice are available at all the major harbors named above and at most large marinas.

BVI charter tax. There are more bunks aboard the charter fleet operating in the BVI than beds in the hotels there, so it stands to reason that the BVI government has instituted a daily tax on visitors chartering both foreign and BVI-registered yachts cruising their waters. The tax applies to any vessel being used for hire or in exchange for any service or reward for a particular period of time. The rate for charter boats based outside the BVI is $4.00 per person per day, year-round. For BVI-registered boats, the rate is $2.00 per person per day from December 1 through April 30, and 75¢ per person per day from May 1 through November 30. The tax must be paid in cash or travelers checks. There is a 10¢ stamp duty charged throughout the BVI on travelers checks.

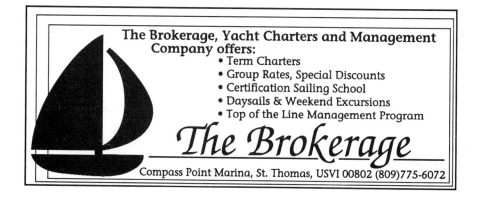

Note: These costs are subject to change when new legislation will be enacted in late 1992; ask your charter company for current information at the time of your cruise.

What to bring. No matter how little you bring, you'll probably bring too much. Duffel bags are easy to handle and store on a boat, where storage space is at a premium. Few marinas will store luggage for you. There are exceptions, but be sure to check ahead of time.

The temperate breeze might fool you into underestimating the fierce tropical sun. Bring lots of sunscreen, a brimmed hat, and something to cover you entirely when you need extra protection, like an old pair of summer pajamas, a scrub suit, or a white long-sleeved shirt. You'll need more than one pair of sunglasses, preferably with polarized lenses to help you spot reefs.

Clothing should be light-weight and light-colored. You'll need a couple pairs of shorts, T-shirts, sweat socks, two pairs of non-skid shoes (deck shoes are preferable) and a cotton sweater for winter evenings. Bring extra swimsuits and some old sneakers for slogging around in shallow water. Gloves will protect your hands when anchoring, diving, or snorkeling. You'll probably want to do some hiking and exploring, so bring a pair of long pants to protect your legs from underbrush and bugs. Some charters supply snorkeling gear, but you might want to bring your own. Men probably won't need a jacket and tie, although these are required for dinner at a very few of the more elite resorts. Women should bring a skirt or simple dress.

Check with your charter company about whether they supply fishing gear, towels, and foul-weather gear. Also inquire about what electrical appliances you can use on board. If your boat will have a cassette player, you might want to bring some tapes.

Guns are not allowed in any of the islands, American or British, without a permit. For further information in the USVI, write the Commissioner of Public Safety. In the BVI, write the Government of the British Virgin Islands, Road Town, Tortola, BVI.

Don't assume that camera equipment or film will be cheaper in the Virgin Islands. Film especially is likely to be more expensive, so bring plenty along.

Check with your doctor about prescriptions or medication you might require. Don't depend on being able to find what you need once you're here.

And don't forget to pack some bug repellent. Be aware that some of the commercial brands contain an ingredient that can damage synthetic fabric and plastic camera parts.

WHAT THE SKIPPER SHOULD KNOW

*Anchoring, Buoyage, Charts, Collection of Coral and Shells,
Communications, Cruising Etiquette, Currency, Customs and
Immigration, Depths, Drugs, Holidays, Navigation, Reefs, Security,
Sunset, Tides, Water Safety, Weather,
Where to Find It: Fuel, Ice, Water, and Provisions*

Good navigation requires judicious use of all resources available. Use government charts, be aware of weather and tide conditions, and use your eyes in reading reefs and assessing any chart in comparison to what's in plain sight. Conditions at sea and on land are constantly changing, and landmarks and other features are likely to change unpredictably. Even markers, especially those that are privately main-

**MORE POWER TO YOU
and your BOAT!!!**

Established 1950

Marine Industries Association

South Florida's Most Complete
MARINE ELECTRIC SPECIALISTS

EQUIPMENT			**SERVICES**
Wire & Cable	Switches	Light Fixtures	Electrical & Corrosion
(Spooled or Cut)	Converters/Inverters	Custom Panels &	Surveys
Battery Chargers	Enclosures	Engraving	Repairs
Shorelines & Adapters	Panel Meters	Transformers	Modifications
Circuit Breakers	Wiring Devices	Capac Systems	New Installations

Ward's Marine Electric, Inc.

**630 SW Flagler Ave., Ft. Lauderdale, FL 33301
1-800-545-9273 • (305) 523-2815 • FAX 305-523-1967**

Missing Navigational Marks

At the time of our survey in November 1991, the light just off the north end of Steven Cay, just west of Cruz Bay, was missing.

In addition to government marks, there are many marks in the Virgins Islands that are privately maintained. Remember, there is always the possibility that any navigational mark can be missing or off station at any time. Also, authorities or private interests may add new marks, which won't show up in the Guide until the next edition.

tained, can disappear and not be replaced for months, if ever.

Even so, there are few places in the world where navigation is as simple as it is in the Virgin Islands. Except for Anegada, all the islands are high and easily spotted. (While eyeball navigation here is easy, use of a hand bearing compass will make things easier for people in these waters for the first time. Before you get to know the area, perspective often makes it hard to tell if a land mass is one island or a group of islands. The hand bearing compass will help you sort things out.) The clarity of the water is another advantage.

The magnetic variation is about 12° west, give or take a few minutes, depending on your location in the group.

Anchoring. If you are accustomed to the Bahamas or the low-lying Atlantic shore of the U.S., where the prevailing winds get little interference from the terrain, the mountains of the Virgin Islands will play tricks on you. Anchoring in the lee of a mountain for protection from the prevailing trades will surprise the newcomer when the boat seems to swing upwind of the anchor and fetch up stern to shore with bow pointed west. Locally this phenomenon is called *backwinding*. The prevailing wind is deflected upward by the mountain and then descends down the lee slope in a rolling motion with reverse currents rushing back in to fill the void. The stronger the wind, the more brisk the backwinding. Under strong conditions, use two anchors, especially if your stern lies close in to the shore. Backwinding is common at Great Harbour, Jost Van Dyke; The Bight, Norman Island; and Manchioneel Bay on Cooper Island.

Ground swells are a vital consideration in anchoring, especially between November and April, when they are most prevalent. The swells originate in heavy weather thousands of miles away, and although they usually create no problem for boats under way, they can break with some violence on the coasts of islands, making otherwise calm anchorages untenable and dangerous. It's important to remember that they can build any time of night or day.

Buoyage. There are a number of fairly recent alterations in the

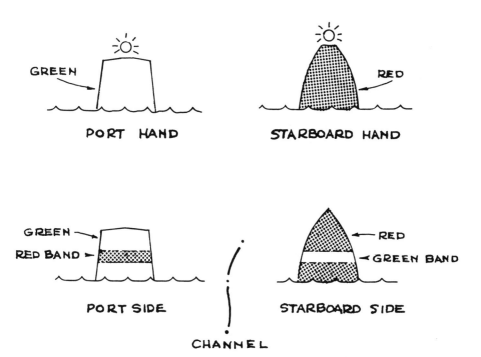

RED RIGHT RETURNING

GREEN — PORT HAND

RED — STARBOARD HAND

GREEN, RED BAND — PORT SIDE

RED, GREEN BAND — STARBOARD SIDE

CHANNEL

buoyage systems of both the BVI and the USVI that you must be prepared to encounter. In 1984, the BVI changed over from the International System of buoyage to the "red, right, returning" system used in the United States. In 1982, the United States signed an agreement to convert its buoyage system to the IALA (International Association of Lighthouse Authorities) system. This changeover has now been completed. The change to the IALA system required that: (1) all black buoys be painted green; (2) all red-and-black horizontally banded buoys be converted to red and green; (3) all black-and-white vertically striped buoys be red and white. This applies to Coast Guard maintained buoys and not necessarily to privately maintained markers. Since this conversion has been completed, any buoys still identified as black in this book's sketch charts should have been painted green by this time.

To stay current on these and other changes, subscribe to the Local Notices to Mariners for this area, available from the Coast Guard District Office, 909 SE 1st Ave., Room 400, Miami, FL 33130-3050.

Charts. In many of the large, busy harbors the water is not clear

Government Charts Useful for Cruising the VIs
National Ocean Survey (N.O.S.) Charts
25641: U.S. and British Virgin Islands eastward to Gorda Sound.
25649: St. Thomas Harbor and surrounding area.
25645: Christiansted Harbor, St. Croix.
25644: Frederiksted, St. Croix.
25647: Eastern end of St. Thomas, Pillsbury Sound, and western end of St. John.
Defense Mapping Hydrographic Office (U.S.)
25609: Tortola to Anegada.
25610: Approaches to Gorda Sound.
25611: Road Harbour and approaches.
Admiralty Hydrographic Office (British)
2019: Road Harbour and Sir Francis Drake Channel.
2452: St. Thomas, St. John, western Tortola. Excellent detail.
2008: Northeast Virgin Gorda to Anegada. Shows area not on N.O.S. 25641.
485: St. Croix.
2016: Gorda Sound and Sir Francis Drake Channel.

enough to depend on eyeball navigation. Here you must rely on close scrutiny of your government charts, with the help of directions found in this *Guide*, and the use of your sounding lead. N.O.S. Chart 25641 is the only government chart that covers the U.S. and British Virgin Islands, except Anegada. Charts that you will find useful are listed on this page.

As an additional service to yachtsmen, Tropic Isle Publishers provides 11 x 17-inch enlargements of the sketch charts in this *Guide* (see order form in back of book).

Collection of coral and shells. There is a delicate ecological balance in the sea that is disturbed by thoughtless destruction. Helmet conch, which feed on sea urchins, have almost disappeared from some areas in the island because their beautiful shells are coveted by collectors. An explosion in the population of sea urchins has resulted, endangering snorkelers and swimmers.

Shell and coral collectors are welcome to pick up specimens from the beaches, but never take live coral or fans from the reefs or shallows. It isn't worth it, and many people have misgivings when they discover that coral smells dreadful for a long time as it dries. Enjoy these creatures alive in their natural states, where they're most beautiful.

Communications. For communications within the island area, a VHF set will suffice, although yachts cruising to the Virgin Islands from the Florida coast should have a single side band set as well. If you are shoreside in the USVI and want to contact a boat, call Virgin Islands Radio

Great Harbour, Jost Van Dyke. (Fields photo)

at 776-8282; in the BVI call Tortola Radio at 494-3425. The same procedure can be used from the States by those who may need to get in touch with you. Before you leave, give them these telephone numbers and the name of the boat you'll be on, and they can leave messages for you. If a message is left for you, your boat's name will be read during traffic hours (every hour on the hour for Virgin Islands Radio and at 7 a.m., 11 a.m., 3 p.m., and 6 p.m. for Tortola Radio.) From your boat, you can make local and international telephone calls or have messages held via Virgin Islands Radio or Tortola Radio. Virgin Islands Radio, or WAH (Whiskey Alpha Hotel), is tied to Vitelco, the USVI telephone company, and also acts as agent for Western Union International. If you're planning to make an international call from your boat, you should make arrangements beforehand through your marina with Virgin Islands Radio or Tortola Radio. All this can be charged collect or to your telephone credit card, MasterCard or Visa.

It's easy to dial U.S. numbers from the BVI by using "USA Direct," an AT&T service: Dial 1-800-872-2881 and you'll be directly connected with a stateside operator.

Recommended VHF frequencies are:

Channel 16: Distress, safety, and calling. Once contact is made, switch to another channel to keep Channel 16 open.

Channel 6: Intership safety. Do not use for other exchanges.

Channel 22A: Coast Guard.

Calling for Restaurant Reservations

Most restaurants in the Virgin Islands require reservations for dinner and sometimes for lunch. Most stand by on Channel 16, and some in the BVI also monitor Channel 68. As an alternative, you can call Tortola Radio or Virgin Island Radio and patch into the telephone system. Use of Channel 12 to make reservations is discouraged.

It's a good idea to call for dinner reservations early, especially in the winter season. The most popular spots fill up quickly, and smaller establishments often need to know your order ahead of time so the cook can make sure the necessary ingredients are on hand.

Also, if you are cruising off-season (from May through October, approximately), be aware that a number of bars, restaurants, and accommodations close down during these months. If in doubt, call ahead to verify.

Channel 12: Port operations, harbors.
Channel 68: Intership communications, ship to coast (marinas).
Channel 27: Tortola Radio.
Channel 28: Virgin Islands Radio.
Channel 70: Intership, private yachts.

Cellular telephone service, now available in the Virgins Islands, allows you the option of a telephone at hand on board for local and long distance access. Check with your charter company about installing one on your boat. If you must keep tabs on the office, the baby sitter, or the comings and goings of your teenagers while you're away, a cellular telephone might give you peace of mind.

Cruising etiquette. Bear in mind that many beaches in the islands are private property. Respect "no trespassing" signs, and don't venture inshore from the beach on privately owned property. Never leave garbage on the beach. Carry it back to your boat if there no facilities for disposal ashore.

Don't ever throw garbage into the water. Ask any charter company or marine facility where government-maintained refuse collection centers are located. Many charter companies provide plastic bags for storage of refuse until reaching a center. Yachting interests have joined together to report any instances of dumping refuse into the water or littering the beaches. Visiting yachtsmen are asked to cooperate in reporting violations and collecting any bottles or cans to take to the nearest disposal center.

HARKEN

Available Throughout the Virgin Islands

Exclusive Distributors :

BRITISH VIRGIN ISLANDS – RICHARDSON'S RIGGING
Box 97, Tortola, British Virgin Islands
Telephone: (809) 494-2739 • Fax: (809) 494-5436

US VIRGIN ISLANDS – ISLAND RIGGING AND HYDRAULIC, INC.
#6 Long Bay Road, St. Thomas, US Virgin Islands
Telephone: (809) 774-6833 • Fax: (809) 774-5024
Independent Boat Yard
Telephone: (809) 779-2960

When at anchor, be considerate of neighboring boats and keep noise to a minimum in the evening and early morning.

Currency. United States currency is used in both the U.S. and British Virgin Islands. Credit cards are honored in most large hotels, shops, and restaurants in major harbors. However, don't depend on using your credit cards everywhere, especially in the smaller harbors. Acceptance of credit cards at fuel docks is generally left up to the dealer, so you might want to check with the company's overseas department if you plan extensive use of this service. Travelers checks are generally accepted, but there is a 10¢ stamp tax on travelers checks in the BVI. Don't expect to write a personal check anywhere.

Customs and immigration. All boats must clear when entering and leaving American and British territory, with one exception: U.S. flagships need not clear when leaving U.S. waters provided there are no aliens aboard and the vessel is not carrying passengers for hire. These procedures are simple but necessary. The heavy penalties for not carrying them out can include confiscation of your vessel. Note the hours customs is open and plan your cruise accordingly. There is an overtime charge for customs clearance outside of regular hours, including Sundays and public holidays.

When clearing, be prepared to present your ship's papers and passports, voter's registrations, or birth certificates for all members of your crew. Those who are clearing with voter's registration cards may be asked to present picture IDs as well. Drivers' licenses alone are *not* sufficient identification. All members of the crew must be present to clear immigration (except in the BVI). You should also present papers from your last port cleared.

Customs/Immigration Locations

St. Thomas: Customs and immigration formalities may be completed at the customs and immigration offices located by the ferry dock toward the west end of the waterfront. Provided there are no foreign nationals aboard, U.S. pleasure craft and foreign-registered craft with valid cruising permits may phone 774-5539 daily from 8 a.m. to 5 p.m. (Sunday hours vary somewhat) and request telephone entry through customs and immigration. This is sometimes granted, sometimes not, for various reasons as these authorities see fit. Foreign-registered vessels which do not carry valid cruising permits must appear at the customs office to clear.

St. Croix: Wharfside, Gallows Bay (Christiansted). If you are clearing here on a weekday, notify customs (773-1011) between 9 a.m. and 5 p.m. of your arrival into Gallows Bay, and they will give you instructions on how to proceed. On weekends, you must upon arrival call customs officials at the airport at 778-0216 for instructions. In either

Note: Expected Changes in BVI Customs Charges

As we go to press, BVI customs officials inform us that the current cruising taxes as detailed below in our text are subject to change, and that new recreational vessels legislation is expected to come into effect by late 1992. They suggest that vessel operators ask for information at customs at the time of their cruise. Your charter company will probably also be able to fill you in.

case, you must also notify immigration (778-1419), so that an inspector can come down from the airport to inspect you.

St. John: Cruz Bay waterfront.

Tortola: Government dock at Road Town or ferry dock at West End.

Jost Van Dyke: Great Harbor.

Virgin Gorda: Virgin Gorda Yacht Harbor.

Hours

U.S. customs office hours are from 8:00 a.m. to 5:00 p.m., Monday through Saturday. At Cruz Bay, the office is closed for lunch between noon and 1 p.m.

BVI customs are open from 8:30 a.m. to 3:30 p.m. Monday through Friday and from 8:30 a.m. to 12:30 p.m. on Saturdays. Note: There is some variation in these hours, subject to change, depending on location. Any time outside customs business hours, including Sundays and holidays, will cost you overtime charges.

Charges

U.S. clearance is free.

BVI customs and immigrations charges *(see box above for important additional information)* include harbor dues, ship's dues, and form charge. This usually will amount to between $7 and $15 (more for overtime), depending on the size of your boat. Also, at time of clearance, charter boats registered outside the BVI must pay a tax of $4 per person per day. Charter boats registered in the BVI must pay $2 per person per day from December 1 through April 30 and 75¢ per person per day from May 1 through November 30. In addition, visiting crewed boats will be assessed a departure tax of $4 per passenger. If you plan to use the mooring system that the BVI National Parks Trust has installed for limited day use only over many dive sites in the BVI, you must obtain a National Parks Permit for a fee payable when you clear customs. These charges are subject to revision as we go to press. For information at the time of your cruise, consult your charter company or call the National Trust at 494-3904 or 494-2069.

Depths. The edges of most of the islands drop away very sharply, so you cannot rely on your lead line or depth sounder to warn you of impending danger. In shallow areas you will have to judge depth by the color of the water. If you're accustomed to northern waters, the clarity of the waters in the islands will be deceiving at first. Experience alone can best teach you how to read depth by water color, but we can offer some general guidelines, applicable only in calm waters when the light is high and behind the observer. In depths of over about 60 feet, the water has a deep, inky, blue-black color. Over sand, this color takes on a lighter but still deep-blue color, and if the bottom is rocky, the color is more dark green. On coming into water of about 15 to 30 feet deep, a sandy bottom will show as light green or blue. A rocky bottom at this depth will be more of a mottled brown color. As you enter shallower water, a sandy bottom will reflect a very pale green at about 10 feet. Over rock or coral at about 10 feet, the water will take on a yellow-brown, mottled tinge and you should be able to distinguish the outlines of the rock.

Drugs. Penalties for illegal drug possession in the USVI match those in the United States. In the BVI, penalties are even more severe.

Holidays. Virgin Islanders see to it that there's time to enjoy life in the islands. All federal U.S. holidays are observed in the USVI, but there are also many local holidays, some of them seemingly impromptu. There are also a whole different set of holidays celebrated in the British Virgin

The Narrows. (Tropic Isle photo)

Watch out for fast-moving ferries. (Fields photo)

Islands. At our press time these dates cannot be confirmed for the upcoming year. Check your calendar and make inquiries when you arrive in the islands to determine which holidays occur during your stay, and remember that on many of these days shops and services are closed and you will have to pay overtime charges to clear customs.

Navigation. With regard to preventing collisions, the main rule seems to be: Stay out of everyone else's way. Realize, however, that this is a simplistic approach and, in complex situations, can be easier said than done. You must be familiar with the *International Regulations For Preventing Collisions At Sea* as they apply to you. The portion of these entitled *Part B, Section II — Conduct of Vessels In Sight Of One Another,* contains the rules of the road and the rules of right-of-way. These state who must give way to whom in all circumstances, and they work well if everyone plays by the same rules. But be aware that in these waters it may be that not all other sailors know the rules, in which case the following from *Part B Section I — Conduct Of Vessels In Any Condition Of Visibility* are important:

> *Rule 7 Risk of Collision* states, in part: *Every vessel shall use all available means appropriate to the prevailing circumstances and conditions to determine if risk of collision exists. If there is any doubt such risk shall be deemed to exist.*
> *Rule 8 Action to Avoid Collision* states:
> (a) *Any action taken to avoid collision shall, if the circumstances of the case admit, be positive, made in*

ample time and with due regard to the observance of good seamanship.

(b) Any alteration of course and/or speed to avoid collision shall, if the circumstances of the case admit, be large enough to be readily apparent to another vessel observing visually or by radar; a succession of small alterations of course and or speed should be avoided.

(c) If there is sufficient sea room, alteration of course alone may be the most effective action to avoid a close-quarters situation provided that it is made in good time, is substantial and does not result in another close-quarters situation.

(d) Action taken to avoid collision with another vessel shall be such as to result in passing at a safe distance. The effectiveness of the action shall be carefully checked until the other vessel is finally past and clear.

(e) If necessary to avoid collision or allow more time to assess the situation, a vessel shall slacken her speed or take all way off by stopping or reversing her means of propulsion.

Boat traffic can be heavy in the Virgin Islands, especially on weekends and holidays. Exercise extreme caution in navigating and anchoring, and remember that there is an enforced 6 m.p.h. speed limit in U.S. and British harbors.

The ferries that operate between the islands are heavy, powerful, and very fast. Don't cross them unless you are absolutely certain you can safely clear both them and their often huge wakes.

Never sail at night. Many local trading boats don't use running lights at night, and even the most experienced yachtsmen in the Virgin Islands restrict their sailing to daylight hours.

An additional caution: Do not pick up a mooring unless you're sure it's safe and available for your use. Many yachts have been damaged after depending on moorings that were rotten, improperly secured, or had anchors that were too small.

Reefs. No matter how clear the water and cloudless the sky, a watchful eye and common sense are necessary. There are many shallow and reefy areas, notably in Gorda Sound and the Camanoe Passages but also present throughout the islands. These require special attention, an alert watch at the bow, and good light above and behind you. Do not enter these areas in overcast weather or in other conditions that make visually reading water depth difficult. Of course, you should not sail at night under any circumstances.

Approximate Sunset/Standard Time/Beginning of Each Month

JAN	FEB	MAR	APR	MAY	JUN	JUL	AUG	SEP	OCT	NOV	DEC
5:54	6:15	6:25	6:32	6:40	6:53	7:00	6:53	6:32	6:06	5:46	5:41

Security. Unfortunately, the attractions of the Virgin Islands have lured a number of boat bums to whom random thefts have been attributed. Unattended boats should always be locked up and secured at anchor as well as dockside. Valuables such as outboard motors and scuba gear should be kept below or locked up.

In view of the sharp rise in international drug traffic, the U.S. Coast Guard advises owners of yachts cruising offshore to be very careful about taking on hitchhikers and paid hands. Thoroughly check the background and reference of anyone you employ. Even a rescue at sea should be approached with caution. Skippers who will be at sea for an extended time should file a Float Plan with someone who could alert the authorities in case of overdue arrival.

Sunset. On this page is a table of approximate standard times for sunset for the beginning of each month so that you can be sure to be tucked into your anchorage before dark. On the water, and especially in these southern latitudes, twilight is quite short, so don't count on being able to navigate after sunset. When the light goes, it goes all at once.

Cane Garden Bay. (Tropic Isle photo)

Tides. Tides are something of an enigma in the islands. They are diurnal (one high and one low per day) on the south side of the islands, while there are four tides (two high and two low per day) on the north side. Tides in Magens Bay, on the north side of St. Thomas, are referenced on the tides at San Juan, while the tides in St. Thomas Harbor are referenced on those in Galveston, Texas, more than 2,000 miles away.

Tide rise is negligible, generally less than a foot, so if you go aground, don't expect the tide to get you off. The main significance of the tide is its effect on the direction and intensity of the current, which runs in a westerly direction with the winds. Since the tide is difficult to predict and because the easterly trades have a great effect on the currents, generally count on a westerly flow. The currents will always be strongest in that direction, reaching as much as 3-4 knots in such places as The Narrows (north of St. John), and Current Cut (between the eastern tip of St. Thomas and Great St. James Island).

The highest tides of the year are in September and October. The lowest are in April, May, and June.

Water safety. Shark, barracuda, and moray eels are probably the most feared denizens of the tropical deep. Many more injuries are sustained from sea urchins and fire coral than from these predators, but it's true that they are not predictable and should not be underestimated. Don't swim too far from your boat, and never swim alone. Sharks, barracudas, and morays don't like to be provoked, so never tease them. They'll usually leave you alone if you treat them with respect. Barracuda will often linger in the water to watch you. Leave them alone and they'll leave you alone. Don't stick your hand or foot into crevices in the reef, where you could easily frighten a moray who will retaliate with a severe bite. Shiny objects attract fish, so don't wear a lot of jewelry unless you want to be mistaken for a giant lure.

The larger, more dangerous varieties of shark seem to swim in deep water off the northern shores of the major islands, particularly St. Thomas and Tortola. They are fewer and smaller south of the islands. Sharks aren't attracted to you so much are they are to garbage thrown overboard or the blood of speared fish. If you must spear a fish, get it out of the water immediately.

Weather. The constant temperature and weather conditions are among the reasons the Virgin Islands are considered by many to be the best cruising area in the world. The islands are so close together that they break the swell of the ocean from the north. The ever-present trade winds, prevailing from the east, are not deflected by the islands.

Although the islands lie in the region of what is called the northeast trade winds, the wind in reality is more to the E, ENE to ESE. During the winter months, the wind averages about 15 knots, but yachts

Squall over Cane Garden Bay. (Tropic Isle photo)

should be rigged and sails made to withstand the 20-to-25-knot winds that frequently occur for weeks at a time, particularly during the "Christmas winds," usually around late December through January.

Rain may come in squalls that last for 10 to 15 minutes and are gone. Very occasionally there may be an easterly wave accompanied by rain and plenty of wind, lasting a day or two. At times the wind goes back to the northeast and north, and very rarely it will back west of north. When it does, it usually does so slowly and diminishes in intensity.

The annual rainfall in the islands is only about 40 inches and water is precious. Most of the water supply is harvested from the roofs of the houses and stored in cisterns. Road Town, St. Thomas, St. Croix and a few of the very large hotel developments in other islands have wells or desalinization plants. In any case, water is expensive and adequate water storage on yachts is a must.

For daily weather reports, listen to any of the local broadcasts:

St. Thomas: WIVI FM 99.5 MHz; WVWI 1000 kHz; WSTA 1340 kHz.

St. Croix: WSTX 970 kHz.

Tortola: ZBVI 780 kHz.

NOAA weather is now available from St. Thomas on 162.475 MHz, weather channel 3 on your VHF radio. There are also frequent daily broadcasts on *Virgin Islands Radio,* announced on VHF 16 and read on VHF 28. At 6 a.m., 2 p.m., and 10 p.m. there are detailed Caribbean weather reports.

Hurricanes strike the Virgin Islands infrequently. Generally, the U.S. Weather Bureau in San Juan does a fine job of weather forecasting and locating hurricanes. Klaus, in November 1984, was an exception, striking with winds of up to 60 knots with only a few hours' warning. Normally, though, there is time to find a hurricane hole. In September 1989, Hurricane Hugo demonstrated that the trick is to pick the right one.

Where to Find It: Fuel, Ice, Water, Provisions

This listing is intended as a general reference to where you are most likely to find these necessities throughout the Virgin Islands. It is not a comprehensive list, and what is offered at different facilities is always subject to change. "Provisions" can range from the most basic of food supplies to gourmet groceries, either on site or within easy walking distance.

Facility name	Fuel	Ice	Water	Provisions
St. Thomas				
Yacht Haven	•	•	•	•
Sugar Reef Marina	•	•	•	•
Crown Bay Marina	•	•	•	•
Tropical Marine	•	•	•	
La Vida Marina	•	•		
Independent Boatyard		•		
Fish Hawk Marina	•	•		
Saga Haven Marina	•	•	•	•
American Yacht Harbor	•	•	•	•
St. Thomas Sportfishing Ctr		•	•	•
Vessup Point Marina	•	•	•	•
St. John				
Caneel Bay Shipyard	•	•	•	•
Cinnamon Bay Campgrounds		•		•
Coral Bay Marine	•	•	•	•
St. Croix				
St. Croix Marine	•	•	•	•
Green Cay Marina	•	•	•	
St. Croix Yacht Club		•	*(members of accredited yacht clubs)*	
Salt River Marina	•*(24-hour notice)*	•	•	•

Facility name	Fuel	Ice	Water	Provisions
Jost Van Dyke				
Harris' Place		•		•
Tortola and nearby islands				
Sopers Hole Marina	•	•	•	•
Sunsail	•	•	•	•
Prospect Reef Resort	•	•		•
Fort Burt Marina	•	•		•
Road Reef Marina		•	•	
Village Cay Marina	•	•	•	•
Inner Harbour Marina	•	•	•	•
Cane Garden Bay Beach Hotel		•	•	•
Tropic Island Yacht Charters	•	•	•	
Seabreeze Yacht Charters	•	•	•	•
Last Resort (Beef Island)		•		•
Marina Cay	•	•	•	•
Islands to the South of the Sir Francis Drake Channel				
Peter Island Yacht Harbour	•	•	•	
Cooper Island Beach Resort		•		
Virgin Gorda				
Virgin Gorda Yacht Harbour	•	•	•	•
Pusser's Leverick Bay	•	•	•	•
Biras Creek	•	•		
The Bitter End	•	•	•	•

Diving in the Virgin Islands

The geography, weather, and accessibility of the Virgin Islands make them the ideal vacation spot for diving as well as cruising enthusiasts. If you're both, you couldn't ask for a better location to combine your interests. Calm seas, especially in late spring through summer, make for impressive underwater visibility of up to 120 feet, and the surface water temperature averages around 80°. The sea is generally no higher than 2 to 3 feet, with some higher swells in unprotected areas, especially during the winter. Local dive guides can clue you to spots to avoid where tidal current can be dangerous and they can also advise you about sea conditions for diving on any given day.

There are more than 100 charted dive sites in the Virgin Islands, and you'll find that almost every anchorage is near a reef good for diving or snorkeling. These shallow coral reefs are alive with sponges and schools of tropical fish. For the experienced diver there are dramatic drop-offs, caves, and canyons, and hundreds of ghostly shipwrecks, notably that of the *R.M.S. Rhone* off Salt Island. Off Anegada, as many as 300 ships lie sunken at the bottom of the sea, inspiring the imagination as well as the ambition of treasure seekers.

The *Rhone,* featured in the movie *The Deep,* was a 2,434-ton mail steamer that sank in a hurricane in 1867. Having skirted St. Thomas, which was ravaged by an epidemic of cholera and yellow fever that year, the *Rhone* had just completed transfer of mail and cargo at Salt Cay and was preparing to return to England when the storm took her. Bert Kilbride has provided us with the following account of the demise of the *Rhone,* taken from the "Royal Mail," a centenary history of the Royal Mail Line from 1839 to 1939:

On the morning of October 29, 1867, R.M.S. Rhone was at anchor near Peter Island taking on cargo and stores for her return crossing. The stillness of the tropic day was undisturbed. The sun blazed down from a clear sky upon a perfectly calm sea. At about 11:00 a.m. the barometer suddenly fell to 27.95 [inches], the sky darkened, and with a mighty roar a fearful hurricane blew from the N.N.W. With engines going at full speed the ship rode the storm.

At noon there came a lull and the captain weighed and stood away to the southeast where there would be more sea room in which to meet the second onslaught. He had negotiated most of the rocky channels in safety and was rounding the last point when the sky again darkened and a fearful blast struck the Rhone, forcing her upon the rocks of Salt Island. She broke her back, parted amidships and instantly sank, taking 125 of her company with her.

Diving Facilities

There are full-service dive shops on all the major islands, many located at marina complexes or nearby. Most rent and sell any equipment you might need for snorkeling or SCUBA, including masks, snorkels, fins, buoyancy compensators, regulators, tanks, and weight belts. Novices can arrange for a short "resort" or introductory courses or they can take full-certification courses lasting about a week. It's hard to imagine a more inspiring environment for learning. Tours offered by most dive facilities include day and night dives. Some will send a guide with

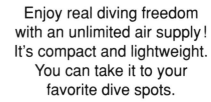

Anchoring Over BVI Dive Sites

The BVI National Parks Trust is in the process of creating a system of daytime, limited-use, permanent moorings at BVI dive sites, to protect the underwater ecology from further damage and to provide a marine environment of sustainable use for the future. A fee for use and maintenance will be charged. If you plan to use the mooring system, you must have obtained a National Parks Permit, either from your charter company in the BVI or, if your boat is not based in the BVI, when you clear BVI customs. Mooring buoys are color-coded as follows:

Red buoys: *Non-diving, day use only.*
Yellow buoys: *Commercial dive vessels only.*
White Buoys: *Non-commercial vessels for daytime dive use only on first-come, first-serve basis. (90-minute time limit).*

It is important to remember that many if not most of the areas where these moorings can be found are exposed and, in some cases, in the vicinity of shallow rocks or reefs — so keep an eye on your weather conditions and check your government charts for possible hazards. Do not mistake these buoys for guides to navigation. *Since anchoring at these sites is restricted, you should check with your charter company or the Trust in Road Town at 494-3904 or 494-2069.*
Locations of National Parks Trust moorings include:

The Caves	*Dead Chest Island*
The Indians	*Blonde Rock*
Pelican Island	*The Wreck of the Rhone*
Carrot Shoal	*Dive sites at Cooper Island*
Dive sites at Peter Island	*Dive sites at Ginger Island*
Dive sites at Norman Island	*Dive sites at The Dogs*
The Rhone's anchor	*Snorkeling sites at The Dogs*
The Wreck of the Fearless	*Guana Island*

equipment to rendezvous with your boat and take you on a tour tailored to your specifications. Many dive shops also rent underwater camera and video equipment, and can develop your film on the premises.

Diving Emergencies

In the event that you find yourself in a dive-related emergency, contact the U.S. Coast Guard immediately (Channel 16, telephone 729-6770 or 722-2943). The St. Thomas Hospital Recompression Chamber can be reached at 776-2686. There is also a recompression chamber at Roosevelt Roads in Puerto Rico, but it is restricted to military use except in cases of extreme emergency.

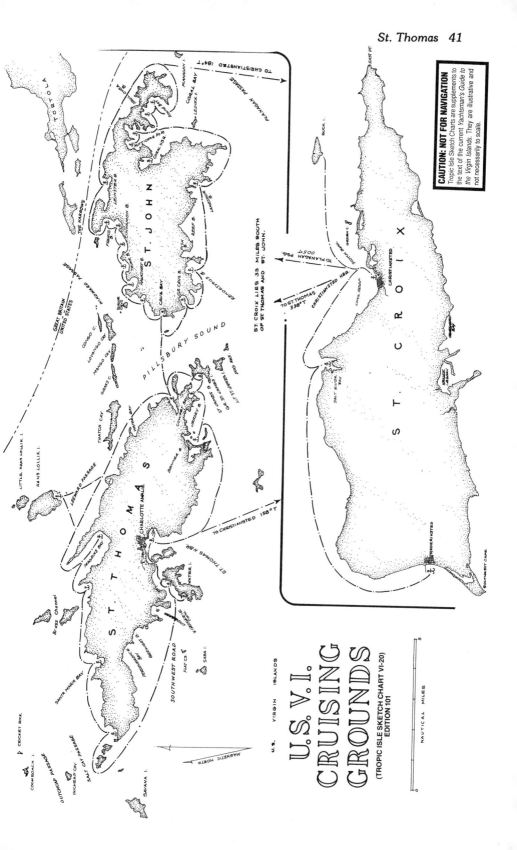

U.S.V.I. CRUISING GROUNDS
(TROPIC ISLE SKETCH CHART VI-20)
EDITION 101

U.S. VIRGIN ISLANDS

CAUTION: NOT FOR NAVIGATION
Tropic Isle Sketch Charts are supplements to the text of the current *Yachtsman's Guide to the Virgin Islands*. They are illustrative and not necessarily to scale.

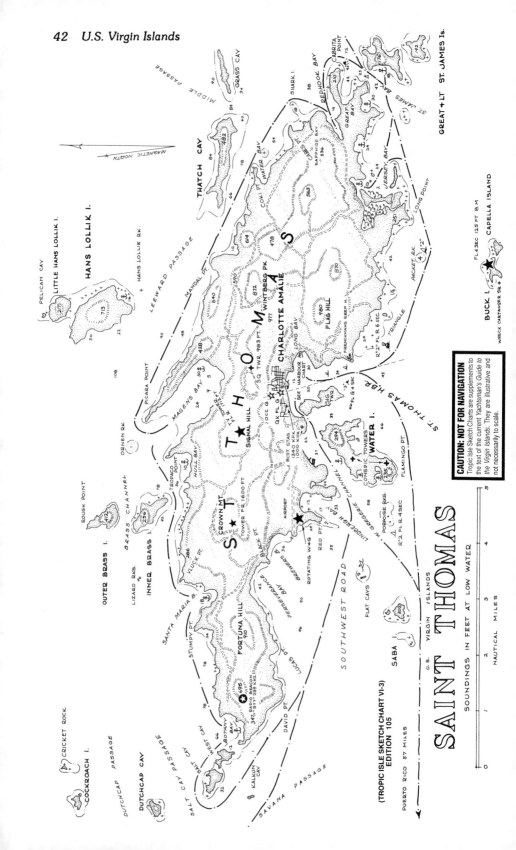

SAINT THOMAS

(TROPIC ISLE SKETCH CHART VI-3)
EDITION 105

CAUTION: NOT FOR NAVIGATION
Tropic Isle Sketch Charts are supplements to the text of the current Yachtsman's Guide to the Virgin Islands. They are illustrative and not necessarily to scale.

SOUNDINGS IN FEET AT LOW WATER

NAUTICAL MILES

St. Thomas

N.O.S. Charts: 25641, 25647. Tropic Isle Sketch Charts: VI-1, 3, 4, 5, 20.

Among the Virgin Islands, St. Thomas was and still is the lusty rogue of the bunch. With the advantage of one of the Caribbean's best harbors, economic opportunity in all guises has knocked here for almost 400 years. It is noisier, more crowded, more volatile, and in many ways the most tangible reminder of the Virgin Island's history as a trade emporium and melting pot. All things considered, it's where the action is, whatever that might be at the time.

St. Thomas is the most densely populated island of the Virgins. Within its 28 square miles lives a population of 48,000, with houses scattered haphazardly over the steep hillsides. There are those who seem to think that St. Thomas has been spoiled, an aberration from the way the Virgin Islands are supposed to be. But the nature of St. Thomas hasn't changed much in 300 years — through prosperity and setbacks, it has propelled itself forward with high hopes, greed, and a certain amount of ruthlessness. It was the only island whose economy continued to thrive after the collapse of plantation life — most of the other islands were all but abandoned for many years except for a few descendents of slaves who chose not to pursue opportunities elsewhere. Those islands remain relatively uncrowded, idyllic for the visitor who imagines an uncomplicated way of life — but don't be deceived into thinking that the history of all of these islands is not intertwined, and largely driven by the restless energy of St. Thomas.

St. Thomas Harbor. (Tropic Isle photo)

Street vendors along the Charlotte Amalie waterfront. (Tropic Isle photo)

Outside its many expensive, insulated resorts, St. Thomas resists the neutered prettification of the Caribbean that Madison Avenue likes to portray — but magnificent raw beauty persists, especially in the mountains, with spectacular views and a profusion of lavender bougainvillea and ginger thomas (the official flower of the USVI, also known as yellow elder). Beaches include the world-famous and popular variety as well as hard-of-access and remote stretches of sand with cliffs and pounding surf. For visitors interested in the complex texture of Caribbean social fabric and history, there is much to see, with buildings still in use that years ago served as fortifications, watchtowers, government offices, or the mansions of the wealthy.

The administrative center, Charlotte Amalie (pronounced A-mahl'-ya), bustles with government employees, townspeople, waterfront characters, and tourists clutching armloads of free-port bargains. When there are four or five cruise ships in the harbor, which is almost all the time, a trip through town can be like negotiating a Moroccan bazaar. Shoppers struggling with pocketbooks, cameras, and shopping bags crowd the narrow sidewalks, and on street corners hawkers hand out tokens for free rum punches or even samples of "gold" jewelry if you visit the establishment they represent. A procession of cars, taxis, and tour buses clogs the one-way streets, where the speed limit of 10 m.p.h. is seldom approached. It's busy, rude, noisy, and hot outside, in abrupt contrast with elegant shop interiors where air-conditioners blow cold and clerks are soft-spoken, curried, and perfumed. There are unique crafts and specialty stores, the usual souvenir and T-shirt joints, pretty walking streets closed to traffic, and lots of places to eat or drink. Some of the waterfront shop buildings were warehouses in the 1600s and 1700s, with back doors on the beach for the convenience of smugglers. The harbor, a twinkling fairy-tale sight at night, is a festive parade of vessels by day. Cruise ships bellow their arrivals and mightily make their way in, dwarfing hundreds of sailboats and motor craft. Colorful old cargo boats loaded with fruits and vegetables from down island jostle for space along the waterfront with party boats and catamarans advertising day trips.

The first colonization attempt on the island was in 1666 when the Danes arrived in St. Thomas, most interested in the large, protected harbor but also in planting sugar and tobacco. However, less than two years later, after supply shortages, repeated attacks by English privateers, a hurricane, and losses to disease, the survivors returned to Denmark. In 1671, The Danish West India Company was granted permission to re-establish a colony on St. Thomas. The boatload of almost 200 people that left Denmark was made up almost entirely of indentured immigrants and recruited prisoners. By the time the ship arrived at the deserted harbor, nearly half of the passengers had died of poor conditions on board. Within seven months of arrival, less than 30 Danish settlers remained. From this sparse beginning the Danes occupied St. Thomas for almost 250 years.

By 1674 Fort Christian had been built and the town was named *Taphus*, which one source translates to mean *House of Drunkenness*. The rapidly growing population had already exceeded 800, the greater part made up of slaves brought to work the plantations, which cultivated primarily cotton but also tobacco, sugar, and indigo. Dutch planters had

Fort Christian. (Tropic Isle photo)

joined the Danes on the island, with smaller numbers of other nationalities (even today, the patois spoken by many islanders reflects English, Irish, and Scotch, the language of many of the plantation overseers).

Piracy flourished off and on depending on the cooperation of the governor of the time. One infamous English pirate, Bartholomew Sharp, retired from his life of pillaging to become a planter on St. Thomas in 1696. When he found himself in debt, he attempted to sneak out of town one night, but was captured. His subsequent threats to wreak havoc in St. Thomas sent him to jail for life.

By the mid-1700s, many plantations on St. Thomas had been abandoned due to a decline in prices, soil erosion on the island's steep terrain, and inefficient production methods. The harbor, however, continued to thrive. After the American War of Independence, commerce got a boost when trade opened up with the fledgling country. St. Thomas was also internationally famous for its slave market, which attracted buyers from other islands and the American colonies. In these years of frequent wars between nations with interests in the Caribbean, privateers commissioned by governments to attack the shipping and commerce of their enemies frequented St. Thomas' neutral harbor. Smuggling was big business too in this period of heavy trade restrictions. Many people were in debt and needed quick cash, and customs regulations were irregularly enforced by easily bribed officials.

In 1839, the harbor became the base for the Royal Mail Steam Packet Company, so most visitors to the Caribbean had to pass through

Hassel Island ruins. (Fields photo)

St. Thomas, contributing to its cosmopolitan nature. One census around this time turned up almost 140 nationalities. A major coaling station, maritime dockyard and repair facility on Hassel Island helped St. Thomas to remain a major shipping center for many years, and during the Civil War, Confederate blockade runners used St. Thomas as a supply base.

By the mid-1800s, however, prosperity was waning. Between 1853 and 1867, epidemics of cholera and malaria killed thousands of people in St. Thomas. During 1867, a hurricane, earthquake, and tidal wave destroyed many harbor facilities, followed by another even more devastating hurricane in 1871. These disasters, along with availability of lower-priced services elsewhere in the Caribbean, contributed to the decline of St. Thomas as a trade center. Post-emancipation efforts to secure labor for remaining plantations were not successful and the instability of dislocated freed slaves and former slave owners in a plunging economy provoked anger, violence, and social disorganization that lasted through the remainder of the century.

In 1917, the United States purchased the island along with St. Croix and St. John, and it was under control of the Navy until 1931. After the end of World War II, increased tourism stimulated a boom in economic development that has included, in the past 20 or 30 years, rapid growth of the yachting industry.

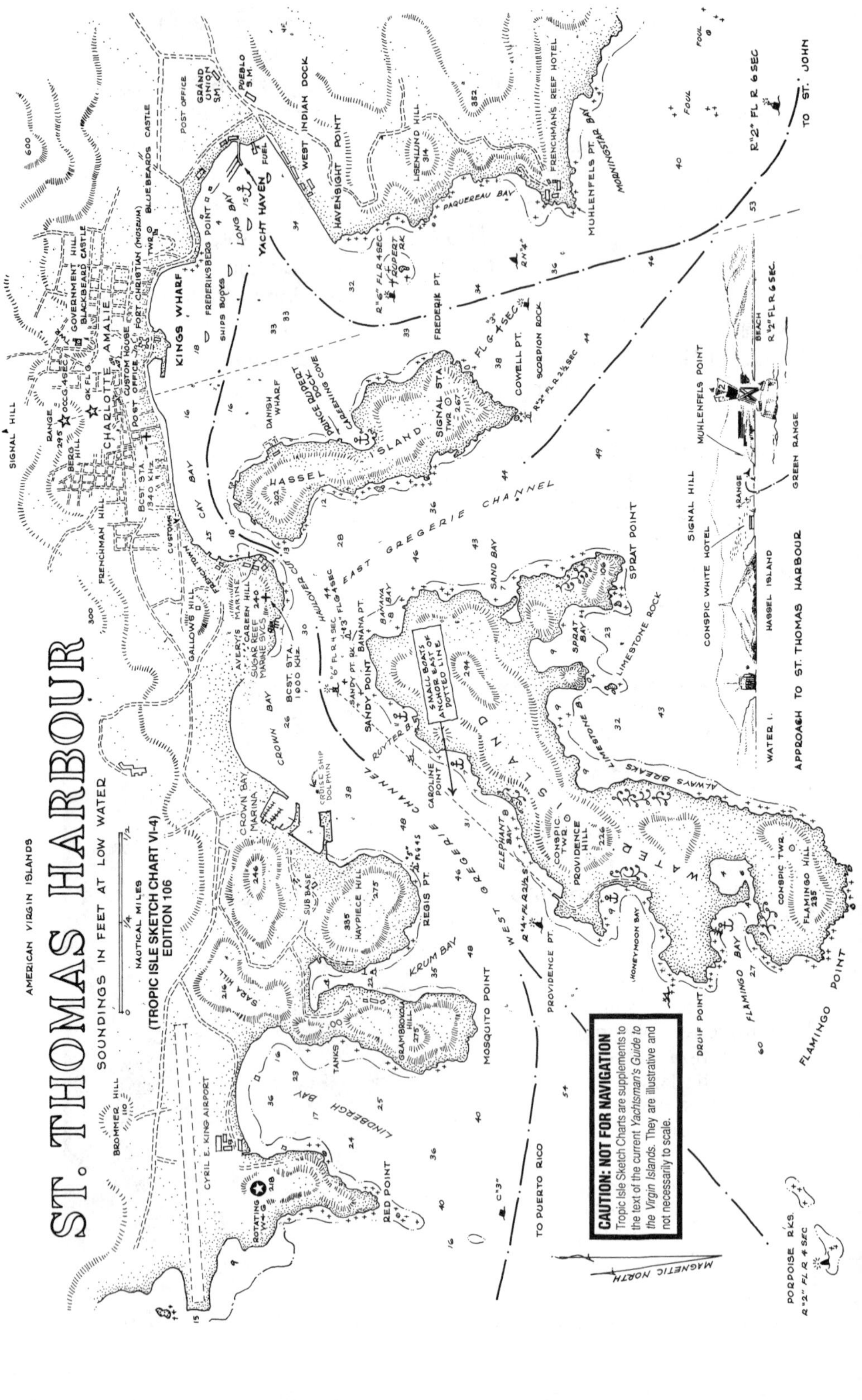

ST. THOMAS HARBOUR
AMERICAN VIRGIN ISLANDS
SOUNDINGS IN FEET AT LOW WATER
NAUTICAL MILES
(TROPIC ISLE SKETCH CHART VI-4)
EDITION 106
CAUTION: NOT FOR NAVIGATION
Tropic Isle Sketch Charts are supplements to the text of the current Yachtsman's Guide to the Virgin Islands. They are illustrative and not necessarily to scale.
CHARLOTTE AMALIE
KINGS WHARF
YACHT HAVEN
LONG BAY
WEST INDIAN DOCK
HAVENSIGHT POINT
FREDERIKSBERG POINT
BLUEBEARDS CASTLE
GOVERNMENT HILL
BLACKBEARD CASTLE
FORT CHRISTIAN (MUSEUM)
CUSTOM HOUSE
POST OFFICE
SIGNAL HILL
BERG HILL
FRENCHMAN HILL
FRENCH TOWN
GALLOWS HILL
CAY BAY
HASSEL ISLAND
DANISH WHARF
PRINCE RUPERT DOCK
CAREENING COVE
SIGNAL STA
COWELL PT.
SCORPION ROCK
FREDERIK PT.
LISENLUND HILL
PAQUEREAU BAY
FRENCHMAN'S REEF HOTEL
MUHLENFELS PT.
MORNINGSTAR BAY
EAST GREGERIE CHANNEL
HAULOVER CUT
AVERY'S MARINE
CAREEN HILL
SUGAR REEF MARINE SVCS
CROWN BAY
CROWN BAY MARINA
CRUISE SHIP DOLPHIN
SUB BASE
HAYPIECE HILL
REGIS PT.
KRUM BAY
SARA HILL
GRAMBROKOLA HILL
MOSQUITO POINT
LINDBERGH BAY
RED POINT
CYRIL E. KING AIRPORT
BROMMER HILL
TANKS
WEST GREGERIE CHANNEL
SANDY POINT
BANANA PT.
BANANA BAY
SAND BAY
SPRAT POINT
SPRAT BAY
LIMESTONE ROCK
LIMESTONE B.
RUYTER B.
CAROLINE POINT
SMALL BOATS ANCHOR EAST OF DOTTED LINE
ELEPHANT BAY
PROVIDENCE HILL
PROVIDENCE PT.
HONEYMOON BAY
FLAMINGO HILL
FLAMINGO BAY
FLAMINGO POINT
DRUIF POINT
ALWAYS BREAKS
WATER ISLAND
PORPOISE RKS.
TO PUERTO RICO
TO ST. JOHN
MAGNETIC NORTH
APPROACH TO ST. THOMAS HARBOUR
WATER I.
HASSEL ISLAND
CONSPIC WHITE HOTEL
SIGNAL HILL
MUHLENFELS POINT
GREEN RANGE
BEACH
R"2" FL R 6 SEC.

St. Thomas Harbor/Charlotte Amalie

Although St. Thomas Harbor is considered ideal for large vessels, the surge can be an occasional discomfort for smaller boats. As in most commercial harbors, the water isn't recommended for swimming.

For the Skipper

Caution: Packet Rock, south and west of Long Point, breaks only in heavy weather. Approaching from the east, give the nun buoy marking Packet Rock a wide berth, staying well offshore toward Buck Island.

Entrance into the harbor is easy and straightforward. The best landmark is Frenchman's Reef Hotel, on Muhlenfels Point. Continuing in, honor the markers and you'll have no problems. There are two hazards to avoid. Stay well south of red flasher buoy no. 2, southeast of Muhlenfels Point, to avoid foul ground south and east of the entrance. Also, you can go between Prince Rupert Rock and the mainland, but avoid the water between Prince Rupert Rock and red flasher no. 6, which is shallow.

VI Charter Yacht League show, Yacht Haven. (Tropic Isle photo)

Coming out of St. Thomas Harbor and heading east to the cruising grounds, you must beat to windward or slog it out under power. If you're sailing, take a series of short tacks between Buck Island and the shore, being careful to avoid Packet Rock. Or go out past Buck Island, leaving it to port, and tack into Christmas Cove and Current Cut.

Anchorages and Facilities

You can anchor stern-to along the waterfront for a reasonable charge but it's usually crowded with tourist boats. Also, be aware that the surge here can be uncomfortable and at times dangerous. There is a dinghy dock on the waterfront inside King's Wharf.

Customs and immigration. Customs and immigration formalities may be completed at the customs and immigration offices located by the ferry dock toward the west end of the waterfront. Provided there are no foreign nationals aboard, U.S. pleasure craft and foreign-registered craft with valid cruising permits may phone 774-5539 daily from 8 a.m. to 5 p.m. (hours on Sunday vary somewhat) and request telephone entry through customs and immigration. This is sometimes granted, sometimes not, for various reasons as these authorities see fit. Foreign-registered vessels that do not carry valid cruising permits must clear at the customs office.

Yacht Haven Marina. Inside St. Thomas Harbor, the Yacht Haven marina complex, adjacent to the Ramada Yacht Haven Hotel, is one of the largest and most complete yachting service facilities in the Caribbean. Fuel, electricity, cable TV, water, and showers are among the dockside facilities. Services include Island Marine Supply, a canvas shop, a laundromat, a provisioning shop and liquor store, Underwater Safaris dive shop, a hair salon, and boutiques. The V.I. Charteryacht League headquarters are also here. Charter companies at Yacht Haven include CYOA (Caribbean Yacht Owners' Association), with 25 sailboats from 30 to 52 feet (they also run the International School of Sailing here), Caribbean Adventures' extensive variety of bareboat and crewed charter boats, and Caribbean Sailing Charters' fleet of Beneteau and Morgan yachts. Open every day for breakfast, lunch, and dinner, the Bridge bar and restaurant is a good vantage point for watching dockside comings-and-goings during the day, and at night it's loud and lively. Across the street from Yacht Haven, Island Rigging and Hydraulics offers complete rigging services and hardware.

King's Wharf. West of Yacht Haven and opposite Fort Christian, you'll often spot the U.S. Coast Guard vessel *Point Whitehorn* and smaller government boats alongside King's Wharf, next to the Coast Guard headquarters. Recreational boats are not permitted to dock here. Incidentally, it's routine these days to be boarded and searched by the Coast Guard in U.S. waters.

Avery's Marine, Inc. In the far western curve of the harbor is Avery's Marine, Inc., known for many years as Avery's Boathouse. This charter operation, which has a long and loyal following, is run by Dick Avery, who founded the Virgin Islands bareboat business way back in 1958. Avery's has moved a few doors south of its recent location back to its original address overlooking Haulover Cut, with over 500 feet of waterfront and plenty of parking space. Avery's has a bareboat fleet of about 10 boats and also books crewed charters, sells Cabo Ricos, Sunfish, and Lasers, and does boat repairs. Even do-it-yourselfers stop by to ask Dick for advice. The restaurants and nightlife of Frenchtown are

Avery's Marine, Inc.

Bare Boat Virgins

Pearson Sailboats From 30' to 39'

Charter the Easy Way! We're in Town...

⚓ 5-minute taxi ride from airport and supermarket.

⚓ Easy to shop for duty-free bargains.

⚓ Dick's chart orientation is the best in the business.

⚓ Our boats are complete, clean, functioning, and insured.

⚓ Same location since 1959.

⚓ Vessels with Captain and Crew in either
the Virgin Islands or Down Island.

⚓ Tell us what you need and where you
need it – we'll get it for you.

Veterans Drive Station P.O. Box 5248, St. Thomas, USVI 00803
Marianne Avery, Charter Manager
Phone/Fax 776-0113 or call 775-2773 (evenings)

within walking distance, and nearby, overlooking the Charlotte Amalie waterfront, the Hook, Line, and Sinker serves good food for lunch and dinner. The atmosphere is informal — it's a sailor's kind of place, good for hanging around, listening to and telling lies.

Sugar Reef Marine Services. Just beyond the west end of Haulover Cut, at the eastern end of Crown Bay behind a prominent breakwater, Sugar Reef Marine Services is a compact facility for visiting yachts. There is dockage for boats with up to 20 feet of draft, but visitors should radio ahead to *E Z Shopper* to make sure space is available. Diesel fuel, showers, ice and water, laundry facilities, and provisioning are available on site. Various types of repair facilities are located nearby. The Sugar Reef Cafe serves good American cooking, and the Lucky Strike Bar is a pleasant place to relax. There's also a Chinese restaurant called Wok on Water.

Crown Bay Marina is at the western end of Crown Bay, north of Water Island. If approaching from East Gregerie Channel, be sure to stay north of red light no. 6 marking Sandy Point Rock north of Water Island. The entrance to the marina is immediately north of the northern-most cruise-ship dock in West Gregerie Channel. Be sure to leave the cruise-ship dolphin to your port as you near the marina entrance.

Inside the marina there is ample turning room with 17 feet of water and better throughout except for an area approximately 10 feet deep between D and E docks. The fuel dock and dockmaster's office are to your starboard as you enter. The marina offers 96 slips with all utilities for boats from 25 to 200 feet long. Provisioning, ice, laundry and shower

Crown Bay Marina. (Tropic Isle photo)

facilities, a clearing house, car rental, secretarial services, engine repair, a ship's store, a wood shop and a watersports shop are on the premises. There's a nice bar/restaurant, Tickle's, with a marina view. Controlled access and security personnel provide for your safety around the clock.

This new facility, which is designed with the charter yacht industry in mind, is just five minutes from the airport. Nearby is just about everything you or your boat might need. You can pick up a complete directory of the numerous services in the immediate area from the dockmaster's office. These include banks, liquor shops, supermarkets, a pharmacy, public tennis courts and a video shop. Within walking distance or a short taxi ride are several inexpensive guest houses and inns, and there's a variety of good restaurants in the Sub Base/French Town area.

Haulover Marine Yachting Center, on the western side of Crown Bay, includes Haulover Marine's complete repair facility, Banks Sails Caribbean sail shop, and Offshore Marine, carrying most lines of inflatables and parts.

What to Do

Charlotte Amalie can easily be explored on foot in an afternoon. More than half of the town's buildings are well over a century old and of historical interest. Street names appear both in English and Danish.

On the east side of town near King's Wharf, the rust-red building topped by a clock tower is Fort Christian, built in 1671 by the first Danish settlers. Inside is a museum of Indian relics and remnants of early settlements as well as shell collections and a stuffed wildlife exhibit with a moth-eaten and particularly unattractive mongoose. The fort was used as a jail as recently as 1982, and a step into the dark, stifling cells will remind you of the wisdom of living within the law. The sky is barely visible through tiny barred openings and the walls are scribbled with the graffiti of endless idle hours. In what used to be the municipal courtroom is an art gallery. Across the street is the green Legislative Building, home of the

Haulover Marine Yachting Center

- S/S Fabrication
- Carpentry Shop
- Fiberglass/Paint
- 100 Ton Crane

Tel. 776-2078 Fax 779-8426 Channel 16

The Grand Hotel. (Tropic Isle photo)

Virgin Island Senate. It was built in 1874 as barracks for Danish troops.

Emancipation Park has benches for resting, a statue of King Christian IX and a replica of the U.S. Liberty Bell. The park was built on the spot where Governor Peter von Scholten announced the end of slavery throughout the Danish West Indies on July 3, 1848. From time to time there are band concerts or other forms of entertainment in the gazebo. The trees surrounding the park are lignum vitae, bright blue when in bloom and valued by ship-builders for hundreds of years for the strength and hardness of the wood.

The Grand Hotel, near the waterfront, was built in 1841. No longer the elite guest house it was then, the building now houses shops on the first level and, on the south side of the building, a hospitality suite where you can get information, use the telephone, buy paperbacks and souvenirs, rest your feet, and check luggage or packages.

The Ninety-Nine Steps are one of the few remaining step-streets in the Caribbean. Apparently the original plans drawn for the city did not take the steepness of the hills into account, and several streets that were laid out running vertically from the waterfront had to be built as stone steps. The bricks of the steps were ballast on merchant ships. At the top of the Ninety-Nine Steps is Crown House, an opulent 18th-century home with Oriental wall hangings, West Indian furniture, and a crystal chandelier said to be from Versailles. Several USVI governors lived here, including Peter von Scholten in 1827.

On Kongens' Gade is the Government House, built in 1867, where the governor of the USVI works and lives. Up the street to the west is Hotel 1829, once a sea-captain's mansion. Across the street, Quarters "B," built as a private home in 1816, was for some time a German consulate and now houses government offices. The mahogany stairs inside were once the staircase of a grand sailing vessel.

Religious tolerance attracted members of many religions to make a new life here. The 18th-century Frederik Lutheran Church, the Dutch Reformed Church, and the St. Thomas Synagogue are notable among the many historically significant churches in the Caribbean.

At 17th-century Fort Skytsborg is the five-story Blackbeard's Tower. Here in the early 1700s, the story goes, pirate Edward Teach (otherwise known as Blackbeard) kept lookout, drinking rum spiked with gunpowder. The pyrotechnic Mr. Teach reportedly also braided his beard around his ears and wore lighted candles in his hair when he attacked passing ships. He's probably best known, however, for his disposal of fourteen successive young brides. Whether Blackbeard ever really used this tower isn't documented, but the tower, along with Bluebeard's Castle on Government House Hill, did serve as a fortified watchtower to back up Fort Christian. Both are now part of privately owned properties.

Charlotte Amalie is probably the best city for free-port shopping in the Caribbean. There are more than a hundred stores specializing in fine watches, cameras, crystal, perfume, liquors, designer clothing and jewelry, as well as the usual souvenir and T-shirt concessions. Havensight Mall, next to the West India Docks near Yacht Haven, has branches of many of the same stores. Be advised that you should take the same safety precautions in St. Thomas that you would in any area where a large number of tourists present a temptation to the less privileged.

Camille Pissaro, the father of French Impressionism, was born in St. Thomas in 1830 and lived on Main Street, above where the Tropicana Perfume Shop now stands, before moving to Paris. His

In the 1830s, Impressionist painter Camille Pissaro lived above where the Tropicana Perfume Center stands now . (Fields photo)

parents are buried in the town cemetery. Some of his paintings hang in Government House.

You can buy fresh produce, including the more exotic Caribbean varieties, at Market Square at the end of Main Street (Saturdays are the best day, when many of the boats arrive). This was once the site of the busiest 19th-century slave market in the world. The metal roof was originally part of a European railway station in the 1800s. You might also bargain for coconuts and other fruits and vegetables at the docks, where boats bring food and supplies from down island.

A frequently recommended place in town for elegant dining and accommodations is the Mark St. Thomas, a restored 1785 mansion that stands high above the harbor. The dining room and veranda have splendid views, and the chef has earned a reputation for innovative and excellent food.

Frenchtown is a short ride or 20-minute walk from town (drive or take a taxi after dark because there are some isolated stretches along the way). Many of the people here are descended from French laborers who left St. Barts in the mid-1800s for St. Thomas. They became fishermen, naming their settlement *Carenage* because of the sailboats careened in the harbor. It has been and remains to some extent an insulated community, where a dialect of Norman French is still spoken. Some of St. Thomas's best restaurants are in Frenchtown or the nearby Sub Base area, including the romantic Cafe Normandie, Alexander's for German food, and Barbary Coast, a dark, cheerful pub with an Italian/West Indian menu. Famous is popular for Italian and seafood dishes, and Victor's New Hide-Out serves excellent West Indian fish and lobster. The Chart House is a traditional steak-and-seafood establishment overlooking Haulover

Frenchtown waterfront. (Fields photo)

Cut. L'Escargot serves French specialties, and Barnacle Bill's, impossible to miss with the immense lobster clinging to its roof, serves dinner, usually with lively entertainment.

It's a shame that so many visitors to St. Thomas rush into town to shop and then beat a hasty retreat, missing the rest of the island. Up in the hills, the fragrance and hues of the tropical foliage are vivid, the air is cool, and the people laid-back. There are also some great places to eat (on Mafolie Road, Sib's Mountain Bar and Restaurant is one of our favorite places to eat in the islands, with its small bar crowded with friendly locals and an intimate dining area nestled outside in the peeping woods). If you can, rent a car, get a map, and explore. Don't be discouraged by the prospect of driving on the left side of the road. Just take it slow. Avoid the rush hour in the morning and late afternoon when traffic backs up on some of the roads approaching Charlotte Amalie, and expect some delays when islanders might suddenly stop their vehicles in the street to have conversations with passing drivers. This is the way it's done here, so be patient. The view of the harbor from Mafolie Hotel is spectacular, especially at night. You might also head up Crown Mountain Road to the highest point of the island, an elevation of 1,547 feet, from which you can admire a magnificent view of Magens By and up the Sir Francis Drake Channel. There is a tourist attraction here called Mountain Top, closed down by Hurricane Hugo in 1989 but now rebuilt in West Indian architectural style and reopened with a number of new upscale shops including a Pusser's store, a museum shop, a coin store, and several shops selling local crafts.

Yachtsmen who'd like to stay awhile on St. Thomas will find the Island View Guest House a refreshing alternative to overpriced tourist traps. Perched way up in the hills with a breathtaking view, it's still within minutes of town and the airport. Rooms are comfortable and relatively inexpensive, and there's a pool and laundry facilities for guests. They've added a very good restaurant, The View, overlooking the harbor and serving continental and Caribbean food at moderate prices. The restau-

ISLAND VIEW GUEST HOUSE

The best little guest house in St. Thomas for before or after your charter. Casual atmosphere, spectacular harbor view. 5 min. to town/airport. Free continental breakfast, cable TV on premises, coin-operated washer/dryer. For brochure write ISLAND VIEW, P.O. Box 1903, St. Thomas, USVI 00803 or call locally (809) 774-4270. For info and reservations only call 1-800-524-2023. Fax (809) 774-6167.

Now featuring The View Restaurant for your dining pleasure.

Magen's Bay. (Fields photo)

rant is open for dinner only and reservations are required.

There are plenty of beaches on St. Thomas. On the north coast, Magens Bay has been called one of the most beautiful beaches in the world. When we visited, it was picturesque with its backdrop of sea grapes and coconut palms, with well-oiled honeymooners spread all over the sand, smelling and looking like macaroons baking in the oven. Many of the resorts around the island have pretty beaches, some more crowded than others. The more secluded beaches usually take a jeep and some hiking to find. On the western end of the island, Sandy Bay and Botany Bay, accessible by dirt path, are uncrowded but somewhat rocky. Fortuna Bay has some good snorkeling. Hull Bay is a good surfing spot and also one of the places where fishermen from Frenchtown throw their nets. The beaches at Bordeaux Bay and Stumpy Bay are often empty, and the snorkeling is good if the sea isn't too rough.

West of Charlotte Amalie, at the College of the Virgin Islands, is the Reichhold Center for the Arts, an amphitheater set into a natural valley. A schedule of events and ticket information is available from the college office.

Hassel Island

Hassel Island was a peninsula of St. Thomas until Haulover Cut was dredged in 1865 to expedite ship passage. Much of the island is part of the Virgin Islands National Park, with a small ranger office at the former Royal Mail Inn and an undeveloped trail system and some visitor facilities. Old sea coast fortifications on Cowell Point date back to the early 1800s, when the British briefly held St. Thomas. In World War II the U.S. Navy had a station here. A path leads to the island's highest point and an old signal station, where signals were flown to alert the merchants of Charlotte Amalie to approaching steamers and sailing ships. Hidden in the bush at the north end of Hassel Island are the dangerous ruins of a complex where, in the early 1800s, there were two marine railways,

Hassel Island. (Fields photo)

three coaling docks, and a floating dry-dock for steamers exchanging cargo and taking on fuel. On the western shore there are some pretty beaches.

For the Skipper

There is a small, very crowded harbor in Careening Cove on the eastern side. In passing from Haulover Cut into East Gregerie Channel, keep the flashing green buoy located north of Banana Point to starboard. It's a port buoy on returning.

West Gregerie Channel/Water Island

For the Skipper

Caution: Be sure to pass through the dead center of Haulover Cut. There are rocks on either side.

Emerging from Haulover Cut, go west toward Sub Base, passing Crown Bay to starboard. Keeping north of red flasher no. 6 marking Sandy Point Rock, come around to the west of it, keeping the buoy to port. Avoid Krum Bay, where a cable that crosses the bay from a power plant has fouled a few masts. Lindbergh Bay, further west by the airport, is not recommended as an anchorage. On charts it appears well-protected, but it isn't.

Anchorages

Honeymoon Bay. On the western side of Water Island, Honeymoon Bay (called Druif Bay on N.O.S. Chart 25649) provides a good but frequently crowded anchorage, with a clean, pretty beach. Entrance is straightforward, with the preferred anchorage 100 feet off the beach in 15-20 feet of water.

Flamingo Bay. Don't anchor here overnight. This can be a surgy anchorage.

Lagoon entrance (looking out south). (Tropic Isle photo)

Jersey Bay/Benner Bay

Benner Bay, also known locally as The Lagoon, is the best hurricane hole on St. Thomas.

For the Skipper

Caution: False Entrance. As you approach Jersey Bay from the west, do not enter between Patricia Cay and Cas Cay, where there appears to be clear entrance. A dangerous reef runs the whole way across, making crossing impossible. This area is locally known as False Entrance.

JERSEY BAY

SHALLOW — SAND CAY — SHALLOW — ROTTO CAY

PRIVATELY MAINTAINED MARKERS LEADING IN.

ENTRANCE TO JERSEY BAY N W ½ MILE.

Do not enter Jersey Bay until you can pass the green can buoy, east of Cas Cay, to port. To enter Benner Bay, proceed northwest until you pass Rotto Cay to starboard. From there the channel, reportedly shoaled to 6.5 feet at low water with a width of approximately 50 feet, is marked with red and green buoys. Approaching the channel, don't allow yourself to stray to the west of it, or you'll be aground. Rotto Cay has a small cliff on its south side, and is a landmark of sorts, with Grassy Cay and the land west of the channel being mangrove.

Anchorages and Facilities

Compass Point Marina, on the lagoon's south shore, has 83 slips with marine services available. It's one of the few marinas on the island that encourages live-aboards. The marina is headquarters for

If a hammock
could float

... It would feel like a Neptune cruise in the Virgin Islands

Charter a Grand Banks motor yacht from the newest power boat company in the Virgin Islands.

An extraordinary way to leave the ordinary behind

Neptune CHARTERS

U.S. call toll-free **1-800-637-6402**

Compass Point Marina, St. Thomas U.S. Virgin Islands

SOUTHEASTERN ST. THOMAS

U.S. VIRGIN ISLANDS

AND ADJACENT ISLANDS

SOUNDINGS IN FEET AT LOW WATER

NAUTICAL MILES
(TROPIC ISLE SKETCH CHART VI-5)
EDITION 105

CAUTION: NOT FOR NAVIGATION
Tropic Isle Sketch Charts are supplements to the text of the current Yachtsman's Guide to the Virgin Islands. They are illustrative and not necessarily to scale.

MAGNETIC NORTH

FERRY TO CRUZ BAY

TO ST. JOHN (CRUZ BAY)

PILLSBURY SOUND

ST. JAMES ISLAND

WELK ROCKS

LITTLE ST. JAMES I.

DOG I.

DOG ISLAND CUT

ST. JAMES CUT

CHRISTMAS COVE

ST. JAMES BAY

CABRITA POINT

REDHOOK POINT

SAPPHIRE BEACH RESORT MARINA

REDHOOK BAY

JUMPING BK

GREAT BAY

WATER PT

COWPET BAY

MULLER B.

VESSUP BAY

ST. THOMAS YACHT CLUB

COWPET HEAD

CALF ROCK

THE STRAGGLERS

ST. JAMES I.

ST. JOHN

CRUZ BAY

DEEPEST WATER

COW ROCK

CURRENT ROCK

NAZARETH B.

COCULUS RKS

JERSEY BAY

RED POINT

GREEN CAN

FL R 6 SEC. 20 FT.

GREAT THATCH

AMERICAN YACHT HARBOR

COMPASS POINT

CARIBBEAN YACHT CHARTERS

SECOND WIND CHARTERS

BOATYARD

LA VIDA MARINA

BENNER BAY

SAND CAY

ROTTO CAY

CAS CAY

JERSEY BAY

CURRENT CUT N.E. ¼ MILE.

SHAL. 8 FT CHNL.

JOST VAN DYKE

WATER POINT

BOVONI CAY

TROPICAL MARINE

PRIVATELY MAINTAINED MARKERS LEADING IN

MANGROVE LAGOON

PATRICIA CAY

REEF

LONG POINT

STALLY BAY

TO ST. THOMAS HARBOR

What a Luxury Bareboat Should Be

Frers 51

Sparkman & Stephens 47

Frers 44

Elegant and sleek. Performance, with an accent on luxury only designer yachts could offer before.

Since 1968, providing the discriminating yachtsman with an unparalleled choice of yachts in the Virgin Islands has been an obsession for CYC.

Our fleet consists of contemporary designs which distinguish themselves in all areas: comfort, handling, speed, and reliability. Seventy percent of our business comes by way of referrals and repeats; that's strong testimony.

Fly direct to St. Thomas in the U.S. Virgin Islands, and sailaway the same day on the newest charter boats that will dazzle you.

Inquire about our purchase lease-back investment.

CYC

Caribbean Yacht Charters

P.O. Box 583, Marblehead, MA 01945
Call Toll Free
1-800-225-2520
Fax (617) 639-0216

Compass Point Marina. (Tropic Isle photo)

Caribbean Yacht Charters of Marblehead, Massachusetts, a company always adding exclusively designed sailing yachts to its well-maintained fleet. Nearby is Neptune Charters' fleet of fine Grand Banks motor yachts. Also part of the Compass Point complex are JE Marine Services for outboard sales and repairs, St. Thomas Yacht Sales/Charters, a liquor store, a dive shop, and gift and clothing boutiques.

Tropical Marine, Inc. has water, ice, mechanical services, gas, diesel, dockage for boats up to 40 feet, and the largest dry-stack operation in the Virgin Islands (even bigger now, with a new unit on the west side of the yard). They offer sales and service for Evinrude, Mariner, and Mercruiser motors. Nearby, Ruan's Marine Service, Inc., is the area's exclusive distributor for Mariner and Mercruiser.

La Vida Marina, on the north side of the lagoon, is a full-service

St. Thomas Yacht Sales/Charters
José Garcia Valdivia • Marge Garcia Valdivia
—— BROKER ——   —— BROKER ——

TELEPHONE/FAX (809) 774-3215
TELEPHONE 1-800- 433-2654

MEMBER
BUC
YACHT SALES
NETWORK®

The FAST, convenient way to BUY or SELL your boat!
Se Habla Español
Compass Point Marina
41-6-1 Estate Frydenhoj B-7
St. Thomas, U.S.V.I. 00802

marina offering all petroleum products, ice, beverages, snacks, film, marine supplies, dry storage, and mechanical services. It is also home of First Class Charters.

Independent Boat Yard, Inc. and La Vida Marine Center, on Benner Bay, has 80 slips, a full-service boatyard, a 30-ton travel lift, and a 15-ton crane. They can handle up to 80 boats, with storage space available. Repair facilities include mechanics, a shipwright, rigging, fiberglass, propeller repair, and Awlgrip refinishing. They also do boat lettering and electronics sales and repairs. An Island Marine Store is on the premises (ice is available). The gathering spot hereabouts is Bottoms Up for food and drink from 7 a.m. to 7 p.m.

East End Boat Park, next to Independent Boat Yard, includes a number of businesses dedicated to the marine scene. They have facilities to haul up to 25-foot power boats.

Fish Hawk Marina is headquarters for a fishing charter operation specializing in blue marlin. Diesel fuel, ice, bait, and tackle are available.

Saga Haven maintains about 20 slips for long-term boat storage with 24-hour security. Live-aboards are not permitted. Fuel, electricity, water, ice, supplies, and a covered, locked parking garage are available. Saga Haven is also headquarters for Virgin Island Power Yacht Charters. On the premises are a number of restaurants, shops, and a grocery. Tied at the end of the dock is a riverboat piano-bar called Puzzles, featuring great appetizers, well-made drinks, and every kind of beer imaginable.

What to Do

In the Compass Point/Benner Bay area are several recommended restaurants, including For the Birds, a popular Tex-Mex spot with potent Margaritas. We also like the Windjammer's hearty German menu and comfortably worn, well-upholstered chairs. Raffles has continental-type food and a piano bar. Dottie's Front Porch is a homemade-

Local critter. (Tropic Isle photo)

supper kind of place. Dottie, a nice lady, also fed us some of her excellent pastry — try it.

Since the vicinity is so thick with marine facilities, there are lots of little spots serving drinks and light meals, handy while you're taking care of business on a hot day or for winding down as the day wanes. Fabian's Landing and Bottoms Up (already mentioned) are two such places.

RUAN'S MARINE
SERVICE INC.
EXCLUSIVE DISTRIBUTORS FOR:

MARINER OUTBOARDS
A BRUNSWICK COMPANY
EXCLUSIVE DISTRIBUTOR FOR BRITISH & U.S. VIRGIN ISLANDS

merCruiser
STERN DRIVES/INBOARDS
PARTS & SERVICE
DOCKING SLIPS
DEALERS FOR MAKO & FORMULA
775-6346 • FAX (809)775-2225
Benner Bay • 43 Frydenhoj, St. Thomas

25/20   9.9   Tropical Marine, Inc.
DEALERS FOR:
BERTRAM YACHT • BOSTON WHALERS
EVINRUDE MOTORS SALES & SERVICE
• FULL STOCK OF PARTS & ACCESSORIES
• LARGEST DRY STORAGE IN THE VIRGIN ISLANDS
• GAS, COLD DRINKS, ICE
• MECHANICAL SERVICES
• DOCKAGE
BENNER BAY • TELEPHONE 775-6595
ESTATE NADIR #27, ST. THOMAS, USVI 00801

St. James Island/Christmas Cove

For the Skipper
You'll see Fish Cay in the middle of Christmas Cove as you approach.

Anchorages and Facilities
Anchor on the north or south side of Fish Cay in 15 feet of water, sufficiently close to the shore that the wind will be steadier. North of Fish Cay, be sure to anchor far enough east toward Great St. James Island to be out of the current that sluices through Current Cut. It's too shallow and reefy to pass between Fish Cay and the island. Both anchorages offer good holding ground and sandy bottoms.

Look out for the sea urchins that surround Fish Cay on the east and north sides. The beach is gravel, but there's good snorkeling on the inside of the south end of the cay. When the weather is calm, you can explore the waters surrounding Little St. James and Dog Island and Rocks in a dinghy. Dog Rocks don't always break, so keep careful watch. Snorkeling is good here but be aware of the currents.

A few minutes' dinghy ride will take you into David's, a good, small, moderately priced restaurant on the beach next to the Yacht Club in Cowpet Bay. It's open for breakfast from 8 a.m., lunch, and dinner.

Cowpet Bay/St. Thomas Yacht Club

Across from Christmas Cove is Cowpet Bay, site of the St. Thomas Yacht Club. Members of accredited yacht clubs are welcome, and might want to add their burgees to the impressive collection in the Club's bar. You can use the telephones and docks in an emergency. Don't use the private moorings set out in the bay. The S.T.Y.C. is the home of the Rolex Regatta, held annually on Easter weekend.

Current Cut

Between St. Thomas and Great St. James Island is Current Cut, the passage generally taken to St. John and the rest of the islands. It's best to pass on the eastern side of the light on Current Rock, taking care to avoid the rocks to its south. The western side will carry 8 feet, but it is narrow and rocky. You should motor through the cut particularly if going to windward, as your wind can be blocked by Great St. James Island. There is a current of up to 4 knots running either direction, heaviest to the southwest, depending on the tide.

Red Hook Bay. (Tropic Isle photo)

Red Hook/Sapphire Bay

For the Skipper

When entering Red Hook Bay, favor the north side of the bay where the water is deeper. The marks for the entrance channel have now been replaced. These are privately maintained, and they are red and black nuns (yes black, and yes nuns). Watch out for ferry traffic here.

Anchorages and Facilities

Muller Bay offers some protection from the frequent wind chop in the channel. Here you can also avoid the ferry traffic and the crowded private moorings further up in the harbor.

American Yacht Harbor is undergoing extensive renovation, with shops and all kinds of things in the works (the first new building is open and operating at our deadline). There are over 100 slips with

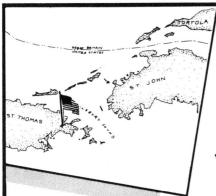

CHART YOUR COURSE TO THE NEW AMERICAN YACHT HARBOR

We welcome you to visit our newly renovated marina offering state-of-the-art docking facilities and an excellent location at the "Gateway to the Caribbean" in Red Hook, St. Thomas.

FOR SAILING OR POWER VESSELS WE OFFER:

- 102 slips
- water, diesel and premium gas
- drafts up to 10 ft.
- electricity (110, 208 & 220)
- in-slip fueling
- central boardwalk
- beam widths up to 22 ft.

WE WILL ALSO BE OFFERING UPON COMPLETION:

- cable tv
- metered (110, 208 & 220)
- phone

AND...FOR YOUR CONVENIENCE:

On Premises...

- restaurants
- marine services
- video shops
- bars
- taxi
- dive shop
- deli
- beauty salon
- boat rentals

Within 100 Yards...

- supermarkets
- shopping
- doctors offices
- veterinarian
- mail services
- notary
- laundry
- travel agent

AMERICAN YACHT HARBOR
RED HOOK, ST. THOMAS

OPEN EVERY DAY, MONITORING CH.16
(809) 775-6454   FAX (809) 776-5970

American Yacht Harbor. (Tropic Isle photo)

controlling depth of 7 feet, all petroleum products, electricity, beverages, water, and ice. Most yachting support services are available on the property. In-slip fueling is available on A, B and C docks. Past the last docks, the bay shoals rapidly, so don't venture too far in. American Yacht Harbor is headquarters for Island Yachts and Ocean Incentives Yacht Charters.

The St. Thomas Sport Fishing Center, next to the ferry dock, has dockage available for 25 boats, electricity, ice, and water. The Piccola Marina bar/restaurant here is one of our favorites for its dockside deck and interesting menu and homemade pasta..

Vessup Point Marina, sister to St. Thomas Sport Fishing Center, is located across the harbor from the Red Hook public ferry dock. If offers relative serenity, deep-draft/wide-beam slips, full service, and plenty of off-street parking. Latitude 18 bareboat charter company is headquartered here.

Sapphire Beach Resort Marina is on the north side of Red Hook Point, southwest of Shark Island. The approach from Red Hook is straightforward. Just stay far enough offshore for the necessary sea room and you'll come to the small marks off the entrance to the marina, where 67 slips are available with fuel, fresh water, electricity, cable TV and telephone hookups (laundry service is available, but not on site). Check ahead for space availability. Also, subject to a spot being open, visitors can tie up for a short visit. There is a $10 charge for this. Marina guests may use the resort's pool, tennis facilities, restaurant and bar, and beach. The marina monitors VHF 16.

Red Hook is St. Thomas' boom town for boating and sportfishing activity, with many marine services available and an ambitious community of entrepreneurs. Red Hook Plaza includes a grocery and pharmacy, ice, an ice-cream shop, and Oceans Tropical Clothing Co. In the parking lot, The Three Virgins Restaurant opens early for breakfast and also serves lunch.

What to Do

Red Hook is a good spot from which to venture ashore, rent a car for the day, and explore St. Thomas. There are some nice resort beaches north and west of Red Hook, none of them a good anchorage but all easily accessible by car. On the north side of Coki Point, Coral World's undersea observatory allows you to study life on a coral reef 15 feet below the surface without getting wet. There's also a reef tank that brings you nose-to-nose with sharks, sting rays, and moray eels. There are no yachting facilities, but there is a bar and restaurant and a small beach.

If you're chartering out of the Compass Point/Red Hook area and you or members of your crew would like to spend sometime ashore before or after your cruise, there are nearby accommodations ranging from super-deluxe resort hotels to more frugal but quite adequate guest houses. There are also lots of great places to eat. Besides the Piccola Marina and the Three Virgins in Red Hook, you can eat at The Frigate, a menu-on-the-bottle type of steak house, or The East Coast Bar & Grill ("where pleasure knows no time"), a local favorite with excellent seafood, an energetic staff, and late hours. All the local bartenders show up here after last call. Horsefeathers (burned down in its old location but relocated next to the East Coast Bar Grill) is still good for pizza, subs, or a snack and a

Coral World. (Tropic Isle photo)

cold beer. Eunice's Terrace serves plateloads of genuine mouth-watering Caribbean cooking. For international gourmet cuisine in an open-air, beachside setting, we recommend dinner at the Eden Restaurant at Secret Harbor. During the day A Bit of Eden here is a good place for breakfast or lunch.

North Saint Thomas

Caution: Most boats don't venture into the waters north of St. Thomas because there are few harbors and most anchorages are untenable with the surge from the north. Information given here is only for experienced skippers who know the dangers. In any case, these waters are not recommended cruising grounds.

Rounding Picara Point will bring you into **Magens Bay,** where there is usually an uncomfortable surge, especially in winter. Beware of Ornen Rock, six feet below the surface, which lies about one-half mile northwest of Picara Point. Going into Magens Bay, watch out for the shoal at the head of the bay. Anchor in the northeast corner in about 30 feet of water.

On **Hans Lollick Island,** to the north and east of Magens Bay, there is a nice beach protected by a barrier reef on its southeast side. Behind the beach and over the ridge are the ruins of an old plantation. Entrance behind the reef can be made by approaching from the south, keeping Hans Lollick Rock to starboard. Be sure the sun is high and behind you so that the reef can be seen clearly. Inside there is 10-12 feet of water over a sandy bottom. Reefs surround Little Hans Lollick Island to the north and the passage between the islands should only be made in shallow-draft vessels in good light. Skin diving is excellent but for experienced divers only.

Off the north shore of St. Thomas is **Inner Brass Island.** There is an anchorage at Sandy Bay on the southeast of Inner Brass. There can be a strong surge when the northerlies are running. There is good water between Inner and Outer Brass Island. Passage should be midway between the two. Passage between Inner Brass Island and St. Thomas should be made favoring the Inner Brass side of the channel. The only hazard in the area is Lizard Rocks to the west of Inner Brass, which are usually clearly seen and steep to.

To the west, farther along St. Thomas's north shore, is **Santa Maria Bay** and at the far end, **Botany Bay,** good only as lunch stops because of the ever-present surge from the north.

The passage between **West Cay** and the western end of St. Thomas should be made with the centerboard up and motoring only. There is a heavy current and the passage is narrow and shallow.

CHART KIT BBA NEWS

Video cruise guide gives real experience of Virgin Islands before you even get there

Now you can visit 46 different harbors and anchorages in the U.S. and British Virgin Islands ... and plan the perfect dream cruise.

■ **"How-to" action video** lets you experience an actual cruise in these tempting waters. Learn the navigational features, the island and reef contours. Read water colors for different depths and see the best anchoring techniques. By watching aerial views, views from the helm, animated course lines with key bearings and superimposed nautical charts, you will experience sailing in the Virgin Islands and be able to enjoy their pleasures to the fullest.

■ **Information-packed Skipper's Handbook.** The VIRGIN ISLANDS VIDEO CRUISE GUIDE comes with a 96-page take-along handbook that illustrates and details with aerial photos and chart inserts the special features to be found at each of the harbors and anchorages visited.

054. Virgin Islands Video Cruise Guide. 45-min. video with 96pp spiral-bound Skipper's Handbook. $79.95 (Add $3.00 for shipping/handling.

CHART KIT BBA — *The Virgin Islands*

Complete full-color navigation charts of U.S. and British Virgin Islands have aerial photos

Perfect companion to the Virgin Islands Video Cruise Guide, THE VIRGIN ISLANDS CHART KIT contains a complete set of full-color reproductions of original government harbor, coastal and offshore charts with updates. There are also more than 50 magnificent color aerial photos of harbors and anchorages.

010. The Virgin Islands Chart Kit, Region 10 (2nd Edition). Complete nautical charts for the U.S. and British Virgin Islands with 51 color aerial photos. $44.95 (Add $3.00 for shipping/handling).

TO ORDER
••••••••••••••••
Visa, MasterCard, or American Express cardholders:
Call toll free 1-800-CHART KIT (1-800-242-7854)
in MA (617) 449-3314
Mon-Fri, 9am-5pm, Eastern time
••••••••••••••••
Or send check or money order (no cash, please) to:
Better Boating Assoc., Inc., Box 407, Needham, MA 02192
*Connecticut, Massachusetts and Rhode Island residents
add your state sales tax on product cost only.*

FREE Chart Kit Catalog
•••••••••••••••••••••
Call toll free 1-800-CHART KIT (1-800-242-7854)
in Massachusetts (617) 449-3314
Mon-Fri, 9am-5pm, Eastern time
•••••••••••••••••••••
CHART KITS—United States, Bahamas & Virgin Islands
VIDEOS—Bahamas & Virgin Islands Cruise Guides
Piloting & Coastal Navigation
Knots & Line Handling
NAVIGATION INSTRUMENTS AND ACCESSORIES

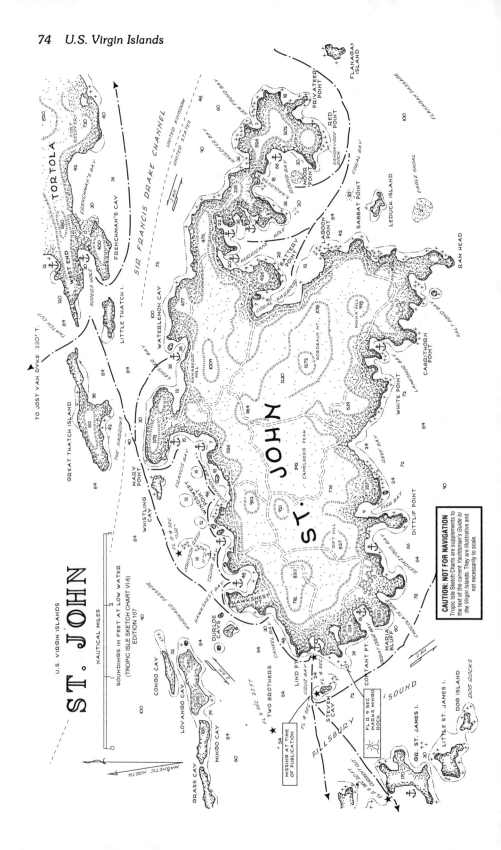

ST. JOHN

U.S. VIRGIN ISLANDS

NAUTICAL MILES

SOUNDINGS IN FEET AT LOW WATER
(TROPIC ISLE SKETCH CHART VI-6)
EDITION 107

CAUTION: NOT FOR NAVIGATION
Tropic Isle Sketch Charts are supplements to
the text of the current Yachtsman's Guide to
the Virgin Islands. They are illustrative and
not necessarily to scale.

ST. JOHN

Charts: 25641, 25647. Tropic Isle Sketch Charts VI-1, 6, 7, 20.

Nine miles long and 5 miles wide, St. John (named by Spanish explorers for St. John the Apostle) is the most densely wooded of the Virgins. In 1954 Laurance Rockefeller bought 5,000 acres of the island to donate to the U.S. Park System, and since then the park has grown to 9,500 acres, about two-thirds of the total area. There are more than 20 beautiful crescent beaches, at least as many hilltop vistas, marked hiking trails, and some of the world's loveliest campsites. The series of bays that circle St. John are among the most spectacular of the Virgins and shouldn't be missed by the cruising yachtsman. Protected by the National Park Service, they remain uncluttered and clean, with a marked snorkeling trail in Trunk Bay and places to explore onshore throughout the park. Wherever you see NPS garbage receptacles, you are welcome to use them — never leave garbage on the beach! Water-skiing, spearfishing, jet-skiing, and disturbing the coral are forbidden within the confines of the park (and not recommended any other place, either).

Hundreds of years ago the hills of St. John were covered with streams, which dried up when the hillsides were deforested by sugar planters. By the late 1700s, almost the entire island was blanketed by sugar cane fields, a sight difficult to imagine today. Throughout the hills are many ruins of sugar factories and manor houses where a discerning observer can spot foundations of grand estates and perhaps the remains of cobblestone driveways lined by tall trees.

Trunk Cay, off Trunk Bay.

In 1717 about 40 people arrived in Coral Bay from St. Thomas to begin settling the island. Although St. John was under the Danish flag, the first settlers were primarily Dutch, joined by smaller numbers of French Huguenots and Danes. Slaves and a few soldiers completed the group, which persevered despite England's attempts to prevent Danish occupation of St. John, too close for comfort to British-occupied Tortola. By 1723, Fredericksvaern (now called Fort Berg) was built on the hill overlooking Coral Bay and, within ten years, over 100 plantations were under cultivation.

In 1733, a census showed 208 whites and 1,987 blacks on St. John. That year, storms, drought, and grasshopper invasions had left the island short of food, and slaves suffered this the most. A number of the most recently arrived slaves claimed royal descent from notably strong-willed African tribes, for whom planting was considered woman's work and an offense to manhood. Many ran away and hid in the wooded areas around Ram's Head and Mamey Peak. Little attempt could be made to recapture them, with no unit organized on St. John to hunt for escaped slaves and only seven soldiers posted at Fort Berg. In an effort to prevent further escapes, the governor in Charlotte Amalie announced particularly harsh punishments, including severing of limbs and "pinching" with red-hot irons.

A rebellion was masterminded by a core of runaways, with plans to kill the governor during his November visit to St. John. When the time came, the governor was called back to St. Thomas earlier than the slaves expected, but they proceeded with the rebellion anyhow, fueled by frustration and anger. Before sunrise on November 13, a group of rebels smuggled cutlasses concealed in firewood into Fort Berg, took the guards by surprise and massacred all except one who hid under a bed and escaped. Then they fired the cannon three times, alerting slaves throughout the island to kill their masters. Not all the slaves complied but, within hours, many white families were murdered. Some of the planters took refuge on Peter Duerloo's plantation, above Caneel Bay, where slaves had been relatively well treated and feared the consequences of joining the uprising. Unrelenting siege by the rebel slaves finally forced the remaining whites to flee to St. Thomas.

The slaves held the island of St. John for six months, fighting off British and Danish forces. French soldiers specially trained in jungle warfare were called in, and they finally succeeded in rounding up some of the rebels. Those who remained killed themselves rather than submit to capture. Some gathered in circles and passed around a gun, shooting each other in turn until the last man shot himself. Others threw themselves off a cliff at Mary Point, near the estate Anna Berg.

Within 40 years of the rebellion, St. John had recovered.

Annaberg ruins. (Tropic Isle photo)

Enormous amounts of money were spent on the construction and furnishing of manor houses high on the hills with views of the bays. However, after emancipation and the failure of the sugar trade, the island's economy plunged.

By 1880 less than 100 people were living on the island and almost all the plantation houses were falling apart while former slaves continued to maintain the old slave quarters and factories for habitation. For almost 100 years, they eked out livings raising cattle or making charcoal or bay rum.

When the United States bought St. John in 1917, it was speculated that Coral Harbor would be the Navy's harbor. However, any plans to this end were scrapped when it was decided that proximity to Tortola made the harbor a defense liability in the event of hostile foreign occupation of the BVIs. Subsequently, not much happened on the island until the mid-1950s, when Laurance Rockefeller developed Caneel Bay into a luxury resort and the National Park areas were established.

Today self-sufficiency and retreat back to nature characterize St. John. The two towns, Cruz Bay and Coral Harbor, are frontiers of the independent spirit, and many who live here will tell you how they left lucrative careers in the States to follow more spiritual pursuits, or in some cases just to pursue more spirits. Aspiring artists, craftsmen, writers, and entrepreneurs easily mingle with those who've come in quest of the mango daiquiri and the total tan.

Rustling in the underbrush or nosing around trash bins, the mongoose is dubiously regarded as St. John's unofficial mascot. Brought to the island in the 1800s to kill rats, these agile little mammals multiplied like crazy and foraged during the day while the island rats were securely asleep in their hidey-holes. So instead of solving the rat problem, the arrival of mongooses only added to the general pest population. They also eat the eggs of some endangered species and have become something of an environmental menace. You can't get rid of mongooses without endangering other species, but one inventive environmentalist suggested a solution: perhaps the rumor could be spread in Cruz Bay that mongoose fur is hallucinogenic when smoked.

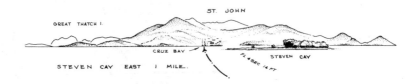

Approaches to St. John

In the passage to St. John, pass on either side of Two Brothers Rocks, which are steep-to and always out of the water. Stay north of Steven Cay, keeping it to starboard. Do not pass through the unmarked channel between Steven Cay and St. John, as it is bordered by coral heads.

On the way over you can anchor south of Thatch Cay, Grass Cay, Mingo Cay, Lovango and Congo Cays to swim. We don't recommend going between the cays, except for Middle Passage between Thatch and Grass Cays.

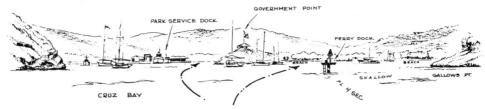

Cruz Bay

Cruz Bay, considerably smaller than Coral Harbor, is the busier harbor on the island only because of its proximity to St. Thomas.

For the Skipper

On your entry, stay well north of the fixed light marking the reef that extends north and west of Gallows Point. This light stands in only one foot of water. Keep the black buoy south of Lind Point to port. Once inside the harbor, you'll see a marked channel leading north of Battery Point to the park service dock to port and the customs office to starboard.

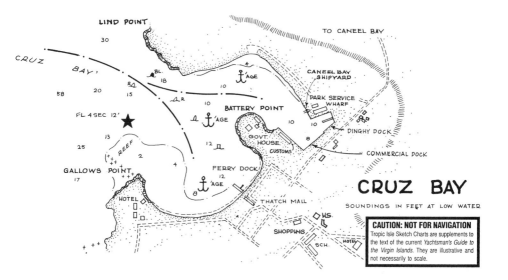

CRUZ BAY

SOUNDINGS IN FEET AT LOW WATER

CAUTION: NOT FOR NAVIGATION
Tropic Isle Sketch Charts are supplements to the text of the current *Yachtsman's Guide to the Virgin Islands.* They are illustrative and not necessarily to scale.

Anchorages and Facilities

Ferry channels preempt much of Cruz Bay's harbor, and most of what remains is occupied by resident and long-term boats. Visitors will discover that finding space to anchor can be difficult. An alternative is to anchor in relatively uncrowded Caneel Bay, within dinghy distance of Cruz Bay. Another reportedly good day anchorage to use while shopping or going through customs is outside the harbor in 15 feet over sand off Lind Point.

Customs and immigration. You'll find the customs and immigration office on the north side of Battery Point. Frequent ferry traffic at the Port Authority dock (in front of the customs building) sometimes makes it advisable to anchor and come into the dinghy dock on the north side of the ferry dock south of Battery Point. If you tie your vessel up to the Port Authority dock, you will be assessed a docking fee of 27 cents per foot, plus a fee of 85 cents per passenger for boats entering from a foreign country and $1.70 per passenger for boats leaving for a foreign country. This fee is collected by Port Authority officials and is not customs-related.

Customs office, Cruz Bay. (Tropic Isle photo)

Notice to Yachtsmen Regarding Disposal of Garbage

St. John residents would like to remind boaters to bag and tie all garbage securely before disposing of it inside designated containers. This is to discourage donkeys, goats, and other animals from rummaging. Cruz Bay has signs posted for container locations, and Coral Bay has a dumpster on the right of way straight off the dock. Throughout the National Park there are park-maintained garbage receptacles that yachtsmen are encouraged to use.

It makes sense, of course, to securely bag and tie all garbage not only on St. John but throughout the islands.

Harbor anchorages. If you anchor off the ferry dock, be sure you stay out of the ferry channel. Anchoring in the channel will result in a visit from the harbormaster, and the ferry skippers have ways of making you feel unwelcome. Be aware that ferries often come in at high speed, causing a roll. Don't tie up at the ferry pier, which is reserved for commercial traffic. There is a dinghy dock at the base of the pier.

Use your lead line if anchoring toward the reef at the entrance to Cruz Bay, as the shoal area extends for a considerable distance toward the dock.

About half the area north and west of Battery Point is inside the Virgin Islands National Park boundary. The boundary runs mid-channel, leaving NPS water to the north. There is usually space to anchor here because of the enforced 14-day anchoring limit that applies to all waters within National Park boundaries. The NPS finger pier has a 15-minute time limit. Don't abuse this limit, as this is the only place in Cruz Bay

Cruz Bay. (Tropic Isle photo)

where noncommercial boats larger than a dinghy can unload. There is a dinghy tie-up area on the bulkhead southeast of the finger pier, with a shoal area in the middle. The rest of the bulkhead is used by freight barges and mini-cruise ships. There are trash bins across the street.

Caneel Bay Shipyard, next to the park service wharf, can supply gasoline, diesel fuel, and water as well as hauling, electrical, refrigeration, fiberglass, and sail repairs. The shipyard is maintained by Proper Yachts, who also run a yacht maintenance service here for those who need boats looked after in their absence. For information, contact the Proper Yachts office upstairs in Mongoose Junction.

Some marine supplies are available at St. John Lumber or St. John Hardware. Grocery and convenience stores and a drop-off laundromat are within walking distance of the docks. Ice is available at St. John's Ice Company or Fred's Cut Rate. At Connections, you can leave messages or have mail forwarded.

What to Do

Cruz Bay is small and informal. You'll see beards, beads, and bare feet reminiscent of the 1960s, and local publications mix astrology, holistic health advice, and poetry with the news. There are lots of pregnant women and bare-bottomed babies, friendly run-down bars, massage therapists, fruit-and-vegetable stands, and four-wheel-drive vehicles, as well as elegant restaurants, vacation villas, and resorts. You can hang around Cruz Bay Park, overlooking the ferry dock, and listen in on local gossip and heated political discussion. Check bulletin boards and trees to find out what's going on while you're there. On weekends there's live music at different spots in town, including rock, reggae,

Caneel Bay Shipyard, Cruz Bay. (Tropic Isle photo)

Cruz Bay shop. (Tropic Isle photo)

calypso, and scratch bands. The first week of July is Carnival Week on St. John, celebrating emancipation of the slaves on July 3, 1848.

On Battery Point, government administrative offices now occupy The Battery, built in 1735 as a fortification after the bloody slave uprising of 1733. There is a small museum where the jail cells used to be. Less than half a mile's walking distance from the dock, a bit out of town, is the Elaine Ione Sprauve Library and Museum. The museum is housed in the restored Enighed Estate manor house, built in the mid-1700s. Indian artifacts from the island's earliest settlements are on display in the museum. Further out of town, the renovated Parish Hall dates back to the 1800s, with old cisterns and Dutch ovens in the adjoining houses. A dirt road leads to the mostly overgrown ruins of Estate Caterinberg, one of the first plantations established on St. John.

Cruz Bay is a great place to shop for unique island crafts, relax for a beer in your oldest T-shirt and beat-up boat shoes, or just wander around absorbing the town's particular brand of funkiness.. Many talented artisans live here who design batik and silkscreened fabric and hangings, clothing, ceramic, and jewelry. (A number of shops have added crystals with "mystical properties" to their retail inventory, apparently to meet new-age demand.) A local licensed massage therapist will make house calls. Among the vacation rentals advertised are one called Villa Joie de Vivre and another called The Lost Chord. There are many shops, restaurants, and bars near the waterfront area and along the short walk through town. A very informative and entertaining St. John Map, designed by local artist/cartoonist/comedienne Linda Smith-Palmer, is available at many of the shops.

Up the road from the docks are Mongoose Junction and Mongoose II, an unusual castle-like complex of studio shops, arcades, restaurants, and open areas with benches. Proper Yacht's headquarters are upstairs over St. John Watersports. They offer for charter 22 sailboats.

South of the ferry dock, the three-story Wharfside Village mall houses more arts-and-crafts shops and boutiques. Upstairs is Pusser's St. John, where the Sports and Oyster Bar is hangout for yachtsmen who need a fix of TV sports, John Courage draft beer, and iced shellfish. You can carry your drink up the stairs to the Pusser's Crows Nest and sit back and survey the harbor scene. Also part of Pusser's St. John is the Terrace Restaurant, overlooking the bay and specializing in steaks, seafood, and West Indian food, and the Late-Night-Club, with music and dancing on the terrace until 2 a.m. Friday and Saturday nights. There's also the largest of branch of The Pusser's Company Store, selling Pusser's line of travel clothing, nautical antiques, and unique accessories and memorabilia.

Good restaurants in town include the Raintree Restaurant for fresh seafood, the Back Yard for its casual, neighborly bar, and Fred's Restaurant, Etta's Place, or Sheila's Pot for inexpensive West Indian food. Cafe Roma serves good Italian food and pizza. The informal Lime Inn is popular for fish, shrimp, and specialty nights. A Lotta Coladas is a bar with Friday night Margarita Madness, a two-for-one deal. You can get Ben & Jerry's ice cream at Luscious Licks & Divine Desserts, inside Paradise Designs.

There are supermarkets, delis, fruit stands, and bakeries for replenishing your provisions or just packing a snack. A laundromat is within walking distance of the dock. A copier and fax machine are available at Connections, on the corner of Routes 10 and 20. You can also make long-distance calls from here.

Before you head up the coast, visit the National Park Service Visitor Center and headquarters for information on the Virgin Islands

National Park Service Visitor Center. (Tropic Isle photo)

Ferry arrival, Cruz Bay. (Tropic Isle photo)

National Park. Inside the small center are exhibits, an orientation video, and a nice collection of nature and wildlife books and maps. Remember that the finger pier at the NPS dock has a 15-minute time limit. The park service sponsors regular programs on island wildlife, culture, and history at Cinnamon Bay and Maho Bay. Park rangers lead seashore walks, and there is a 3-mile Reef Bay hike through a tropical forest down to the south shore cactus woodland, stopping for lunch at the petroglyphs (mysterious rock carvings attributed possibly to early Indian settlers or to slaves). The NPS also offers snorkeling lessons and historic bus tours and hikes. The Annaberg Cultural Demonstrations illustrate subsistence living from the early 1900s, including tropical-plant uses, medicine, charcoal making, and terraced gardening. The park provides a checklist for birdwatchers to encourage the reporting of sightings. In winter, park rangers and volunteers lead bird walks.

When the ferry arrives from St. Thomas, the streets quickly fill with day tourists who pile into tin-roofed jitneys lined with benches seating up to 20 people. Once loaded, each bus lurches out of town and up the steep hills and hairpin curves of the island, halting precariously at vantage points for quick photo opportunities until the next bus roars into line behind it. The destination of this colorful caravan is usually the spectacular beach at Trunk Bay, where passengers are unloaded and picked up. Beyond, the roads are pretty clear.

To explore the island, you can join one of the safari buses or choose a taxi driver from those who gather at the docks. There are several car/ jeep rental companies, but available vehicles are quickly taken, so it's smart to reserve a vehicle ahead of time and get there early. Keep in mind that there are only two gas stations on the island, both in Cruz Bay.

Caneel Bay

For the Skipper

The next stop going east on the north coast of St. John, past some good beaches but poor anchorages, Caneel Bay is part of the Virgin Islands National Park, leased to the Caneel Bay resort. This resort's boundaries extend from Honeymoon Beach to Turtle Bay. Durloe Cays, in the Windward Passage, are part of the National Park.

Anchorages and Facilities

Don't go inside the line of buoys off the bathing beach, and don't anchor in the designated channel. Avoid anchoring in the path of the large cruisers that come in to tie up at the hotel dock. You may not tie up at the dock, but you can bring a dinghy in. Neither supplies nor ice are available here.

What to Do

The grounds of the Caneel Bay resort were once the site of a Danish sugar factory, the remains of which are open to the public. The remainder of the grounds and hotel are private and off-limits to nonregistered guests. You may use Honeymoon Beach and parts of Caneel Beach. The Sugar Mill Restaurant, the Caneel Bay bar, and the gift shop are all open to the public. Shorts and swimsuits are okay for daytime, but at night more formal wear is required. Dinner reservations are required.

Sugar factory ruins, Caneel Bay. (Tropic Isle photo)

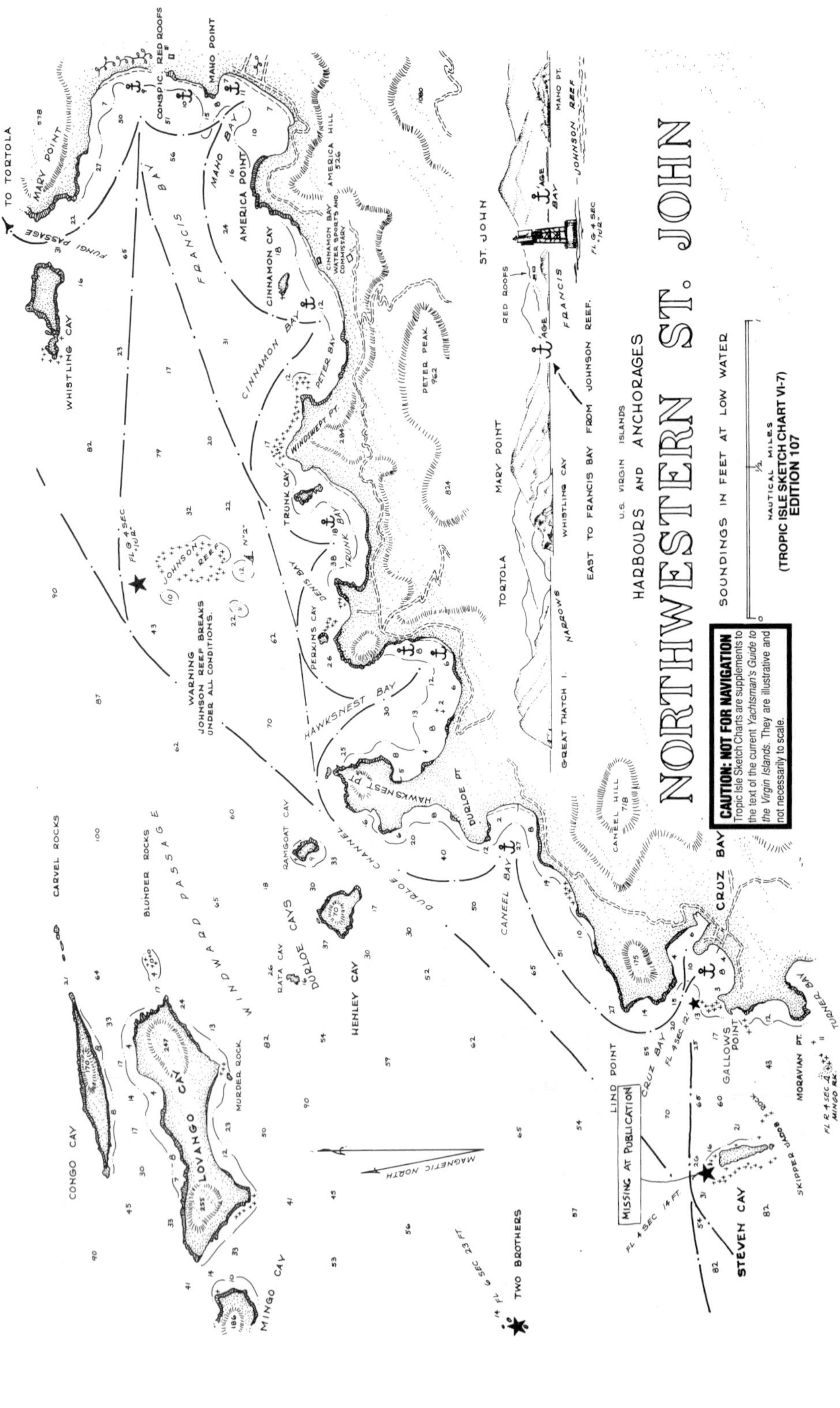

U.S. VIRGIN ISLANDS
HARBOURS AND ANCHORAGES
NORTHWESTERN ST. JOHN
SOUNDINGS IN FEET AT LOW WATER
NAUTICAL MILES
(TROPIC ISLE SKETCH CHART VI-7)
EDITION 107
CAUTION: NOT FOR NAVIGATION
Tropic Isle Sketch Charts are supplements to the text of the current Yachtsman's Guide to the Virgin Islands. They are illustrative and not necessarily to scale.
EAST TO FRANCIS BAY FROM JOHNSON REEF.
ST. JOHN
TORTOLA
MARY POINT
WHISTLING CAY
GREAT THATCH I.
NARROWS
RED ROOFS
FRANCIS
MAHO PT.
JOHNSON REEF
FL G 4 SEC "1U2"
TO TORTOLA
FUNGI PASSAGE
MARY POINT
CONSPIC. RED ROOFS
MAHO POINT
MAHO BAY
AMERICA POINT
AMERICA HILL 526
FRANCIS BAY
CINNAMON CAY
CINNAMON BAY WATER SPORTS AND COMMISSARY
CINNAMON BAY
PETER BAY
PETER PEAK 962
WINDWEPT PT.
TRUNK CAY
TRUNK BAY
DENIS BAY
PERKINS CAY
HAWKSNEST BAY
HAWKSNEST PT
DURLOE PT
CANEEL HILL 718
CANEEL BAY
CRUZ BAY
JOHNSON REEF
WARNING JOHNSON REEF BREAKS UNDER ALL CONDITIONS.
FL G 4 SEC "1U2"
CARVEL ROCKS
BLUNDER ROCKS
WINDWARD PASSAGE
RAMGOAT CAY
DURLOE CAYS
RATA CAY
HENLEY CAY
DURLOE CHANNEL NORTH
CONGO CAY
LOVANGO CAY
MURDER ROCK
MINGO CAY
MAGNETIC NORTH
TWO BROTHERS
FL 6 SEC 23 FT
LIND POINT
MISSING AT PUBLICATION
FL 4 SEC 14 FT.
FL 4 SEC 12'
STEVEN CAY
GALLOWS POINT
SKIPPER JACOB ROCK
MORAVIAN PT.
TURNER BAY
FL R 4 SEC
MINGO RK.

"Christ of the Caribbean" seen from sugar mill ruins. (Tropic Isle photo)

Hawksnest Bay

For the Skipper

The channel between the Durloe Cays and St. John can be choppy from currents created by the wind changing around the headland, so be careful sailing east from Caneel Bay to Hawksnest Bay. It might be wise to motor through.

Anchorages

The beach is closed to boats, as are most north shore beaches. There is anchorage north of the line of buoys marking the swimming and snorkeling area, and NPS moorings are available along the eastern shore. There is an access channel to the beach area, for dinghies only, between the red and the green buoys. Be sure to stay in the designated area. Dinghies approaching west of the marked channel have damaged the reef there. This damages dinghies too.

On the hill inside the northeastern point of Hawksnest Bay, on the old site of the Denis Bay Plantation, is a rough-hewn concrete statue of Christ with outstretched hands (called "Christ of the Caribbean"). It was built in 1953 as a monument to world peace by Colonel Julius Wadsworth. The remains of a sugar mill is nearby. A path leads from the road to the statue, from which point there are some beautiful views.

Trunk Bay/Cinnamon Bay/Maho Bay

For the Skipper

Cautions

1. Johnson Reef is a very hazardous area about one-half mile directly north of Trunk Bay. Although it is well marked, it continues to take its toll of boats each year. A lighted green buoy marks the north end of the reef. When in its vicinity, stay well north of a line drawn east and west from the buoy. You cannot always see water breaking over the main body of the reef. On its eastern side the reef is steep-to, but on the western side it shoals gradually to 6 inches. The south side of the reef is clearly marked by an unlighted red nun with a reflective strip around it. Give the reef a wide berth on all sides.

2. An additional hazard to avoid is Windswept Point, between Trunk Bay and Cinnamon Bay. The reef that projects north of the point claims several boats a year, which run aground and are quickly driven higher by swells. At the time of our survey, it was marked with reef buoys, similar to those that mark swim areas in the park.

Approaching or leaving Trunk Bay, stay well south of Johnson Reef. You should enter or leave Windward Passage on a line drawn from the end of Lovango Cay to Trunk Cay.

If proceeding from Trunk Bay to the east, stay about 200 yards off the north shore of St. John. This passage can be impossible in the winter when northern swells break on Johnson Reef and are carried almost to the shore of St. John. If this is the case, come back west of the

Trunk Bay. (Tropic Isle photo)

Cinnamon Bay beach. (Tropic Isle photo)

reef and pass north of it, taking care again to give it a wide berth.

Anchorages

Trunk Bay, named for the "trunkback" or leatherback turtle, has what is considered one of the most beautiful beaches in the world. For this reason it's popular and often crowded. At times cruise ship passengers on organized tours swell the crowds to well over a thousand visitors.

The anchorage is not recommended for overnight, and there is often a bad swell, especially in winter months. Because of the strong surf, we advise you not to try landing your dinghy. If conditions are unusually calm, you can dinghy in through the channel marked with red and green buoys at the west end of the beach. You may not land dinghies ashore north of the northeast buoy, an area reserved for the swimming beach where the underwater snorkeling trail begins.

The marked underwater snorkeling trail begins in the lee of Trunk Cay. Since this is a preserve within the Virgin Islands National Park, fishing, SCUBA, or dive knives (and, of course, spearfishing gear) are forbidden. Ashore there are picnic grounds, a gift and snorkel-rental shop, and showers and restrooms that close at 4 p.m. Usually there is a lifeguard on duty. Next to the changing facilities is a snack bar selling beer, refreshments, and sandwiches. Fishing is prohibited.

Cinnamon Bay is not an overnight anchorage, and if a northerly swell is running it will be uncomfortable at any time. Cinnamon Cay is part of the park. The land around Peter Bay, on the west side of Cinnamon Bay, is privately owned.

At Cinnamon Bay Campgrounds, cottages, set tents, and tent

sites can be rented, but reservations are required well in advance. A commissary stocked with essential groceries, frozen meats, and ice is open daily and a cafeteria serves breakfast, lunch, and dinner. Concessions rent snorkeling gear, conduct dive trips around the island, and rent windsurfers. At times, park service rangers lead snorkeling excursions in Cinnamon Bay. A self-guided nature trail leads through the site of what was once a sugar factory, and another trail leads up an old plantation road through the woods to Centerline Highway. Along the path are the ruins of a 19th-century estate house and an old Danish cemetery. You might also see a round, flat, raised area, the remains of a horse mill.

Maho Bay is generally quiet and a good day anchorage. Anchor outside the buoy line and bring only your dinghy in through the marked approach, being careful to avoid swimmers and snorkelers. Maho Bay Camps, on Maho Point, is a private ecologically-designed campground.

Although the majority of beaches in the U.S. Virgin Islands are open to the public, most of the shoreline on Maho Bay is acknowledged to be privately owned. Keep in mind that local families own and pay taxes on Maho and Hawksnest beaches, and that visitors are considered uninvited guests in someone's front yard. One contributor advises: If a little old West Indian lady with a machete and very salty language appears on Maho Beach, don't argue and beat a hasty retreat. Tying to the vegetation or littering may provoke a confrontation.

The Francis Bay Trail leads past the Francis Bay Estate House to the beach.

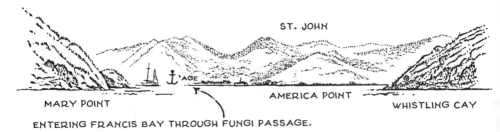

ST. JOHN

MARY POINT

AMERICA POINT

WHISTLING CAY

ENTERING FRANCIS BAY THROUGH FUNGI PASSAGE.

Francis Bay

Francis Bay is a good anchorage in prevailing weather, with excellent holding ground. Mary Point is where 24 slaves are said to have jumped to their deaths rather than submit to capture, after the 1733 slave revolt. One account suggests that the water here is tinged red every year in May on the anniversary of that event (sometimes the rocks below do appear reddish, perhaps from hematite deposits).

Important Note Regarding Francis Bay, Salt Pond Bay, and Great and Little Lameshur Bays

As we go to press with the Guide, the National Park Service informs us that it plans to complete installation of new moorings in Francis Bay, Salt Pond Bay, and Great and Little Lameshur Bays by late summer 1992. At this time, and perhaps before, anchoring will probably be prohibited in Great And Little Lameshur Bays.

The reason for this is that NPS researchers have determined that the sea grass beds, pasture for the threatened green turtle, are under stress, possibly from anchor damage. Shallow areas around the new moorings should be avoided for anchoring, as sea grass monitoring is under way here.

For current information at the time of your cruise, call the NPS offices in Cruz Bay at 776-6201.

For the Skipper

Approaching from any point west, be sure to avoid Johnson Reef (see the Caution in the section in this *Guide* on Trunk Bay).

If you're approaching from the north through Fungi Passage, between Whistling Cay and Mary Point, look for the ruins of an old customs house on the area where Whistling Cay shoals southeast into Fungi Passage. Your wind here may be blanketed by the cliff on Mary Point, so you may want to motor through.

Anchorages

Anchor on the eastern side of the bay, keeping an eye out for the sandbar in the northeastern corner. The breeze may feel deceptively strong because the wind funnels into the slot between the two mountain to the east. Don't hesitate to anchor 200-300 yards offshore to avoid the hungry bugs in the mangroves. If you dinghy ashore any later than 5 p.m., you'll be easy prey. The dinghy access channel is at the southern end of the beach.

Old customs house on Whistling Cay. (Fields photo)

In the northeast corner of Francis Bay is another area closed to anchoring in order to protect endangered sea grass beds. It is marked by a line of white buoys one foot in diameter inscribed "No Anchoring." Boats may enter the sea grass protection areas or land on the shore, but anchoring is prohibited.

What to Do

There is a picnic area with garbage receptacles ashore. You can follow the hiking and service trail beginning at the picnic site to an abandoned plantation house in the middle of the gap in the hills to the east. From this point, a blacktop road runs along the shore of Leinster Bay to the Annaberg Ruins, a pretty walk of .7 mile.

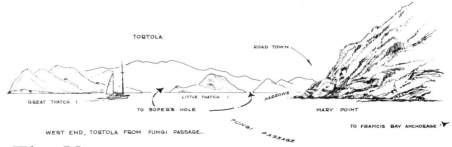

WEST END, TORTOLA FROM FUNGI PASSAGE.

The Narrows

As you leave Francis Bay for Leinster Bay or Tortola, the current will generally be against you in the Narrows. In prevailing winds, you might try tacking just west of Whistling Cay (remember to avoid Johnson Reef) and Great Thatch Island. Then, on the port tack, come back east of Great Thatch and through Thatch Cut. From there you can go between Little Thatch and Frenchman's Cay into Sir Francis Drake Channel.

Leinster Bay

For the Skipper

Enter the eastern side of the bay, called Waterlemon Bay, keeping Waterlemon Cay to port. You can enter and leave between the cay and the shore of St. John in 12 feet of water, but beware the shoal extending from the cay.

Anchorage

Anchor well up into the southeastern corner of the bay in 20-30 feet of water, or just south of the cay, about 200 yards from shore. You will usually be backwinded and will lie with the stern toward the shore.

Annaberg Mill ruins. (Tropic Isle photo)

Anchorage here is well-protected and there is a good, sandy bottom.

Although it's possible to land a dinghy on the rock beach just west of the Annaberg ruins, the rocky trip in could damage your dinghy. Also, it's difficult to secure a dinghy far enough up to prevent the surf from washing it away. We recommend that you land your dinghy on the sandy beach in Waterlemon Bay, bringing the skiff well out of the water and anchoring it securely (the NPS prohibits tying any vessel to vegetation, however). You can also avoid the rock beach by anchoring further west where the bottom is shallow and sandy, and wading ashore.

There are several interesting ruins ashore. On the hillside at the entrance to Mary Creek are the remains of an old schoolhouse. The Annaberg Mill ruins, restored by the NPS, are well worth the walk. These were once the base of an estate and mill built in the 1780s. The prominent windmill tower of the sugar mill and factory, slave quarters, vats for making molasses and rum, storage rooms, and part of a dungeon are visible. The stones were made of ships' ballast, stone, and local coral. There are exhibits with explanatory signs and a scenic overlook. In the early 1900s, a local cattle farmer lived here and used the building remains for storage and livestock pens. East of the bay, the ruins on top of the hill were once an estate house and later a reform school. Much of the structure is intact.

Haulover Bay

East of Leinster Bay, Haulover Bay is a satisfactory anchorage in prevailing conditions, but exposure to northerly seas can sometimes make it uncomfortable. Entrance is straightforward through the center, but avoid shoals to either side. In the very small anchorage in the southeastern corner, the water shoals to 10 feet in sand close to the beach. There is no other shallow water to anchor in, and the remaining depths of 60 feet or more have fragile patch reefs. Off the cobble beach there's good snorkeling.

The middle of the bay is the approximate NPS boundary, west of which all coastal waters to Cruz Bay are protected park areas. In the vicinity of the boundary, a shore path crosses to the road and small sandy beach at South Haulover Bay on the Coral Bay side. Goods, and perhaps boats, were once hauled over to Coral Bay at this point to avoid the upwind sail around East End. From Haulover Bay eastward there are no other anchorages until you reach the south side of St. John and come into Coral Bay.

Coral Bay: Round Bay/Hurricane Hole/ Coral Harbor

Coral Bay, which includes Coral Harbor, Round Bay, and Hurricane Hole, got its name not from coral but from the Dutch word *kraal,* which means "corral." It is where Arawak Indians first came to St. John over 2,000 years ago, and was St. John's main anchorage in the days of slavery, with almost as much commercial traffic as St. Thomas. By early 1733, plans had been drawn to transform Coral Harbor into a grand city in European style. But later that year the slaves had other ideas — this is the site of Fort Berg and the Estate Carolina, where the 1733 slave rebellion began and almost all of the white citizens of Coral Bay were massacred.

For the Skipper

In approaching this area from the east, leave Flanagan's Island to your port. Enter around Privateer and Red Points, keeping them well to starboard. Go in halfway between Leduck Island and Red Point.

Caution: Stay well clear of the rock about 100 yards off Red Point, locally called "Sandavore Rock," where a yacht of that name came to grief in 1984. A more obvious rock lies closer to shore. Often

Boat passing south between Leduck Island and St. John. (Fields photo)

there is no break over the seaward rock (Sandavore Rock) at all.

As you enter, on your starboard is Moor Point (Long Point on some charts), which is the beginning of the outermost harbor, Round Bay.

If you are approaching Coral Harbor from the west or south, you must avoid Eagle Shoal, just below the water and very difficult to see. Either hug (but not so close you hit it or put yourself on ground) the coast to your port when rounding Ram Head, or better yet, stay well south of a line drawn between Ram Head and the northern tip of Norman Island and then head in halfway between Leduck Island and Red Point.

If you use the route west of Eagle Shoal, be sure to favor St. John's eastern shore enough to avoid Eagle Shoal, and then pass midway between Leduck Island and Sabbat Point in deep water. Remember that if you lose your wind on this route, you'll need your auxiliary motor fast, or you may wind up on the rocks. If you lose your steering for any reason, you're in trouble (it's happened). It's too deep to anchor. Having passed Leduck Island, move northeastward until you can approach Coral Harbor as though you'd come in halfway between Leduck Island and Red Point. Give Lagoon Point sufficient berth to avoid its off-lying reefs.

Caution: Fish traps marked with white floats, bleach bottles, and the like lie within 200 yards of the windward side of Ram Head. Stay away from them. A boat fouling these lines would quickly drift onto the rocks.

When entering Coral Harbor, stay in mid-channel and check the depth. The channel is usually marked with red and green buoys maintained by the Coral Bay Yacht Club.

Hurricane Hole. (Tropic Isle photo)

In leaving Coral Harbor, the safest way is to proceed southeast halfway between Leduck Island and Red Point until well over a line drawn between Ram Head and the northern tip of Norman Island. Once over that line, head south and west around Ram Head. This is to avoid getting anywhere near Eagle Shoal.

Anchorages and Facilities

Round Bay. There is a light ground swell at times, but usually this is a comfortable anchorage and the most beautiful spot in the area.

Caution: Beware of Blinders Rocks, which lie well off the point west of South Haulover Bay, and which do not break in prevailing conditions.

Hurricane Hole consists of a series of fingerlike slots with plenty of water. You can stick your bow right into the mangroves without going aground. It's the most protected spot in the islands, although the wind gusting and eddying over the hill can make for twisted anchor lines. There are five ample bays. As you go in from the south, on your starboard are Nathaniel Bay, Water Creek, Otter Creek, Princess Bay, and Borck Creek. Then the coastline follows around Battery Point into Coral Harbor to the west.

Coral Harbor. The channel into Coral Harbor is used at night by returning fishermen and should be kept open. The inner and more sheltered portions of the harbor are largely occupied by permanent moorings. The best anchorage for visitors is in the inner harbor, north of Pen Point and west of the channel.

Caution: Throughout Coral Bay, particularly in the area east of the channel, many boats have mistaken small white styrofoam fish trap markers for available mooring buoys and wound up aground in the middle of the night.

Coral Bay Marine. (Tropic Isle photo)

On the waterfront, Coral Bay Marine Service offers engine and outboard repairs, general marine services, ice but no water, and some supplies and parts. Parts not in stock can be shipped in by air-freight. Coral Bay Marine Service monitors VHF Channel 16. You can buy ice and do your wash at Coral Bay Laundry, and dive trips and tank refills can be arranged by calling Coral Bay Watersports.

What to Do

Coral Harbor is where the people went who found Key West and even Cruz Bay too spiritually confining, the real Margaritaville. A first impression of the settlement may intimidate some newcomers — it has a definite outpost-of-civilization look and feel, with no pretensions of being a tourist destination — but if you hang out here for awhile, you'll find it has a ramshackle, casual, let-it-all-hang-out kind of charm, beloved by a number of the islands' serious sailors and freethinkers. There are good restaurants and places of striking historical interest to poke around.

Skinny Legs Bar, in the old Redbeards building, is the most recent official clubhouse of the Coral Bay Yacht Club, as far as that hyper-bohemian organization has any fixed abode. The yacht club sponsors an annual Thanksgiving race and party. Also in the same building are an auto parts store, a video shop, Caribbean Colors boutique (where you can also rent snorkels), and a pottery shop/gallery called Out A Hand. The Sputnik bar and restaurant, adjacent to Coral Bay Laundry, also houses a small grocery store and Mickey's Pizza. Joe's Discount keeps a good stock of groceries and supplies.

On the northwest shore, The Still, run by Genaviva Rodriguez, has a nice menu that includes grilled seafood. Continuing south around the bay, the Sea Breeze Cafe serves breakfast, lunch, and dinner. We especially like the Shipwreck Landing, a breezy, informal bar with

The Emmaus Moravian church. (Fields photo)

continuous food service and an excellent menu including seafood specials and pasta (dinner reservations are recommended). The St. John Music Festival is held here annually on the second Sunday of February, when close to a thousand people gather to listen to folk music. To find Shipwreck Landing from the water, look for a point with a house atop it on the west side of Coral Harbor where it opens into Coral Bay. You can land your dinghy on the sand-and-rock beach to the south of the point and walk across the road, but don't try this in an eastern or southern swell. Further down the road is Lucy's, with a good gourmet menu and, on some nights, West Indian food.

Most of the Coral Bay gathering places feature bands from time to time. Check bulletin boards and trees to see who's playing where. When there's no live band, there's a lot of Neil Young and James Taylor-type stuff playing. Baby boomers who voted for McGovern will be in nostalgia heaven.

Locals can direct you to some of the local places of historical interest. The sugar mill of the old Estate Carolina and the Emmaus Moravian church, built in 1783 on the site of the old estate, are worth seeing. Rumor has it that a ghostly ram haunts the grounds on full-moon nights, a spectre of the 1733 massacre. If you continue on the lower road, you'll come to the old shore battery, built in the early 1800s during British occupation. The ruins of Fort Berg stand atop the hill protruding into the harbor.

There are endless possibilities for exploration and snorkeling around Battery Point and over into Hurricane Hole. On entering or clearing these bays, be on the lookout for white-buoyed fish pots that will foul your propeller if you run too close.

Other Anchorages on the South Coast

A note of caution when anchoring in isolated spots on the south coast: There have been incidents reported of thieves swimming from shore to rob unlocked unattended boats in these areas. Always secure your boat when going ashore, and also keep your eye on any valuables you take ashore with you.

To protect the area's coral and seagrass beds, please look for a sand bottom when anchoring.

Around the corner west of Ram Head, the first cove is **Salt Pond Bay.** It is an excellent overnight anchorage. In the middle of the entrance is a big reef with deep water on either side. Anchor in the northeast corner on a sandy bottom. Three moorings are provided by the NPS for boats under 60 feet in length. The bay has a beautiful beach, a picnic area, and a garbage can at the west end of the beach provided by the park service. There are hiking trails to Ram Head and the nearby salt pond. The best beachcombing area is at Drunk Bay to the east, accessible by trail ("drunk" is Dutch Creole for "drowned," probably because the bay is rocky and rough, exposed to the wind).

Lameshur Bay, as shown on our sketch chart, consists of Great Lameshur Bay, east of the peninsula that protrudes in the center, and Little Lameshur Bay, west of it. **Great Lameshur Bay** is a well-sheltered

Important Note Regarding Francis Bay, Salt Pond Bay, and Great and Little Lameshur Bays

As we go to press with the Guide, *the National Park Service informs us that it plans to complete installation of new moorings in Francis Bay, Salt Pond Bay, and Great and Little Lameshur Bays by late summer 1992. At this time, and perhaps before, anchoring will probably be prohibited in Great And Little Lameshur Bays.*

The reason for this is that NPS researchers have determined that the sea grass beds, pasture for the threatened green turtle, are under stress, possibly from anchor damage. Shallow areas around the new moorings should be avoided for anchoring, as sea grass monitoring is under way here.

For current information at the time of your cruise, call the NPS office in Cruz Bay at 776-6201.

overnight anchorage (please see note on previous page). The best spots are in the two coves on the eastern side of the bay in good holding ground. A park service dock is in the northwest corner of the bay, with trash cans ashore. Dinghies may tie up temporarily near the shore end of the north side of the dock, clear of the park ranger's boat so that it can be used quickly in emergencies. The end and the north side of the dock are reserved for park service boats. The south side for the Virgin Islands Ecological Research Station, a facility of the College of the Virgin Islands, one of the groups that use the fairly pristine and remote environment of the Lameshur area to study reefs and tropical ecosystems. The white building is the Wet Lab for VIERS.

Just west of Great Lameshur Bay, **Little Lameshur Bay** is relatively well-sheltered except when the wind is in the south. The best anchorage is on the eastern side of the bay. There is a sand beach with picnic tables and garbage cans provided by the NPS. The buildings near the shore were overseers' quarters, a bay rum still, and the ruins of what was briefly a sugar factory.

The radio tower on the hill marks the National Park Ranger Station. Although the station can communicate on VHF, it does not monitor Channel 16. If you need help and want to contact the ranger, call the park office in Cruz Bay (776-6201) through the marine operator to alert the Lameshur Ranger to come up on 16. Emergency telephone and emergency medical services are available, but casual visits are not encouraged, as this is the ranger's home.

From Little Lameshur you can follow a trail that joins the Reef Bay Trail and the trail to the petroglyphs. From this junction the petroglyphs are about .3 mile, or you can turn south to the ruins of the Reef Bay Estate and sugar mills. Nobody seems to know for sure the origin of the

Chocolate Hole. (Tropic Isle photo)

petroglyphs. Some say they are the work of the fierce Carib Indians who took over the island from the gentle Arawaks, but there is some recent evidence that the symbols are of Ashanti origin, carved by slaves. In the rainy season, there is a waterfall here.

Fish Bay and Rendezvous Bay (supposedly once a frequent pirate's meeting place) are the next two bays to the west and, like Reef Bay, are open to the south and are not safe anchorages when the wind veers toward the south. These are poorly charted and seldom visited. Enter with care and good light. Fish Bay is the better protected of the two but is too shallow for anchoring most boats.

Around Bovocap Point is **Chocolate Hole.** This is well-protected, with good holding ground in sand. There is a little beach at the head of the bay.

Great Cruz Bay, site of the Hyatt Regency St. John, is usually a crowded anchorage. Be careful when anchoring here, as the bay shallows about three-quarters of the way in to 10 feet or less. Areas restricted for swimming are marked. A marked channel with a 7-foot controlling depth leads in to the resort's T-dock, which has about 5-7 feet at the end. Be aware, however, that just south of the good water at the end of the dock is an area only 5 feet deep. The front section of the dock is only for pick-up or drop-off traffic or the ferry, and several slips are reserved for hotel use. You may tie up to the dock for lunch or dinner, but you must contact the dockmaster on VHF 16 first for instructions. Space on the far side of the beach is designated for dinghies. Overnight dockage is not permitted. Visiting yachtsmen may use the pool bar and restaurants.

Caution: As you proceed around to Cruz Bay, be sure to stay west of Steven Cay.

Great Cruz Bay. (Tropic Isle photo)

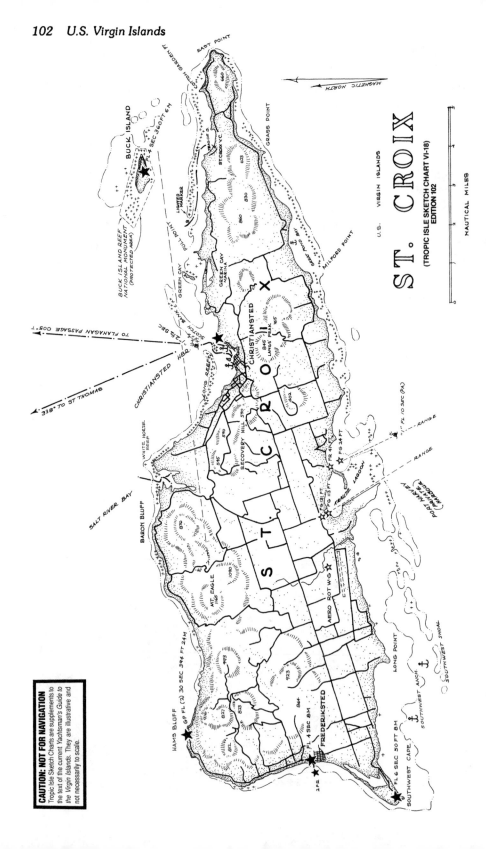

ST. CROIX
(TROPIC ISLE SKETCH CHART VI-18)
EDITION 102

U.S. VIRGIN ISLANDS

NAUTICAL MILES

CAUTION: NOT FOR NAVIGATION
Tropic Isle Sketch Charts are supplements to
the text of the current Yachtsman's Guide to
the Virgin Islands. They are illustrative and
not necessarily to scale.

St. Croix

N.O.S. Charts: 25641, 25644, 25645. Tropic Isle Sketch Charts: VI-17, 18, 19, 20.

Thirty-five miles south of St. Thomas and surrounded by deep water, St. Croix is the largest of the Virgin Islands, with 84 square miles. About 7 miles at its widest point and 20 miles long, it has two main towns, Christiansted, on the north shore, and Frederiksted, at the west end. St. Croix is modest and pastoral, consistently lovely rather than breathtaking. The low rolling hills are dotted with grazing cattle and the ghostly ruins of plantation greathouses and windmills. Danish influence is also apparent in the idiosyncratic, charming city architecture, where stone arcades and arches shade unhurried shoppers. From the southern bluffs of the island, there are some magnificent panoramic views of long deserted beaches.

St. Croix was the earliest inhabited of the Virgins because of level, fertile land and plentiful water. Columbus landed at Salt River in 1493 and was chased away by angry Carib Indians, probably the first conflict recorded between natives of the New World and explorers from Europe.

Fort Christiansvaern. (Tropic Isle photo)

For years the island was fought over by the French, Dutch, English, Spanish, and Knights of Malta. The Danes bought St. Croix from the French in 1733. The land had already been largely cleared by the French, who had burned down the island's forests in hopes of controlling disease and insects that bred in the humid woodlands. Danish settlement began in 1734, a year after the nearly successful slave rebellion on St. John. Within 20 years, almost 400 plantations were thriving, with such evocative names as Jealousy, Upper Love, However Love, Recovery, Solitude, and Wheel of Fortune. As on the other islands, the population of St. Croix was never predominantly Danish. Many Englishmen came from Virgin Gorda, Tortola, Eustatius, and Barbados. A majority of the settlers were members of the upper class, and the island became one of the richest in the West Indies. By 1796 half the island was planted in sugar cane.

Throughout the 1700s St. Croix was a leading exporter of rum, molasses, and sugar. Many Europeans arrived, made fast fortunes, and returned to Europe to live off their profits. However, by the early 1800s when the price of sugar dropped, planters accustomed to borrowing huge amounts of money to finance their luxurious life-styles found themselves deeply in debt.

Unlike the slaves of St. Thomas, many of whom assisted in business ventures and had the opportunity to learn skills, almost all the slaves of St. Croix were field workers. When the slave trade was abolished in 1802, there were already about 30,000 slaves on the island, and they were not freed until 1848. Their accumulated frustration expressed itself in a number of slave revolts. As a result you will see the ruins of sentry houses with slits in the walls for muskets. These were built by landowners who feared that their slaves would set fire to the fields.

Sugar mill ruins. (Tropic Isle photo)

Protestant Cay. (Tropic Isle photo)

Much of Christiansted was destroyed by a fire in 1866, followed within ten years by an earthquake and tidal wave. Labor riots disrupted the island in 1878 and 1892. With the other islands, St. Croix experienced decline until the post-World War II tourism boom. Many immigrants from Puerto Rico arrived in the early 1960s, and now about half the population has its roots in Puerto Rico.

Today St. Croix is known for upscale resort hideaways. There are places to play golf or tennis or go horseback-riding. For visitors, St. Croix is relaxing, comfortable, spacious, and unobtrusive. You won't feel so much a tourist here as a guest, politely left to choose your amusement.

Plan at least three days for a trip to St. Croix. You'll need one day to get over, another to explore, and another to return. A visit to Buck Island will require an additional day, but is well worth the time.

CRUISING GUIDE TO THE
Florida Keys

Cruising Guide to the Florida Keys $18.95

- PLACES TO GO
- THINGS TO SEE
- DETAILED CHARTS
- WEATHER INFO
- AERIAL SATELLITE PHOTOS
- UNDERWATER ACTIVITIES

Send $18.95 To:
TROPIC ISLE PUBLISHERS
P.O. Box 610938
North Miami, FL 33261-0938

Add $3 Postage & Handling for orders inside the U.S., $4 for orders outside the U.S. Florida residents add applicable Sales Tax.

NEW Revised
8th Edition

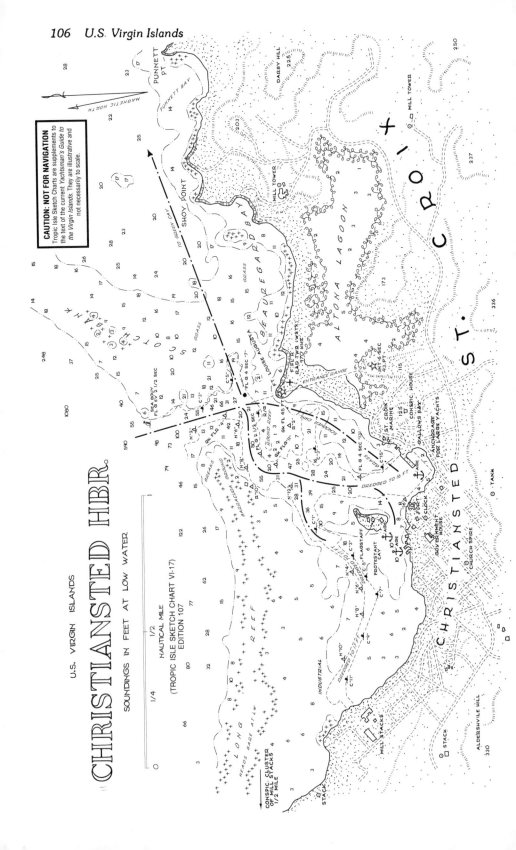

CHRISTIANSTED HBR.

U.S. VIRGIN ISLANDS

SOUNDINGS IN FEET AT LOW WATER

(TROPIC ISLE SKETCH CHART VI-17)
EDITION 107

NAUTICAL MILE

CAUTION: NOT FOR NAVIGATION
Tropic Isle Sketch Charts are supplements to the text of the current *Yachtsman's Guide to the Virgin Islands.* They are illustrative and not necessarily to scale.

LANG PEAK   RECOVERY HILL

CHRISTIANSTED HARBOR

Approaching St. Croix

Start as far east of St. Thomas as you can to avoid beating into the wind. On a clear day you may be able to see St. Croix from St. Thomas, St. John, or Tortola. The sail across can take from 4 to 10 hours. The buoys aren't all lit in Christiansted harbor, so always plan to arrive in daylight. You should leave for St. Croix no later than 8 a.m., preferably earlier. Figure on an average one-half knot current running in a westerly direction. Until you near St. Croix hold your heading toward the eastern end of the island.

When you return from St. Croix to the main body of islands, allow for the westerly set of the current. St. John will probably be the first island you can identify.

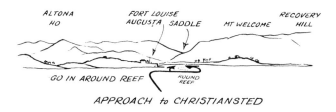

ALTONA   FORT LOUISE   RECOVERY
HO   AUGUSTA SADDLE   MT WELCOME   HILL

GO IN AROUND REEF   ROUND REEF

APPROACH to CHRISTIANSTED

Christiansted

During the French occupation of St. Croix in the 1600s, Christiansted was called *Bassin* (basin or port). At the same time, Protestant Cay was named because it was the only place where non-Catholics were allowed burial by the French.

The town was founded as Christiansted in 1734 by the Dutch West India and Guinea Company, and became the Danish colonial capital in 1755. Among Caribbean towns, it is one of the best preserved.

For the Skipper

Approach St. Croix to the east of Christiansted. Head for the saddle formed between the peaks of Recovery Hill and Lang Peak. Staying north and west of Scotch Bank, which extends out from the

St. Croix Marine. (Tropic Isle photo)

harbor entrance, pass the black sea buoy to your port. As you continue in through the channel toward Fort Louse Augusta, the WSTX radio tower is a possible landmark, although it is harder to see now that it has been replaced — it is now tall, very spindly, and visible but not distinct. The entrance range is now the most visible landmark.

If bound for the schooner channel, ride the range until about 100 yards off Fort Louise Augusta and safely around Round Reef, a major hazard that lies awash west of Fort Louise Augusta. From here, the schooner channel, now dredged and marked to accommodate small cruise ships, leads in to Gallows Bay. A second way around Round Reef is to the north and west of it. Make a sharp turn to starboard before coming to the fixed marker off Fort Louise Augusta. Keeping the channel-dividing marker to port and the red nun to starboard, follow in the marked channel around the west side of Round Reef.

St. Croix Marine and Annapolis Sailing School both stand by on VHF 16 during business hours if you need more information, and after hours there are usually live-aboards listening in. But remember, approaching any landfall at night is difficult and dangerous, so you should be all tucked into whatever anchorage you've chosen well before dark..

Anchorages and Facilities
Do not pick up a mooring in Christiansted Harbor, as all are

privately owned and in use. Any that appear not in use are probably deficient.

Most small craft anchor in the lee of Protestant Cay. Head for the fort east of the cay, round the cay to the south and head west. Anchor off the southwest end in 10 feet of water. Don't go too far west, as it shoals rapidly. Also in heavy weather the sea breaks over Long Reef and creates a strong easterly current against the wind, so it's a good idea to set two anchors here to avoid swinging into another boat.

Customs and immigration. If you are clearing here on a weekday, notify customs (773-1011) between 9 a.m. and 5 p.m. of your arrival into Gallows Bay, and they will give you instructions on how to proceed. On weekends, you must upon arrival call customs officials at the airport at 778-0216 for instructions. In either case, you must also notify immigration (778-1419), so that an inspector can come down from the airport to inspect you.

St. Croix Marine. Vessels over 50 feet long and 8 feet draft should anchor off St. Croix Marine, the largest yard on the island. Dockage and all services are available, and there is a 60-ton lift and 300-ton marine railway that can haul vessels with up to 11 feet draft. There is a well-stocked Island Marine Supply store on the premises. A casual eatery called the Baggy Wrinkle serves breakfast, lunch, and dinner. From

ISLAND MARINE SUPPLY STORE ON PREMISES
Dealers For:
Evinrude, Boston Whaler, Hatteras

ST. CROIX MARINE
· 300 Ton Marine Railway · 60 Ton Travelift
· Hauling To 11 ft. Draft
Fiberglass · Woodworking · Engine Repair · Dockage
Fuel · Laundry · Bar - Restaurant · Yacht Brokerage

Gallows Bay - Christiansted, P.O. Box 24730, St. Croix, VI 00824
809-773-0289 FAX 809-778-8974
We Monitor Channel 16.

Chandler's Wharf at Gallows Bay. (Tropic Isle photo)

St. Croix Marine, easy provisioning is nearby. Most wholesalers will deliver; the office at St. Croix Marine can help you find the phone numbers you need for whatever.

Within walking distance of St. Croix Marine on Gallows Bay is Chandler's Wharf shopping center. The Canvas Loft here does sail repairs and specialized welding. There's also a liquor store and restaurant, among other shops. Nearby are a deli, post office, cleaners, hardware store, bank, and pharmacy. The Rogue's Gallery serves breakfast and lunch, and Baggies Too specializes in West Indian food. Also in the vicinity is The Wreck Bar, a boaters' hangout.

On King Cross Street in town is headquarters for the Annapolis Sailing School, which offers courses from "Become a Sailor in One Weekend" through combination learn-to-sail/cruise packages.

What to Do

A walking tour of Christiansted is easily begun from the harbor. Designated a National Historic Site, the town square and waterfront area include many beautifully restored 18th-century buildings, built by the Danes of imported yellow brick or carved coral. The Scalehouse, facing the waterfront, was built in the mid-1800s for Danish customs operations. The visitor's bureau here has brochures and a free walking tour map. East of the Scalehouse is Fort Christianvaern. It was completed in 1748, but was never invaded. It is uniquely well-preserved and has been restored to the appearance it had in 1850. There is a self-guided tour through the powder magazine, officers' kitchens, dungeons, and cannon-lined battlements. A block away on Company Street is the Steeple Building, the first Lutheran church established on the island by the Danes in 1753. Inside is a museum of Carib and Arawak relics, a model sugar plantation that diagrams sugar-cane processing, and a diorama of Christiansted in the early 1800s. If you look at the weather vane on top of the Steeple Building, you'll be able to see the direction Hugo blew in from in September 1989.

The West India and Guinea Company Warehouse, built in 1749 at the corner of Company and Church Streets to house personnel and supplies, now contains the U.S. Post Office and, upstairs, the customs office. Public restrooms are in the north corner of the courtyard.

The Government House, once capital of the Danish West Indies and home of the Danish governor-general before the U.S. purchase of the Virgin Islands in 1917, still headquarters the St. Croix government offices. In the 1700s it was the largest governor's palace in the Lesser Antilles, furnished so grandly that the Danes packed everything up and took it home when they sold the island to the United States. They later sent fine replicas of the missing pieces as replacements. Across from the Government House, where the Little Switzerland store now stands, was the hardware store where young Alexander Hamilton worked. Hamilton was born on the island of Nevis in 1755 and brought as young child to St. Croix by his mother (she is buried on the island). He grew up on the estate Shoy, where the Buccaneer Hotel now stands, and lived in St. Croix until 1773, when his family sent him to Boston after a hurricane

Downtown Christiansted. (Tropic Isle photo)

nearly wiped out Christiansted.

Shopping in St. Croix is a pleasure even if you don't buy anything. There are branches of the major stores of St. Thomas that offer the same free-port bargains, but in St. Croix the streets don't teem with cruise-ship passengers because of the reefy harbor entrances. You can amble from shop to shop through covered walkways and arcades shaded with flowers, stopping for refreshment in one of the relaxed waterfront bars or restaurants. Many of the shops sell ceramics, jewelry, metal and leatherwork, and furniture made by Cruzan craftsmen. Fresh island produce is for sale at the Company Street Marketplace between Queen Cross and King Cross.

Good restaurants include the Top Hat for elegant Danish cuisine and the Comanche Restaurant for continental food. Try Nolan's Tavern or the Lobster Hole for island-style seafood. Stixx on the Waterfront serves breakfast, lunch, and dinner, with good pizza, seafood and BBQ ribs, a raw bar, and a weekly clambake. There's a dinghy dock for patrons.

You can explore the island from Christiansted by taxi or rental car, but if you rent, be sure to reserve a car ahead of time and get there early. Taxi drivers are good local guides and rates are negotiable.

The prettiest beaches on the island are at Cane Bay and Davis Bay. Cramer Park, operated by the Department of Agriculture, has a picnic area, restaurant, and bar. It's near the east end of the island, also by some reckoning the easternmost point of the United States. Near Cramer Park, the National Radio Astronomy Conservatory has recently completed construction of an enormous antenna (260 tons and 82 feet in diameter), which will be used to explore quasars, pulsars, radio galaxies, molecular clouds, and black holes, as well as other properties of the universe previously unknown. Tours are conducted for visitors; call (809) 773-4448.

Just northwest of Christiansted, Judith's Fancy was once the home of the Governor of the Knights of Malta. From the hill beyond the estate, you can see Salt River, where Columbus first anchored and was attacked by Indians in 1493.

A drive along North Shore Road will take you through some lush, thickly vined forests of mahogany, ferns, and fruit trees. The Cruzan Rum Distillery on West Airport Road offers guided tours on weekdays. Off Centerline Road, near Frederiksted, is the St. George Village Botanical Garden, 16 acres of exotic tropical plants and fruit trees. The gift shop sells an unusual variety of Cruzan crafts and foods.

Along the road to Frederiksted stand ruins of old greathouses, built of rock and coral blocks mortared with a mixture of molasses and seashells. A few have been restored, some as guest houses. Just northwest of Frederiksted, off Centerline Road, the Whim Greathouse is the most interesting and informative of the plantation restorations. Inside the cookhouse is a museum of implements, old photographs and woodcuts, antiques, and a reconstructed pharmacy. A gift shop sells reproductions of antiques, profits of which go to St. Croix Landmarks Restoration.

If you visit Frederiksted, go when no cruise ship is in the harbor so you'll be able to park near the pier at the north end of town. When we were there on this past survey, the town was a bit like a ghost town, with many shops closed or boarded up and relatively few places to get a meal. We were informed locally that crime has been a problem here, so observe caution.

Most of Frederiksted was rebuilt in Victorian gingerbread style after fires destroyed much of the city in the labor riots of 1878. A free map and Walking Tour Guide are available at the Visitors Bureau (also the Customs House) on the corner of Strand and Lagoon Streets. On the other side of Lagoon Street, Fort Frederik is where Danish Governor-General Peter von Scholten proclaimed freedom for all Danish West Indian slaves in 1848. It was a timely decision, as hundreds of slaves were at that moment rioting in Frederiksted and revolt was spreading fast throughout the island. Von Scholten was later court-martialed for his action, but his proclamation was not revoked. There are several interesting 18th- and 19th-century churches of various denominations and designs. On Fisher Street, at the south end of King Street, is one of the largest banyan trees in the Caribbean.

Fredericksted pier. (Tropic Isle photo)

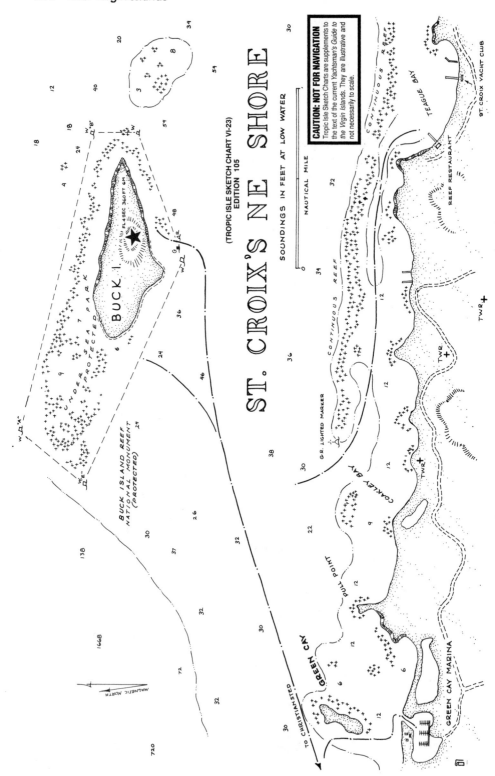

ST. CROIX'S NE SHORE

(TROPIC ISLE SKETCH CHART VI-23)
EDITION 105

SOUNDINGS IN FEET AT LOW WATER

CAUTION: NOT FOR NAVIGATION
Tropic Isle Sketch Charts are supplements to
the text of the current *Yachtsman's Guide* to
the Virgin Islands. They are illustrative and
not necessarily to scale.

Green Cay Marina. (Tropic Isle photo)

Green Cay Marina

For the Skipper

Leaving Christiansted, when off Fort Louise Augusta, leave black can no. 5 to port and head for the northern end of Green Cay. Leave Green Cay to port (see sketch chart VI-23) and keep clear of the scattered reefs in the area.

Green Cay Marina

5000 Southgate
Christiansted, St. Croix
U.S. Virgin Islands 00820
(809) 773-1453
Fax (809) 773-9651

- Fuel Dock
- Power & Water
- Laundry Facilities
- Rest Rooms & Showers
- Yacht Broker
- Restaurant
- Monitoring Channel 16

Anchorages and Facilities

Green Cay Marina, about 3 miles east of Christiansted, has dockage for 140 vessels. Facilities include power and water at each slip, fuel, ice, laundry, and a yacht broker. On the premises, the Galleon Restaurant serves dinner and, nearby, you can get drinks and light meals at the Deep End Poolside Bar.

St. Croix Yacht Club/Teague Bay

For the Skipper

Proceeding about 1.5 miles east from the north end of Green Cay, you will see a lighted green Coast Guard marker. Leave this marker to port and head into the bay toward the windmill. Then head east, keeping close enough to the shore to avoid the continuous reef. Continue no further east than Teague Bay to avoid a shoal studded with coral heads.

Anchorages and Facilities

Members of accredited yacht clubs are welcome at the St. Croix Yacht Club. Skippers are requested to check with the club manager for an anchoring site and official guest card. Light meals and drinks are

St. Croix Yacht Club. (Tropic Isle photo)

available, although the hours are limited, and no provisioning, fuel, or laundry facilities are available. You can, however, get ice, leave garbage, and take a shower.

What to Do

Down the road from the Yacht Club, Duggan's Reef is a casual, friendly restaurant overlooking a swimming beach. Lunch and dinner are served daily. In settled weather you can anchor off and dinghy in for dinner, but watch out for swimmers and snorkelers.

Buck Island

Buck Island, along with its spectacular surrounding coral reef, was declared a national monument in 1961, administered by the National Park Service. The reef attracts snorkelers and divers, and visitors can also enjoy a picnic area and the unusual variety of bird life and vegetation that thrive on the island. If you choose not to sail to Buck Island yourself, excursion boats make day trips from Christiansted, Green Cay Marina, and the St. Croix Yacht Club. Snorkeling instruction and equipment are usually offered.

Dutch settlers in the mid-1700s called the island *Pocken-Ey,* the Dutch word for lignum vitae trees. It later was named Buck Island because of an abundance of goats who kept busy deforesting the island up until the 1950s, when they were removed and the island was allowed to return to its present wooded state.

For the Skipper

Proceed on to Buck Island from a point north of the shoals off the north end of Green Cay.

Anchorages

Buck Island is a day anchorage only.

If your boat draws 5 feet or less, steer for the prominent point on the south side of Buck Island, then proceed eastward along the southern shore, keeping south of the orange-and-white buoys until you see the brown park service sign mounted on the reef. The entrance to the cut is between the red and green buoys and carries about 5 feet. The sign will be a few yards to starboard.

Follow the inside of the reef to the eastern end of the island and take one of the moorings provided by the park service. If all the moorings are taken, anchor well away from the reef in a WNW direction, staying outside the line of traffic. Boats of greater draft can anchor in 15 feet of

Buck Island, seen from the eastern point of St. Croix. (Tropic Isle photo)

water off the sandy beach on the western end of the island.

What to Do

Once your boat is secured you can go over the side with snorkel gear and follow the underwater coral gardens around to the north side. A marked trail guides swimmers through forests of elkhorn and staghorn coral populated with angelfish, parrotfish, and other brilliantly colored creatures. There are many species of birds including frigate birds and pelicans, and over 60 species of trees. A hiking trail leads to the top of the island (an elevation of about 330 feet) from the trees on the beach, about 1.4 miles round-trip. On the west side of the island is a beautiful beach with barbecue pits, picnic tables, and restrooms. Also, on the south side, there is a pier and another picnic area.

Salt River Bay

Salt River has recently been given National Park status, and under this protection will continue to remain much as it appeared when Columbus entered it on his second visit to the New World in 1493. According to his journals, he sent a party ashore here for water, which apparently required raiding a Carib village. The Indians retaliated with bows and arrows until Columbus and his men turned tail and ran. Columbus named the area *El Cabo de Las Fleches* (Cape of the Arrows). The rest of his explorations in the Virgin Islands on that particular voyage were made from a safe vantage point on board.

Salt River really was once a river that divided the island of St. Croix in two. Now dense mangrove growth and protective reefs make the

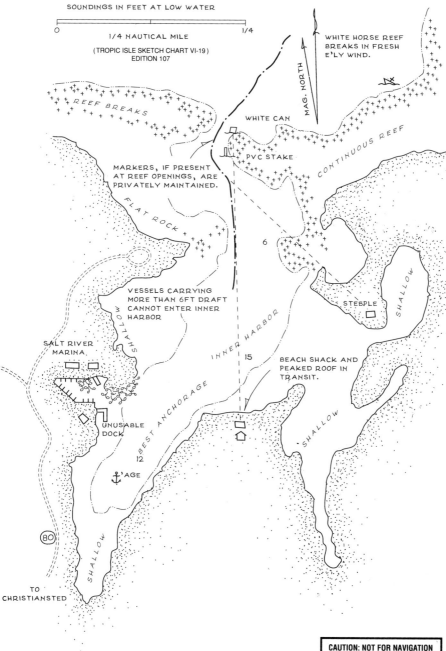

U.S. VIRGIN ISLANDS

SALT RIVER BAY

SOUNDINGS IN FEET AT LOW WATER

0   1/4 NAUTICAL MILE   1/4

(TROPIC ISLE SKETCH CHART VI-19)
EDITION 107

WHITE HORSE REEF
BREAKS IN FRESH
E'LY WIND.

MAG. NORTH

REEF BREAKS

WHITE CAN

PVC STAKE

CONTINUOUS REEF

MARKERS, IF PRESENT
AT REEF OPENINGS, ARE
PRIVATELY MAINTAINED.

FLAT ROCK

6

SHALLOW

VESSELS CARRYING
MORE THAN 6FT DRAFT
CANNOT ENTER INNER
HARBOR

STEEPLE

SHALLOW

SALT RIVER
MARINA

SHALLOW

INNER HARBOR

15

BEACH SHACK AND
PEAKED ROOF IN
TRANSIT.

BEST ANCHORAGE

UNUSABLE
DOCK

SHALLOW

12

⚓ 'AGE

80

SHALLOW

TO
CHRISTIANSTED

CAUTION: NOT FOR NAVIGATION
Tropic Isle Sketch Charts are supplements to
the text of the current *Yachtsman's Guide to
the Virgin Islands.* They are illustrative and
not necessarily to scale.

remaining bay an excellent hurricane hole for boats drawing 6 feet or less.

For the Skipper

Caution: Even experienced locals check and recheck their bearings throughout this area. Be careful. Use your depth finder or lead line, and only enter in good light so the channels through both the outer and inner reefs will be clearly visible.

Because there is only 6 feet of water between the continuous reef outside the reef harbor and the inner reef that protects the inner harbor, deeper-draft boats cannot be carried through this area into the deep inner harbor.

Approaching, keep west of White Horse Reef, which lies to the north and east of the entrance. Enter midway in the break in the outer reef across the mouth of the reef harbor. Once inside, turn to port and parallel the south side of the reef on a heading toward the steeple. Don't go too far or you'll be on shallow sand. At the time of our recent survey, a privately maintained white can and PVC stake marked the east side of the entrance channel through the outer reef. Farther in, additional (also privately maintained) PVC stakes marked the channel through the inner reef opening. Remember, marks (especially those that are privately maintained) can disappear.

The best anchorage is in the inner harbor, as is the marina entrance. The L-shaped dock on the south side of the marina entrance is unusable. It was heavily damaged by Hurricane Hugo.

Anchorages and Facilities

Salt River Marina is a pretty place, nestled in a mangrove forest and surrounded by palm trees and bougainvillea. Alongside both banks of the cove are long docks for mooring. Space is limited, so it's a good

Entrance, Salt River. (Tropic Isle photo)

Salt River Marina. (Tropic Isle photo)

idea to make arrangements in advance or at least check ahead for availability. If there are no slips available, anchoring in the inner harbor is the only alternative. The marina provides all services to dockside customers (fuel requires 24 hours' notice, however), and there is a dive shop, a marine store with limited supplies, and a bar/restaurant. The marina monitors VHF 16 during daylight hours. At this writing, the restaurant and marina office close on Tuesdays.

The water off Salt River's outer reefs is a local surfing and windsurfing hot spot. Experienced SCUBA enthusiasts might want to try the spectacular wall dives of Salt River Canyon.

Frederiksted/South Coast of St. Croix

Frederiksted is an open harbor on the west end of the island, protected from trade winds. It has the only dock for cruise ships in St. Croix, and the very deep water prohibits most yachts from anchoring here. You may be able to anchor south of the town pier, but be sure the water is shallow enough.

Along the south shore of St. Croix are numerous reefs and some anchorages, depending on conditions, between reefs. There are no harbors. Local knowledge should be sought.

Port Harvey is strictly a commercial port.

CHART KIT [BBA]

$130 worth of valuable government publications for only $27⁹⁵!... the new *Reed's Nautical Almanac, East Coast Edition*

ver 900+ pages with a wealth of navigation material from more than six government publications—all carefully organized and indexed for fast, easy reference.
■ Complete tide tables and tidal current charts from Halifax, Nova Scotia,

through the Caribbean and the Gulf of Mexico.
■ Weather broadcasts and forecasting.
■ First aid.
■ Compass corrections.
■ Navigation and nautical astronomy.
■ Radio beacons and other aids

to navigation.
■ Complete nautical almanac for celestial navigation.
■ Over 150 pages of visual navigation aids.
■ Seamanship, distress and rescue at sea.
106. Reed's Nautical Almanac, American East Coast Edition. $27.95. (Add $2.00 for shipping and handling).

TO ORDER
••••••••••••••••••
Visa, MasterCard, or American Express cardholders:
Call toll free 1-800-CHART KIT (1-800-242-7854)
in MA (617) 449-3314
Mon-Fri, 9am-5pm, Eastern time
••••••••••••••••••
Or send check or money order (no cash, please) to:
Better Boating Assoc., Inc., Box 407, Needham, MA 02192
Connecticut, Massachusetts and Rhode Island residents add your state sales tax on product cost only.

FREE Chart Kit Catalog
••••••••••••••••••••
Call toll free 1-800-CHART KIT (1-800-242-7854)
in Massachusetts (617) 449-3314
Mon-Fri, 9am-5pm, Eastern time
••••••••••••••••••••
CHART KITS—United States, Bahamas & Virgin Islands
VIDEOS—Bahamas & Virgin Islands Cruise Guides
Piloting & Coastal Navigation
Ropes, Knots & Line Handling
NAVIGATION INSTRUMENTS AND ACCESSORIES

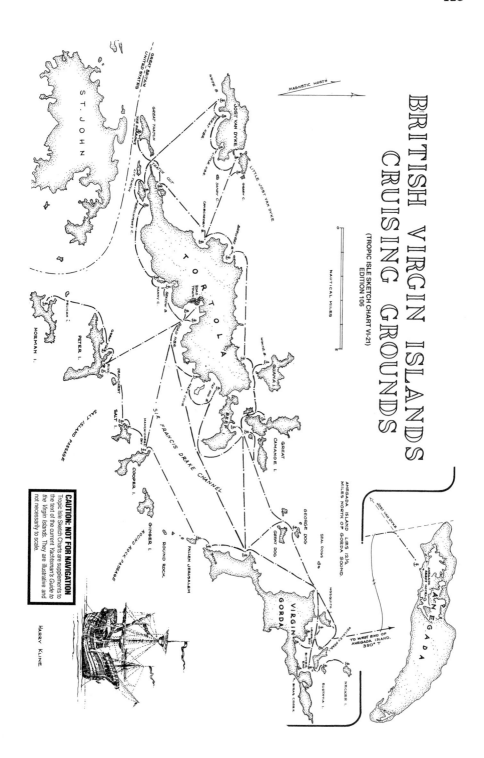

BRITISH VIRGIN ISLANDS
CRUISING GROUNDS

(TROPIC ISLE SKETCH CHART VI-21)
EDITION 106

MAGNETIC NORTH

NAUTICAL MILES

CAUTION: NOT FOR NAVIGATION
Tropic Isle Sketch Charts are supplements to the text of the current Yachtsman's Guide to the Virgin Islands. They are illustrative and not necessarily to scale.

HARRY KLINE

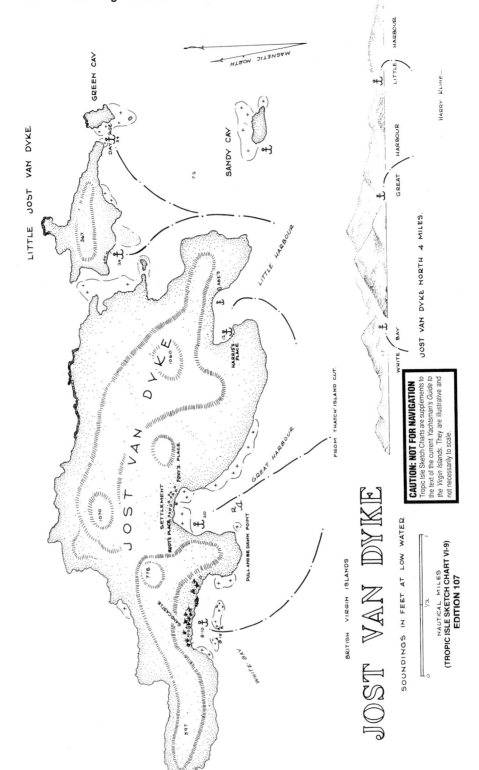

JOST VAN DYKE

BRITISH VIRGIN ISLANDS

SOUNDINGS IN FEET AT LOW WATER

NAUTICAL MILES
(TROPIC ISLE SKETCH CHART VI-9)
EDITION 107

CAUTION: NOT FOR NAVIGATION
Tropic Isle Sketch Charts are supplements to the text of the current Yachtsman's Guide to the Virgin Islands. They are illustrative and not necessarily to scale.

Great Harbour waterfront. (Fields photo)

JOST VAN DYKE

N.O.S. Chart: 25641. Tropic Isle Sketch Charts: VI-1, 8, 9, 21.

Legend has it that Jost (pronounced *Yost*) Van Dyke was named for a Dutch pirate, although research has indicated that the island is more likely named for a planter from Holland who may have owned the island sometime in the late 1600s. In the 1700s, Dutch settlers were followed by Englishmen who built sugar and cotton plantations. A community of Quakers had also established itself by the mid-1700s, with enough people to fill two meeting-houses, one on the East End and another in White Bay. One member of the Quaker congregation, whom Little Jost Van Dyke claims as a distinguished native son, was John Coakley Lettsom. He was born the youngest of seven sets of male twins (perhaps no particular accomplishment of his own but certainly a credit to the perseverance of his mother). Sent to England to learn medicine in the 1700s, Lettsom became the foremost physician of the times and the founder of the Medical Society of London. He returned to the islands in 1767, took over family's land, when he freed all the slaves of the estate. A clever and popular fellow, Lettsom penned this often-quoted poem:

Foxy's, Great Harbour. (Tropic Isle photo)

I John Lettsom
Blisters bleeds and sweats 'em
If in spite of this they die
I John Lettsom

When the plantations failed and their owners left the island, those people who remained turned to fishing, charcoal production, or smuggling for income. Easy access to St. Thomas created opportunities not only for legitimate trade, but for illegal transport of slaves from the emancipated British islands to St. Thomas (later Jost Van Dyke served as a bootlegging station during Prohibition). In the early 1800s, the population of Jost Van Dyke, which exceeded 500 (at least 400 of which were slaves), began to shrink as people left for St. Thomas or Tortola and others fell victim to cholera, smallpox, or hurricanes.

Today there is little on this rugged island except a few small settlements with perhaps 130 people altogether. There are next to no vehicles, none of the roads are paved, and electricity was acquired only in the past few years. Drinking is what people do when they visit Jost Van Dyke, embellished by good food, dancing, and general carousing. The beach bars, most run by islanders, are long-time favorites of chartering as well as local yachtsmen and famous for long happy hours and competitive brews of "painkiller" rum punches. According to a news item in the November 1990 *Caribbean Boating,* two Navy men who were drinking heavily on a bareboat in Cane Garden Bay decided to swim over to Jost Van Dyke. VISAR, the BVI's excellent search-and-rescue unit, launched a thorough land-and-sea search for the two men, finally finding them, drinking again, at a Jost bar. VISAR understandably was not amused.

There is also excellent hiking — a trail leads from White Bay to Great Harbour to Little Harbour to East End, with many beautiful views from on high and a chance to check out all the beach bars to decide your evening itinerary. There are some lovely beaches on the south shore with good snorkeling. You might also explore the ruins of a Quaker settlement and what remains of an old fort. Ask locals for directions.

Great Harbour

Great Harbour is the main settlement of the island and the port of entry. As you go in, don't get too close to either shoreline. You'll see a distinct change in water color to a darker hue at the head of the bay. This is a reef, so anchor just before you get to it, about 300 yards off. The holding ground is good in 15-20 feet of water over a sandy bottom. You'll get a change of wind from the hills, so at anchor you won't face east. Make sure you're securely anchored, and then take your dinghy into the dock through the break in the reef.

Customs and immigration offices are together in the building at the head of the dock. You can clear in and out of the BVI here.

What to Do

In the afternoon the town sleeps and the pretty beach is tranquil — children splash in the shallows while mothers keep watch, and old men wade out to stand in the cool water. It could be a hundred years ago, if you can manage to overlook the T-shirt concessions set up at lunch time.

Customs house, Great Harbour. (Tropic Isle photo)

Things liven up as evening approaches. Hand-lettered signs off the dock direct you to several beach bar/restaurants, all within a short walk up or down the beach. At the western end of the harbor is Rudy's Mariner's Rendezvous, where there are frequent pig roasts, weekly live music, good home-cooked food, and a not-inexpensive guest house. The next establishment east of Rudy's is Dorsey Chinnery's Club Paradise, where lunch and dinner are served daily, with live entertainment on Saturday nights. The extensive menu when we visited included black bean soup, sherried shrimp, Cornish hen, and lobster. Also at this end of the beach is "Christine" Bakery. Two spots further east on the beach are Happy Laurry and Ali Baba's, both with recommended seafood specialties. At the eastern end of the harbor, Foxy's Tamarind Bar and Restaurant has been a legendary yachtsman's hangout for over 25 years. Foxy, a seventh-generation Jost native, is a calypsonian and entreprenuer of renown, as well as the host of Foxy's Wooden Boat Regatta and the founder of the Jost Van Dyke Preservation Society. The food is good (but be prepared to wait for it awhile). Foxy entertains in the bar daily and there is a live local band Friday and Saturday nights. On New Year's Eve (known for these purposes as Old Year's Night), up to 300 yachts crowd into the anchorage for heavy-duty partying at Foxy's.

A 20-minute walk following the path over the hill west of Rudy's will take you down to White Bay. There's a nice view from the hilltop.

White Bay

White Bay is named for its beautiful white sandy beach. In calm sea and normal wind conditions, it's an excellent day anchorage and a great snorkeling and swimming spot. However, a ground swell can build at any time of day or night (especially in winter), and the anchorage can become uncomfortable or untenable. If you're not experienced with

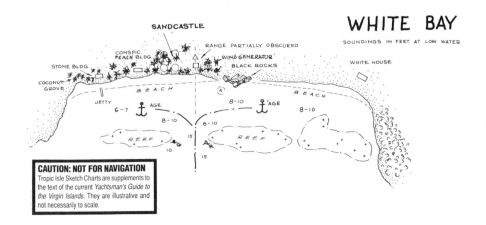

CAUTION: NOT FOR NAVIGATION
Tropic Isle Sketch Charts are supplements to the text of the current *Yachtsman's Guide to the Virgin Islands*. They are illustrative and not necessarily to scale.

Sandcastle, White Bay. (Tropic Isle photo)

ground swell conditions, we suggest you anchor elsewhere and make the short and scenic walk over the hill to the White Bay Sandcastle for a meal and enjoyable visit. The management of the White Bay Sandcastle invites you call them on VHF 16 for their advice or help anchoring.

Enter only in good light when you can clearly see the two large reefs across the entrance, as well as another one close to the shore on the eastern side of the bay. The recommended entrance between the reefs is now marked by a pair of privately maintained red and green buoys at the center reef entrance. The old 12° range can still be used as a backup, but it's hard to find. Although the channel carries a bit more, inside you'll find about 8-10 feet of water over a sandy bottom. Anchor to port (a bit shallower) or starboard, halfway between the reef and shore. Stay clear of a shoal spot to starboard off Black Rocks. Don't block the channel, and make sure your hook is dug in because there isn't much swinging room.

What to Do

Right on the beach, the Sandcastle is the dream spot for independent souls who prefer their tropical paradises tranquil, uncrowded, and unpretentious. Four quiet cottages are available with pretty views, and there's a casual bar and restaurant, hammocks for snoozing, and perhaps a pinochle game in progress. Reservations for lunch and dinner are required.

Snorkeling is excellent, with outstanding formations of elkhorn coral. You can also follow paths over the hill to see the tumultuous waters of the north shore.

Little Harbour

For the Skipper

Entrance is wide and deep in the center, but beware of shoals on both shores. Anchorage is off the western end of the bay in about 12 feet. It can get crowded on nights when a pig roast is under way on shore.

What to Do

There is a small settlement ashore. On the east shore of Little Harbour, Abe's has moorings available and serves a tasty menu of local fish, chicken, or lobster, with cheap drinks at happy hour. Across the bay,

Abe's. (Tropic Isle photo)

Sidney's Peace and Love. (Tropic Isle photo)

Harris' Place is run by Harris Jones, a Jost native who lived in New York for many years and, for awhile, worked in a liquor store in Harlem. Harris has moorings for visitors and serves breakfast, lunch, and dinner. Ice, groceries, cottages are available. Harris' daughter Cynthia runs Tula's Campgrounds, where bird-watching and snorkeling are encouraged. Sidney's Peace and Love is another good place to eat, drink, and on occasion enjoy live music. You can leave your autographed T-shirt or business card here for posterity.

Little Jost Van Dyke

A good anchorage can be found on the southwestern end of the island. Entrance is straightforward from the south. There is a 450-foot concrete dock that appears to be in bad repair, with 6 feet at the seaward end. Anchorage off the dock is over a good-holding sandy bottom. This anchorage can be choppy when the wind is out of the south, and if a big northerly swell is running there can be an inhospitable surge. Don't risk anchoring here overnight.

You'll find good snorkeling and gunkholing in the vicinity, but do your exploring by dinghy. There is no passage north between Jost Van Dyke and Little Jost Van Dyke. Between the two islands are shallow reefs.

Harris' Place. (Tropic Isle photo)

Adjacent Islands

Another good snorkeling spot is on the south end of the cay south of **Green Cay.** You can anchor in the lee of Green Cay, due west of the sandbar where the water is about 20 feet deep. Stay close to the bar because the depth increases sharply.

Sandy Cay, owned by Laurance Rockefeller, is a botanical garden with an encircling path and a kaleidoscope of beautiful views. The pretty beach is a good spot for a picnic lunch. Anchor on the southwest side of the cay, close to shore. The bottom is steep-to with some coral, so be sure you're securely anchored before going ashore. Here again, a heavy winter ground swell can cause breaking waves on the beach that will make landing impossible. This is strictly a good-weather, day anchorage. In the winter, humpback whales migrating from the south Atlantic to the cold northern waters have been sighted near the island.

Suggestions for next year's Guide?

We'd like to hear them! Send your notes to the Editor, Yachtsman's Guide to the Virgin Islands, P.O. Box 15397, Plantation, FL 33318 before March 1993. Please include your name and address. Thanks!

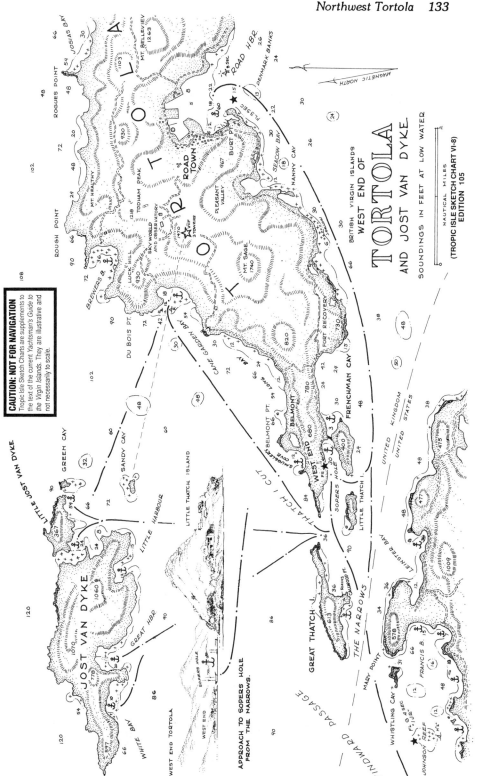

CAUTION: NOT FOR NAVIGATION
Tropic Isle Sketch Charts are supplements to the text of the current *Yachtsman's Guide to the Virgin Islands*. They are illustrative and not necessarily to scale.

BRITISH VIRGIN ISLANDS
WEST END OF
TORTOLA
AND JOST VAN DYKE
SOUNDINGS IN FEET AT LOW WATER
NAUTICAL MILES
(TROPIC ISLE SKETCH CHART VI-8)
EDITION 105

APPROACH TO SOPERS HOLE FROM THE NARROWS.

NORTHWEST TORTOLA

N.O.S. Chart: 25641. Tropic Isle Sketch Chart: VI-18.

The north shore of Tortola has some of the Virgin Island's most gorgeous beaches, long, white, and for the most part uncrowded. They're all the more brilliant in late afternoon when the sun turns the backdrop of overgrown hills to a rough emerald cloak. The climate is more humid here than on the south side of the island, and sea grape and coconut trees thrive, as well as such interesting bird life as the ruddy duck and the blue-faced booby. The northerly swells that make for risky anchorages in the winter months also make this area among the top Caribbean destinations recommended by the travel agency of the Association of Surfing Professionals.

The pretty little settlements that meander close along the shoreline, Carrot Bay and Apple Bay, are usually quiet except for the rhythmic wash of surf over sand and the occasional crow of a rooster or braying of a donkey. Further east, the carnival charisma of Cane Garden Bay has been praised in song by Jimmy Buffett.

In summer 1989, Tortola's northern coast was the site of the filming of the television movie *The Old Man and the Sea,* apparently

Bomba's Surf Shack. (Tropic Isle photo)

Long Bay (Fields photo)

satisfying the filmmaker's requirements for recreating a Cuban fishing village in the 1930s. Smuggler's Cove, Carrot Bay, and Brewer's Bay (using mechanical sharks and marlins) were all used extensively for locations in the film, which starred Anthony Quinn.

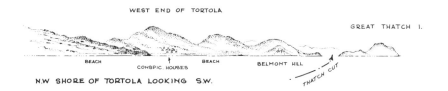

Smuggler's Cove

Just north of Sopers Hole, this is a daytime anchorage only. If a northerly swell is running, don't attempt it at all. The entrance through the reef is directly in the center of the opening of the bay in line with the center of the beach. Don't go in unless you can see the reef. Holding ground is good on a sandy bottom in 8 feet of water. There is a small hotel and bar/restaurant for lunch and dinner by reservation.

Long Bay

You can't anchor here, but it's worthwhile when the northerly swells are running to visit Long Bay by land or view it from a safe distance off in your boat to see the magnificent surf. Apparently the slope of the beach here is ideal; it produces awe-inspiring combers that are famous among the big-time, industrial-strength surfing set. If you want to meet some of the surfers who spend the winter here, find Bomba's Surf Shack along the road between Smuggler's Cove and Long Bay. Drinks and sandwiches are served and there's usually something going in the evenings, from full moon parties to live reggae music to barbecue.

Another reason to visit Long Bay by land – you can taxi up from Sopers Hole or rent a car in Road Town – is to visit some of the best places to eat on the island. The Sugar Mill, owned by Californians and gourmet writers Jeff and Jinx Morgan, serves fine food in a romantic 300-year-old setting. Their excellent cookbook is worth purchasing. Further east, in the settlement of Carrot Bay, is a roadside eatery called Jules' Place with good inexpensive patés. At the foot of the steep hill west of Cane Garden Bay is Mrs. Scatliffe's Restaurant (and home), where she and her family will cook and serve you a multi-course feast of island dishes, made with fresh produce and foods, some gathered from her yard. Between courses, members of the Scatliffe clan often reconvene into a scratch band. Reservations are required.

Cane Garden Bay

For the Skipper

Enter between the buoys, the red buoy to starboard. These marks are often reported missing. If there is any ground swell at all, don't anchor in Cane Garden Bay. It would not only be uncomfortable but also possibly dangerous. Remember that a swell can build any time, day or night.

Anchorage

Once inside, the northern end is the better protected part of the anchorage. Be sure to avoid the swimming area, which is sometimes but not always marked by buoys. Make sure your anchor is secure and allow your boat swinging room. Remember that wind often changes direction near the mountains. Rhymer's has moorings available for a fee. When you go ashore, pull your dinghy well up on the beach. Many dinghies have been set afloat by the tide or the surge here, so you're advised to tie up to a tree.

Some groceries and supplies can be purchased at Mr. Callwood's liquor store, and Rhymer's stocks various sundries.

What to Do

Cane Garden Bay is something of a cross between Shangri-la and Coney Island, leaning toward Coney Island. It isn't pristine or quiet, but its lush tropical beauty and carefree amusements can bring out the hedonist and calypso dancer in just about anyone. The beach bars, restaurants, and associated enterprises are owned by islanders whose families have been here for well over a century. Stanley's Welcome Restaurant, which claims to have been around the longest, about 20 years, has a landmark tire swing hanging from a palm tree out front. Big platters of wonderful barbecued lobster, chicken, or fish are the specialty. A steel band plays on most evenings and a crowd of islanders and visiting yachtsmen sway their inhibitions away in no time. Just west of Stanley's, Mona on the Beach sells T-shirts and jewelry. She'll also French-braid your hair if you like. Next to Stanley's to the east, Rhymer's unmistakable pink beach hotel and restaurant features frequent all-you-can-eat barbecues. Showers, umbrellas, pedal boats, ice, water, groceries, and liquor are available. Further down the beach, Loriel Henley runs the Paradise Club, a bar/restaurant with Saturday night pig roasts and music. He also rents motorized dinghies, windsurfers, and snorkeling and fishing equipment. In the back of the Paradise Club, Sigrid Leslie (who works at

Cane Garden Bay. (Tropic Isle photo)

Callwood's Distillery. (Tropic Isle photo)

Stanley's in the evenings) has a little shop called Distinctively Natural, with T-shirts, coral jewelry, and spices, among other things. Next door, the Gazebo, an open-air wooden pavilion serving food and drink, is owned by Quito Rymer, an accomplished singer and guitarist who entertains frequently with his pleasant combination of Caribbean and folk music. Across from the Gazebo, Quito has the Ole Works Inn, with eight rooms with baths and air-conditioning. At the far west end of the beach is De Wedding Bar & Restaurant, and also The Elm, a small inn and gift shop.

At Callwood's Distillery, you might be able to watch rum-making in progress but check with Mr. Callwood before exploring. If you buy a bottle or so, he may be willing to give you a tour. We were told the building is 400 years old.

Brewers Bay and Eastward

Brewers Bay, almost completely isolated, has one of the most beautiful uncrowded beaches in the islands and fine campgrounds. However, it's a difficult, reefy anchorage and not to be risked in even a slight ground swell. It's also not for overnight, especially in winter when there's a heavy surge.

Further along the north side of Tortola are more lovely beaches,

Cane Garden Bay. (Tropic Isle photo)

none recommended for anchorages. In the late winter, swells from the north break in spectacular surf that would make anchorage impossible and beaching a dinghy disastrous.

For the Skipper

It's safest to slowly and carefully motor into Brewers Bay, keeping a lookout at the bow as there are many reefs and the bottom drops away very steeply. Take care again when you anchor because a submarine cable comes into the bay. You can anchor in the southeast corner between the reef that runs all along the southwest shore and the reef that protrudes into the center of the bay, but be careful getting in there. There is a frequent roll. The bottom is sandy with 15-20 feet of water.

What to Do

In season, there are a couple beach bars and a small restaurant that sometimes serves breakfast and lunch. If you have time, you can poke around ashore and explore some distillery ruins along the beach. Around the salt pond are reportedly the remains of a fort built to cope with pirates. A 30-minute hike up the road are the ruins of a windmill and an old distillery on Mount Healthy.

Overlooking Road Harbour. (Tropic Isle photo)

SOUTH TORTOLA

D.M.A. Chart: 25611. N.O.S. Chart: 25641. Admiralty Charts: 2019, 2452. Tropic Isle Sketch Charts: VI-1, 8, 10, 11, 21.

Tortola got its name ("turtle dove") from the Spanish in the 1500s, who stopped here en route to their copper mines on Virgin Gorda. For years, pirates used the bays of Tortola as hideouts and replenishing points, and plenty of pirate legends date back to this era. In 1966 a rumor spread that the skeletons of seven pirates had been found buried in a T-formation near West End, perhaps a clue to buried treasure. It's also said that unearthly voices can be heard near some of the old haunts on moonless nights.

In 1648 the Dutch settled on the island but were chased off by pirates 20 years later; they were followed by the English, who were chased off by the French, and in turn re-chased off by the English, all within six years. By this time England and Denmark were emerging as the occupying powers of the various Virgin Islands, with the British moving quickly to acquire whatever the Danish didn't already have. Like the other islands, Tortola attracted planters, who were moderately successful. A

Tortolan who found a degree of fame in these times was William Thornton, a self-taught architect who heard from a passing ship captain in 1792 that a contest was under way to select a design for the new Capitol Building in Washington, D.C. Thornton drafted some ideas and brought them to the States. His designs were judged the best, and he was awarded $500 and a home in the new capital city, where he moved and was later appointed the first Commissioner of Patents.

By the early 1800s Tortola had entered an economic decline that lasted for more than 100 years. Many of the white residents left Tortola after a slave plot to murder them all was uncovered in 1831. In 1834 slavery was abolished. Labor problems and a cholera epidemic during the next thirty years left even fewer people able to make a living here, and the island retreated into relative anonymity until the yachting industry brought tourism to the BVIs in the 1960s.

Tortola remains a beautiful sleeping giant of an island, inscrutable and intriguing. Burros still serve as transportation for some Tortolans who live up along the narrow ridges in the hills, and cattle plod down the main road, Drake's Highway, with bleating nanny goats clambering alongside. Succulents and shrubs thrive on this dry, hot side of the island, and in spring the bushy golden blooms of century trees dot the hillsides. Time seems to move at a previous century's pace, as though history slowed with no desire to catch up to the 20th century.

Despite this enticing surrender to languor, the south shore of Tortola has a very active marine community, excellent services, and a good deal of civic pride. There is a close community of British, American, and Canadian expatriates and native Tortolans who appreciate and intend to preserve Tortola's simplicity and at the same time attract the type of visitors who won't abuse it.

West End

Sopers Hole was the first settlement on Tortola, used by pirates in the 1600s as a location to repair vessels, stock up on fresh water and

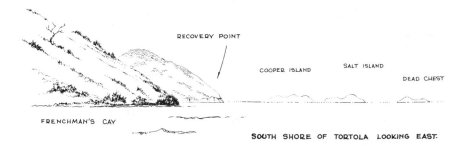

RECOVERY POINT

COOPER ISLAND   SALT ISLAND

DEAD CHEST

FRENCHMAN'S CAY

SOUTH SHORE OF TORTOLA LOOKING EAST.

food, and spot unwary approaching boats from the surrounding steep hills. Today Sopers Hole is internationally famous among wooden-boat devotees for its excellent building and repair facilities. Vessels of unusual beauty, fame, or historical significance can often be seen undergoing refurbishing here.

Ferries from St. Thomas, St. John, Virgin Gorda, and Jost Van Dyke stop here, so depending on whether one of these is at the dock, you may or may not clear customs and immigration quickly. If members of your group want extra time shopping or exploring in Road Town, you can easily send them ahead by taxi from West End and then sail up to meet them. Drake's Highway winds along the water from West End to Road Town and is a pretty drive. Along the way is Fort Recovery, built in 1660 by the Dutch and now part of a private resort.

For the Skipper

Entrance is through Sopers Hole in very deep water, with a current of up to 3 knots. Watch out for various buoys, ropes, and markers that change positions in the vicinity of West End Slipway, put there for their own boat works.

Anchorages and Facilities

Sopers Hole offers good overnight protection. The eastern end of the bay is the only area shallow enough for anchoring, but moorings have been placed there by both Sopers Hole Marina and West End Slipway. Since it's difficult if not impossible to anchor on your own tackle without swinging into a moored vessel or running over a buoy, you're probably best off taking a mooring. If you're only clearing customs, inquire about short-term mooring rates. West End Slipway maintains about 20 moorings painted orange and marked "Shipyard," with fees payable at West End Slipway. Sopers Hole Marina has 18 white-topped moorings near Pusser's, payable at the marina (monthly mooring rates are available).

Customs office and ferry dock, West End. (Fields photo)

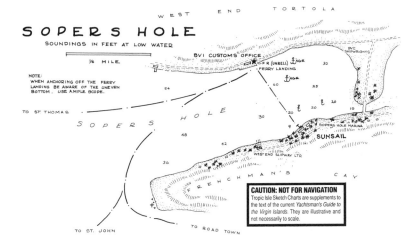

Customs and immigration offices are together upstairs in the building right on the government wharf/ferry dock, on the north shore about 300 yards from the eastern end of the harbor. There is ample water alongside to tie up, but constant ferry traffic makes this inadvisable. Anchor off to the east or pick up a mooring and bring your dinghy in instead. Nearby are snack bars, ice machines, a fruit stall, and a post office.

Sopers Hole Marina is on Frenchman's Cay, across from the customs wharf. There are 18 deep-water slips averaging 25 feet deep, with fuel, ice, water, and electricity available. The adjacent complex houses a convenient Ample Hamper provisioning shop as well as some unique gift shops and boutiques. Baskin in the Sun has a full-service dive shop here with SCUBA repair facilities and an air compressor (they can usually fill your air tanks while you wait). Two dive trips are offered daily. Baskin in the Sun monitors VHF 16.

Sunsail, just west of Sopers Hole Marina, has dockage available for boats with up to a 9-foot draft, with 13 feet available at the end of

YACHTSMEN
FOOD & LIQUOR PROVISIONING
in the BRITISH VIRGIN ISLANDS

With over 18 years experience
we set the STANDARD all
others try to follow.
Do yourself a favour
CALL, FAX or WRITE for our
25 page CUSTOM order form.

ENSURE YOU GET ONLY THE FOOD YOU WANT

THE AMPLE HAMPER

Inner Harbour Marina   Soper's Hole Marina
Road Town, Tortola   West End, Tortola
(809) 494-2494   (809) 495-4684

Fax: (809) 494-5349
Box 73, Road Town
Tortola, British Virgin Islands

Sunsail at Sopers Hole. (Tropic Isle photo)

the T-dock. Sunsail maintains a fleet of 50 yachts, bareboat or crewed, from 32 to 53 feet. Radio ahead to make sure that slips are not all in use. Fuel, water, ice, and electricity are available at the dock, and there is a laundry.

West End Slipway, owned and run by Morgan Sanger, is immediately west of Sunsail. The only yard of its kind between San Juan and Antigua, it's a full-service facility with a complete machine, fiberglass, and carpentry shop specializing in design and rebuilding. The 200-ton marine railway can haul up to 110-foot vessels with 14-foot draft. If the dock is unoccupied, boats can tie up there at night. Also under West End Slipway management on Sopers Hole are the Sandy Spit Boatyard and BVI Shipwright.

The Wood Works, Ltd. rebuilds and designs classic yachts and also specializes in the construction of masts, booms, and custom interiors. Some dockage may be available.

Serving the Caribbean's Finest Yachts
WESTEND SLIPWAY, LTD.
SOPERS HOLE, TORTOLA, BRITISH VIRGIN ISLANDS
(809) 495-4353 FAX (809) 495-4678
200-Ton Marine Railway • 50-Ton Sidetrack Facility
• Boat Building • Woodwork • Cabinetry
• BVI Shipwright • Sandy Spit Boatyard
Reconstruction of larger wooden vessels our specialty.
YACHT MAINTENANCE
ANY MAJOR OR MINOR REPAIRS ON ALL
TYPES OF YACHTS AND EQUIPMENT

Sopers Hole. (Fields photo)

What to Do

You can dinghy in to The Pusser's Landing, next to Sopers Hole Marina, for lunch, dinner, or just a drink and a snack. Weekly specialties include all-you-can-eat shrimp on Tuesdays, West Indian night on Wednesdays, and a Sunday BBQ. The Pusser's Company Store sells sports and travel clothing, sport watches, luggage and nautical accessories and, of course, Pusser's Rum.

A short walk east, Frenchman's Cay Hotel and Restaurant offers a variety of cuisines for lunch or dinner, served on a spacious terrace. On the other side of the harbor, the Jolly Roger bar serves good island food, sandwiches, and pizza, and keeps late hours for high-spirited customers. You can also take a cab for the briefly precipitous but scenic ride over the hill to Long Bay, Carrot Bay, and Apple Bay, where there are several recommended places to eat.

Great Thatch/Little Thatch Islands

Great Thatch and Little Thatch Islands may be named after Edward Teach (sometimes written as Thatch), also known as Blackbeard. Little Thatch Island is said to have been the retirement spot of another famous pirate with the operatic-sounding name of Gustav Wilmerding and a group of his pirate cohorts.

Take care approaching the anchorage just west of Callwood Point on Great Thatch Island. A native boat is sunk in the middle of it.

Frenchman's Cay

Continuing east, leave Sopers Hole between Frenchman's Cay and Little Thatch Island. The passage between Frenchman's Cay and Tortola is for dinghies only. On the northeastern shore of Frenchman's Cay is a good day anchorage for vessels drawing 7 feet or less. Do not anchor here overnight.

Great Thatch and Little Thatch Islands. (Tropic Isle photo)

Pegleg's prominent white roof at Nanny Cay. (Tropic Isle photo)

Nanny Cay

For the Skipper

As you near Nanny Cay, you'll see masts, and the white roof of Peg Leg Landing restaurant, perched on stilts, is a prominent landmark. Red and green channel markers lead you in. Inside the harbor, the green buoys to port mark shoals that run all along the western shore. The marks here are privately maintained, and the outer pair is lighted. Nanny Cay

---

Nanny Cay Resort And Marina

A Haven For Mariners

The well protected harbor at Nanny Cay contains a 200 slip marina offering dockage, fuel, water, ice and repair services.

The boatyard at Nanny Cay can lift boats up to 50 tons and has room to store 140 boats. Available services include fibreglass repairs, woodwork, refinishing, engine repairs, rigging, electronic and electrical work as well as long term storage.

A hotel, two restaurants, a diving service, a laundry, a yacht brokerage and a food and liquor store make Nanny Cay Resort and Marina a fine place for a long or short term stay.

Box 281, Roadtown, Tortola, British Virgin Islands

Tel: (809) 494 - 2512   Fax: (809) 494 - 3288

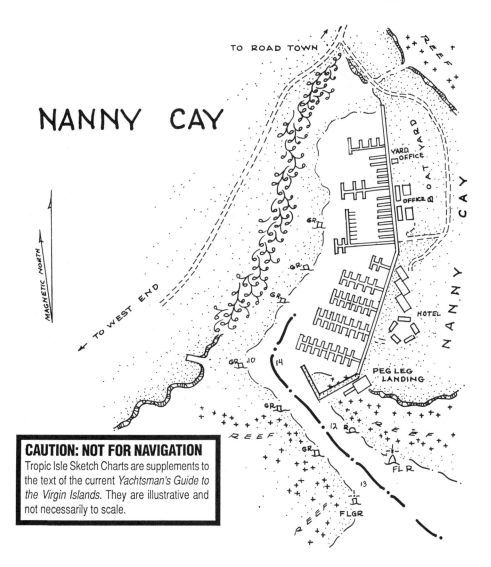

NANNY CAY

TO ROAD TOWN

CAUTION: NOT FOR NAVIGATION
Tropic Isle Sketch Charts are supplements to the text of the current *Yachtsman's Guide to the Virgin Islands.* They are illustrative and not necessarily to scale.

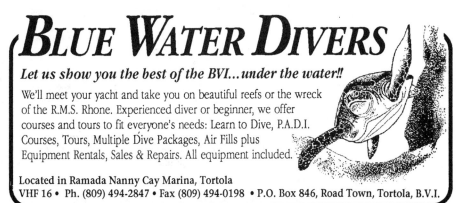

ʃBLUE WATER DIVERS

Let us show you the best of the BVI...under the water!!

We'll meet your yacht and take you on beautiful reefs or the wreck of the R.M.S. Rhone. Experienced diver or beginner, we offer courses and tours to fit everyone's needs: Learn to Dive, P.A.D.I. Courses, Tours, Multiple Dive Packages, Air Fills plus Equipment Rentals, Sales & Repairs. All equipment included.

Located in Ramada Nanny Cay Marina, Tortola
VHF 16 • Ph. (809) 494-2847 • Fax (809) 494-0198 • P.O. Box 846, Road Town, Tortola, B.V.I.

management reports that the harbor has been dredged to a controlling depth of 12 feet.

Anchorages and Facilities

You may not anchor at Nanny Cay. Call them on VHF 16 or tie up to one of the first two docks when you enter and ask for the harbormaster. Nanny Cay is no longer a port of entry.

Nanny Cay Resort and Marina, three miles west of Road Town, has 200 slips and dockage available for boats up to 170 feet long, with electricity and water meters at each berth, and full shower facilities available to yachtsmen. Long-term in-water/out-of-water storage can also be arranged. Call ahead if you need assistance in docking. Reservations are welcome.

There is a boatyard with a 50-ton hoist, dry storage for 140 boats, a full-service fuel dock, a chandlery with engineering and repair facilities, and a shop that does refinishing and fiberglass work. Also at Nanny Cay are a provisioning store, a laundry, Castaways Boutique, a video store, a cafe and a resort hotel. At Blue Water Divers, Mike and Keith Royle offer dive tours, refills, and dive equipment rentals and repairs. Nearby is a boardsailing instruction and rental concession. Charter companies based at Nanny Cay include North South Yacht Charters, Discovery

Nanny Cay Resort and Marina. (Tropic Isle photo)

Yacht Charters, and Offshore Sail & Motor Yachts. Peg Leg Landing restaurant has a raw bar with fresh seafood and a beautiful view westward up Sir Francis Drake channel. Resort facilities include fresh-water and sea-water pools, a swimming beach, and tennis courts.

Prospect Reef Resort

For the Skipper

About a mile east of Sea Cow Bay and around Slaney Point lies the Prospect Reef Resort and Marina. The harbor will take boats only up to 40-45 feet long with 5.5 feet draft or less. There are reefs on both sides of the entry into the harbor. Don't attempt to enter without first calling *Baskin in the Sun* on Channel 16 for instructions and information on available dockage. On the starboard side is a stone breakwater curving out beyond the shore. Once through the breakwater, be ready to make a sharp bend to port.

Prospect Reef is *not* a port of entry.

Facilities

Ice, diesel fuel, showers, and overnight berthage are available with full hook-ups. Anchoring in the harbor is not allowed. You can buy provisions at Robin and Liz Smith's compact, well-stocked Little Circle. Resort wear is sold at their adjacent shop, On the Beach, and the Pink Pineapple has colorful fabrics and gifts. Baskin in the Sun runs two dive trips daily and will fill your tanks while you wait. They monitor VHF 16.

Prospect Reef offers a complete roster of resort-type activities.

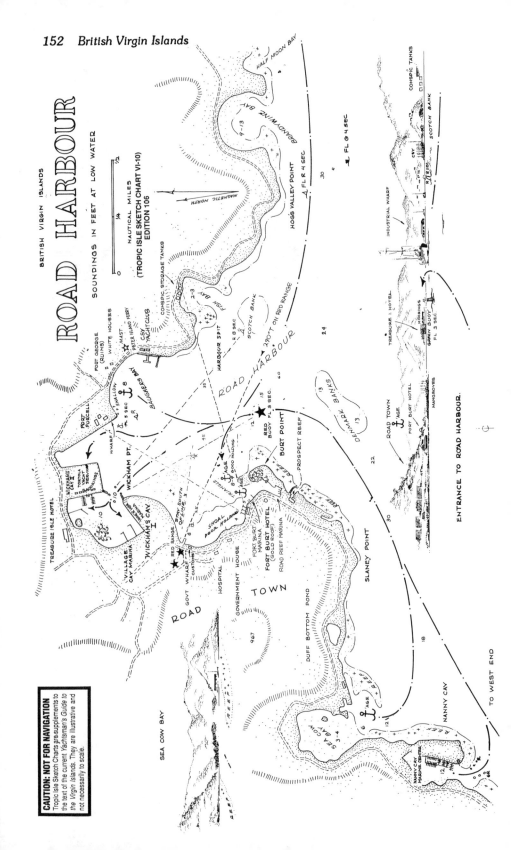

ROAD HARBOUR

BRITISH VIRGIN ISLANDS

SOUNDINGS IN FEET AT LOW WATER

(TROPIC ISLE SKETCH CHART VI-10)
EDITION 106

NAUTICAL MILES

CAUTION: NOT FOR NAVIGATION
Tropic Isle Sketch Charts are supplements to the text of the current Yachtsman's Guide to the Virgin Islands. They are illustrative and not necessarily to scale.

ENTRANCE TO ROAD HARBOUR.

Road Harbour

Road Town is the administrative capital of the British Virgin Islands and the center of its marine community.

For the Skipper

Entering from the west, look for the silver gas tanks in Fish Bay on the eastern side of the harbor entrance. Take the green sea buoy (Fl. gr. ev. 3 sec.) off Burt Point to port. This marks the deep water lying off the reef that juts east from Burt Point. On the east side of the harbor you'll see a red conical buoy flashing red every 8 seconds. This marks Scotch Bank. There are usually some large freighters in the harbor and occasionally a cruise ship.

As you continue in, opening up on your left is the Fort Burt Marina and Island Marine Store, directly below the round roof of the old Fort Burt Hotel. Do not steer for it immediately as there is a sandbar with only 3-4 feet of water over it extending north of Burt Point for about 100 yards. Instead, head for the government dock in Road Town until the north end of Fort Burt Marina is abeam. Then steer in for a point north

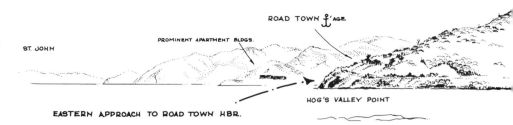

ROAD TOWN ⚓'AGE

PROMINENT APARTMENT BLDGS.

ST. JOHN

HOG'S VALLEY POINT

EASTERN APPROACH TO ROAD TOWN HBR.

of the Fort Burt Marina dock, where you can anchor in sand in 8-10 feet of water.

Caution: *In spite of clear directions, boats continue to go aground on the sand spit that projects north from Burt Point. To avoid this, go a little further north even when you feel you are far enough in past the buoy, before turning to port.*

Note: Approaching Road Harbour from the east, there is a newly marked channel for large freighters and cruise ships which bears 278° T on Fort Burt Hotel. It is marked with a green buoy flashing green every 4 seconds about .5 mile southeast of Hog's Valley Point and a red buoy flashing red every 4 seconds about 200 yards south of Hog's Valley Point. Don't let these confuse you.

Anchorages and Facilities

Road Harbour doesn't have the best holding ground and, although there's usually no swell, it can be choppy and uncomfortable. If the wind is in the south, the harbor can be untenable. Be sure you're well-anchored because if you drag, you'll go right up on the shore. If you want to stay overnight, tie up at one of the marinas.

Customs and immigration offices are together at the town dock. Procedures here in the capital of the British Virgin Islands tend to formality. All yachts arriving from foreign ports must anchor off the town dock and check with customs and immigration before proceeding to any

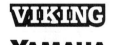

Fort Burt Marina. (Tropic Isle photo)

marina or nearby anchorage. The surge is often strong, so you'd best not lie alongside. Dinghy in instead, but take care tying up.

Fort Burt Marina. Anchor about 250 feet north of the marina docks. The anchorage is in 8-9 feet of water. Don't go closer unless your draft is under 5 feet, and don't anchor too far north, where the bottom is grassy and poor holding. If you stay within the limits of the small dotted triangle on the Road Harbour sketch chart, you'll be in good water. Fuel and ice are available at the marina and there is an Island Marine Store on the premises. Conch Charters, headquartered upstairs, offers charter boats from 30-50 feet. There's also woodworking, outboard, and equipment repairs available, and a grocery nearby. The Pub (now officially called the Paradise Pub and run by ex-Denver Bronco Mike Dunafon) is a good place to drink and eat, with a big-screen TV for football junkies. Across the street, the Fort Burt Hotel restaurant is excellent.

Road Reef Marina is south of the Fort Burt Marina docks in the cove (known as Careening Cove) inside of Burt Point. This is the base of Tortola Marine Management. There is 7 feet in the approach to their facility and better than that at the docks. Pass just off the Fort Burt Marina docks. Leave the small green floats, which mark the inside of the reefs, to port as you enter (these floats were missing at the time of our recent survey). Slips are available with electricity, water, and ice, and there is a marine electronics sales and repair facility. Call *TMM* on VHF 12 for more information or help on entering. Road Reef Marina is headquarters for VISAR, the Virgin Islands Search & Rescue organization.

Wickham's Cay

For the Skipper

Head for the masts you'll see beyond a stone breakwater. The entrance to the inner harbor is well-buoyed and marked. Leave the red buoy to your starboard and proceed inside the breakwater. The channel is 80 feet wide and will carry a draft of 10 feet. Inside is another set of markers that must be carried.

Anchorages and Facilities

Village Cay Marina and Hotel, to your port after entering, has berths for 106 yachts up to 200 feet long with 11 feet draft, stern-to or along finger piers. Electricity, water, telephone, and cable TV facilities are available dockside, and ashore in the marina complex are hot

Village Cay Marina. (Fields photo)

VILLAGE CAY

VILLAGE CAY
MARINA · HOTEL
TORTOLA · B·V·I

RESTAURANT · HOTEL · MARINA

Centrally located in the heart of Road Town

- *Full Service Marina*
  106 slips all with full facilities for boats up to 200ft, security dawn to dusk, 110/220 power, water, cable, IDD phone, garbage removal, chandlery, clearing house, fuel, ice, laundry, showers.
  All general services within 5 minutes of marina.
- *Restaurant on the waterfront*
  Open all day 7:30 am – 11:00 pm
  Lunch served 11:00 am – 6:00 pm daily
  Featuring fresh fish, aged meat and daily specials
  Weekly buffet; check local press for details
- *Hotel*
  Recently refurbished rooms with a/c, color and cable tv, daily maid service, dry cleaning, laundry and swimming pool.

Village Cay, Wickhams Cay I, Road Town, Tortola, BVI
Tel: (809) 494-2771   Fax: (809) 494-2773

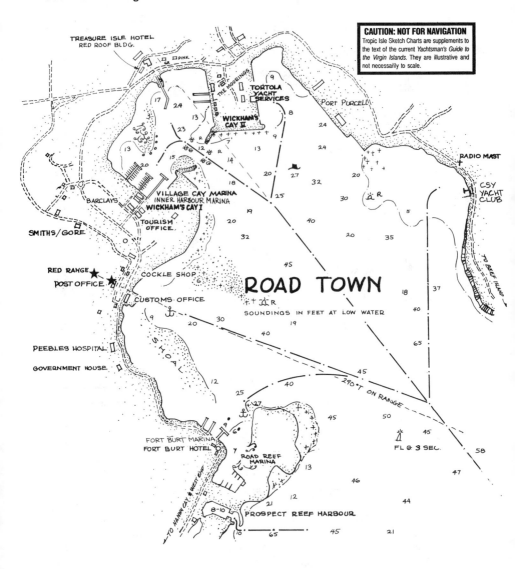

CAUTION: NOT FOR NAVIGATION
Tropic Isle Sketch Charts are supplements to the text of the current *Yachtsman's Guide to the Virgin Islands*. They are illustrative and not necessarily to scale.

ROAD TOWN

SOUNDINGS IN FEET AT LOW WATER

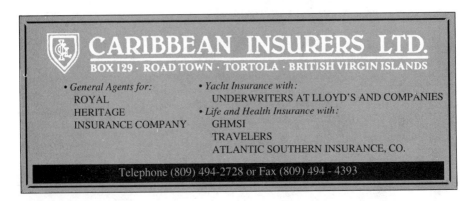

CARIBBEAN INSURERS LTD.

BOX 129 · ROAD TOWN · TORTOLA · BRITISH VIRGIN ISLANDS

- *General Agents for:*
  ROYAL
  HERITAGE
  INSURANCE COMPANY

- *Yacht Insurance with:*
  UNDERWRITERS AT LLOYD'S AND COMPANIES
- *Life and Health Insurance with:*
  GHMSI
  TRAVELERS
  ATLANTIC SOUTHERN INSURANCE, CO.

Telephone (809) 494-2728 or Fax (809) 494-4393

Inner Harbour Marina. (Tropic Isle photo)

showers, ice, a laundromat, restaurants, hotel rooms, an Ample Hamper provision shop, and clothing and gift shops. The Mill Mall, next to Village Cay, includes a boutique, car rental, and chandlery. Road Town's main shopping area is just a few minutes' walk across the street.

Inner Harbour Marina is located just south of Village Cay Marina. Slips are available for 22 boats, with fuel, water, ice, and electricity, plus a car rental agency on site. Call ahead on VHF 16, let the dockmaster know your needs and draft, and see if space is available. The

INNER HARBOUR MARINA

Water, Electricity, Phones
Showers, Cable TV • Duty Free Fuel
Restaurant & Bar • Diving Facility • Beauty Salon

• Wrangler 4-Wheel Drive Jeep
• Suzuki 4-Wheel Drive Jeep
• Discounts Marina Guests

AIRWAYS CAR RENTAL

Visa, Mastercard, AMEX
Wickhams Cay I
P.O. Box 852
Road Town,
Tortola
Tel:
809 - 494-4502
VHF 16

marina is headquarters for BVI Bareboats, offering sail and power boats from 32' to 51', with yacht management and brokerage among their services.

Treasure Isle Hotel's dock is to your starboard after entering. Call on VHF Channel 12 to see if dockage is available.

The Mariner Inn, on Wickham's Cay II, has some slips available to visiting boats. Contact the dockmaster on VHF Channel 12 for instructions.

Tortola Yacht Services, also on Wickham's Cay II, has two 37-ton TAMI lifts, an 80-ton railway, dry storage for 40 boats, Awlgrip refinishing facilities, the Golden Hind chandlery, and Tortola Yacht Sales. TYS is also headquarters for the Caribbean Refinishing Group, offering fiberglass repair and Awl-Grip refinishing. Within walking distance is Tradewind Yachting Services, for inflatable sales and repair, outboards, and batteries. Nearby are machine and electronics shops, a sailmaker and repair loft, and a marine power services shop.

What to Do

If you stay in the Road Town area more than a week, you'll begin to recognize familiar faces and, in fact, you'll become a familiar face yourself. This is not to say it's a sleepy little harbor town — quite the

---

VIRGIN ISLANDS SEARCH & RESCUE is ...

- **SAVING LIVES** of people in distress at sea.
- **RENDERING ASSISTANCE** as necessary to vessels and persons in distress at sea.
- **ASSISTING INTERNATIONAL ORGANIZATIONS** in the search for missing vessels, aircraft, and people.
- **TRAINING AND EDUCATING** the public in safety at sea.
- **HELPING COORDINATE** the response of the private and government sectors in the BVI in the event of a marine, air, or natural emergency under the guidelines established by the National Emergency Committee.

MEMBER'S BENEFITS AND ANNUAL DUES

Individual $25 Receives semi-annual newsletter and decal
Family $40 Receives semi-annual newsletter and decal
Friend $100 Receives semi-annual newsletter and decal
Benefactor $250 Receives semi-annual newsletter, decal and VISAR burgee
Life Member $500 Receives semi-annual newsletter, decal and VISAR burgee

To become a member or for more information, contact:

VIRGIN ISLANDS SEARCH & RESCUE LTD.
P.O. Box 3042, Road Town, Tortola
British Virgin Islands
(809) 494-4357 FAX (809) 494-5166

Road Town street. (Tropic Isle photo)

contrary. Each year we notice a remarkable proliferation of new businesses, shops, and restaurants.

The local boat crowd hangs out in the afternoons at The Pub, overlooking the Fort Burt Marina. Across the street and a short climb up the slope, the Fort Burt Hotel is built over the ruins of a 17th-century Dutch fort. You can have a drink on the patio overlooking the harbor, and the hotel restaurant's excellent food is enhanced by a panoramic view when the enormous shutters are thrown open. Further up the road, on your way into town, are Government House, Peebles Hospital, and the BVI Tourist Board Office, where you should pick up a copy of the *BVI Welcome* tourist magazine.

Homemade pizza with assemble-your-own-pie trimmings has been added to the menu at Pusser's Road Town, where drinks, sandwiches, and traditional English dishes are also served. At The Pusser's Company Store a collection of nautical antiques is on display and unique

gift items are for sale, including Pusser's own line of travel and leisure clothing and fine luggage. Upstairs is the new, elegant Pusser's Outpost Restaurant, with a Victorian formal dining room and terrace overlooking the harbor. Reservations for dinner are recommended, and dinner guests are requested to not wear T-shirts or shorts.

The post office is on Main Street. Philatelists will be interested in the colorful sheets of BVI stamps, often featuring local fish and plant life depicted by local artists. Downtown are many small, cheerfully painted shops selling island crafts and imports. Ooh La La stocks novelty items, postcards, clothing, and imported toys. Bonkers Gallery has an eclectic variety of tropical clothing. Past and Presents is a book lover's paradise, with a large selection of excellent paperbacks, including many English editions of books no longer available in most American bookstores. Owner Madge Collins is an authority on literature, antiques (also sold in the store) and local wildlife. The little Virgin Islands Folk Museum has well-researched exhibits on island history and sells a variety of literature including collections of folklore, songs, and personal accounts. The Sunny Caribbee Herb and Spice Company is a good place to buy some easily packed gifts and souvenirs. At the Courtyard Gallery, humming-birds, hibiscus blossoms, and leaping fishes are exquisitely molded from pink coral. Further up the street, Little Denmark is a conglomeration of odds and ends, Scandinavian imports, and gold and silver jewelry. Off the traffic circle, TICO stocks wines and liquors. An adjoining boutique, The Turtle Dove, sells perfume and fashionable clothing.

One of our favorite places for lunch in town is the tiny garden patio sloping up the hill at Carib Gardens, where the West Indian dishes are hot and spicy. On Main Street, Elena's is a pretty garden restaurant with an exotic menu. A *Guide* contributor told us the Roti Palace was one

Road Town town square, overlooking the waterfront. (Fields photo)

Road Town. (Tropic Isle photo)

of their best stops for the good island cooking and warm hospitality. Spaghetti Junction is very good but small, so reservations are a good idea. Behind Village Cay Marina, The Wharf is excellent, with barbecue nights a couple times a week. The Virgin Queen bar has live music on weekends.

We recommend renting a car or jeep to explore. You must show your driver's license and pay a fee at the rental agency to be issued a temporary BVI driver's license, good for three months. The winding roads climb at alarming angles, but with experience you'll find them easier to negotiate than they appear. Take it slow on all roads, shift to low gear going downhill, and stay on the left-hand side of the road. The roads aren't well marked and some are in bad shape. You can ask for directions, but it's also fun to just get lost and wander around the island. This is probably best done by daylight, though — no one likes to still be "lost" at dinner time.

Once you have transportation, you can visit the J.R. O'Neal Botanic Gardens, four acres of tropical foliage. Another worthwhile trip by car or taxi is to Sky World, a roller-coaster climb up the mountain for a magnificent view all around the surrounding islands. Choose something from the interesting drink menu (the Misty Mountain or Soursop Daiquiri are good) and watch the sun go down. From up here the clouds, the islands, and the surrounding water can seem animate and brooding, especially after a Misty Mountain or two. There's also a nice gift shop and art gallery. From here you can drive down to Cane Garden Bay or back to Road Town. Brandywine Bay restaurant, about 6 miles east of Road Town on a bluff overlooking Brandywine Bay, is another out-of-town restaurant with a lovely view and Florentine cuisine. Proprietors are Cecelia and Davide Pugliese.

Baugher's Bay

For the Skipper

Farther around the north end of the harbor and just east of Wickham's Cay II is Port Purcell and the deep-water harbor used by large cargo ships delivering goods to Road Town. To the south is Baugher's Bay (pronounced *Bogger's*).

Anchorages and Facilities

There is good protected anchorage off the southern end of the filled area on a sandy bottom in 8-9 feet of water. In normal conditions this is a good overnight anchorage.

CSY Yacht Club is no longer in business, but there are plans afoot to open a new full-service marina with a commissary and gift shop in CSY's old location, so you might want to check this out. The dock to the north is reserved for the Peter Island ferry. Nearby, the Port Purcell Market has a good selection of groceries (at the time of our survey they offered delivery service). There's also K-Mark's Cash & Carry, a liquor store, a fish market, and the Beach Club West Indian restaurant and bar.

Brandywine Bay

Brandywine Bay's entrance is toward the center, between shallow reefs extending out considerable distances from the points of land which bound the eastern and western sides of the bay. Approach only in good light so you can clearly see the opening and the mooring area inside. Brandywine Bay Restaurant keeps three moorings for dinner guests in the center of the bay. These should be comfortable in settled easterly conditions. Other moorings situated in front of the apartments are private — do not pick them up. You can call the restaurant on VHF 16 after 2 p.m., or by telephone any time for mooring instructions or reservations. The center of the bay, where the restaurant's moorings are, is the deepest part, with about 10 feet of water. The bay shoals rapidly if you go too far toward shore, in any direction. Don't go inside the innermost of the restaurant's moorings.

Be aware that there can be a surge in Brandywine Bay.

John, I really need to shop! All we have left is peanut butter.

Gert! Did you forget to pack my *Yachtsman's Guide?*

Dad, you promised we could go scuba diving today!

I wanna go home.

Plan ahead...

If that fails be sure you have the latest *Yachtsman's Guide* on board. The source of indispensable information for generations of yachtsmen cruising the Bahamas.

- Updated Annually
- What The Skipper Should Know
- Island Profiles
- What To Do
- Sketch Charts
- Tide Tables And More !

Call (305) 893-4277
or write to: Tropic Isle Publishers
P.O. Box 610938
North Miami, FL
33261-0938

YACHTSMAN'S Guide
to the **Bahamas**

When you're cruising the Islands you should support the local Search and Rescue Units. They could save your Life.

When you are out in the Islands, the Coast Guard is far away. The local volunteer rescue unit is Virgin Islands Search and Rescue (VISAR). They need your money to be ready to help you.

SEARCH (Search and Rescue Charitable Foundation), a U.S. tax-exempt foundation, is devoted to improving and expanding all the volunteer search and rescue units in the Caribbean and the Bahamas.

SEARCH

Send your TAX-DEDUCTIBLE donation today to:

SEARCH,
1316 S.E. 17th Street,
Fort Lauderdale, FL 33316

[ ]   I wish to make a tax-deductible donation to SEARCH of $50/$100/more ($..........) My check is enclosed . Please send my contributor's certificate and recognition decal to my address below.

[ ]   Please send me more information.

Name _____ Date _____

Address _____ _____

City _____State _____Zip _____

Yacht's name/Aircraft Type & Reg No. _____

Please make checks payable to SEARCH and mail this form with your generous donation.

YOUR MONEY SAVES LIVES - MAYBE YOURS.

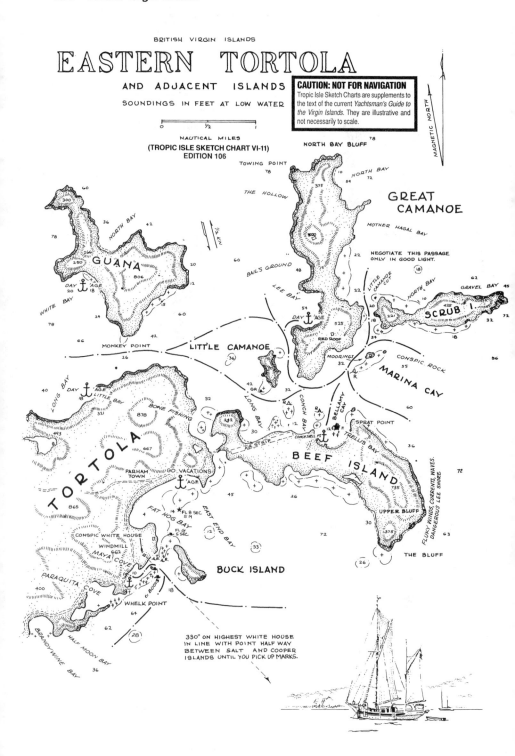

BRITISH VIRGIN ISLANDS

EASTERN TORTOLA

AND ADJACENT ISLANDS

SOUNDINGS IN FEET AT LOW WATER

CAUTION: NOT FOR NAVIGATION
Tropic Isle Sketch Charts are supplements to the text of the current *Yachtsman's Guide to the Virgin Islands*. They are illustrative and not necessarily to scale.

NAUTICAL MILES
(TROPIC ISLE SKETCH CHART VI-11)
EDITION 106

330° ON HIGHEST WHITE HOUSE IN LINE WITH POINT HALF WAY BETWEEN SALT AND COOPER ISLANDS UNTIL YOU PICK UP MARKS.

EASTERN TORTOLA

N.O.S. Chart: 25641. Tropic Isle Sketch Chart: VI-11.
The bays of eastern Tortola and the Camanoe Passages offer some dramatically beautiful cruising at the feet of Tortola's dark slopes and Beef Island's scrubby hills. As you progress through the shifting light and shadows within the surrounding collection of islands, the scenery opens up in constantly changing formations. There are some nice overnight anchorages with possibilities for memorable evenings ashore.

Maya Cove

Maya Cove is east of Whelk Point and west of Buck Island on the southeastern coast of Tortola. It is relatively bug-free, cool, sheltered, and one of the best anchorages on the coast.

For the Skipper

Entrance to and exit from Maya Cove should be made by motor. No more than 7 feet can be carried through the entrance channel at low water. Approach Maya Cove on a heading of 330° M on a line drawn from the center of the passage between Cooper and Salt Islands to a point between the two pink houses close together high on the hill that forms

Tropic Island Yacht Charters at Maya Cove. (Tropic Isle photo)

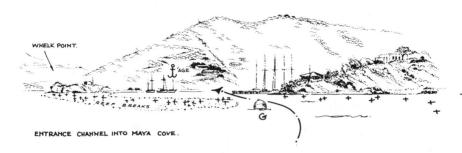

ENTRANCE CHANNEL INTO MAYA COVE.

the cove's eastern perimeter. Be careful to avoid the reef that projects westward from the highest point of Buck Island. This approach will lead you to the buoys that mark the northeast point of the reef that bounds Maya Cove on its south side. Take the green buoys to port and, once around the end of the reef, turn to port and parallel the inside of the reef into the anchorage. Keep a good lookout.

Anchorages and Facilities

Maya Cove offers excellent protection in 10 feet over a good holding bottom. Don't go too far in past TIYC's dock, because the water shallows fast from 8 feet just past the dock to 4 feet and less.

To pick up a mooring, call Tropic Island Yacht Charters, whose base is here, on VHF 12. If you take a mooring, TIYC will take your garbage. Diesel fuel, ice, water, and some supplies are available. There is a pleasant dockside restaurant and bar, the Pelican Roost.

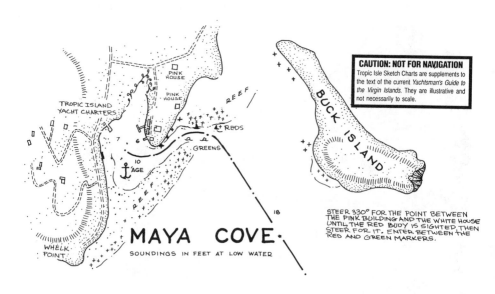

CAUTION: NOT FOR NAVIGATION
Tropic Isle Sketch Charts are supplements to the text of the current *Yachtsman's Guide to the Virgin Islands.* They are illustrative and not necessarily to scale.

STEER 330° FOR THE POINT BETWEEN THE PINK BUILDING AND THE WHITE HOUSE UNTIL THE RED BUOY IS SIGHTED, THEN STEER FOR IT. ENTER BETWEEN THE RED AND GREEN MARKERS.

MAYA COVE
SOUNDINGS IN FEET AT LOW WATER

Fat Hog's Bay

Fat Hog's Bay was the site of a large Quaker community and also for awhile the capital of the British Virgin Islands. There still exists the remains of an old Quaker cemetery here.

For the Skipper

East of Maya Cove is Fat Hog's Bay. Entrance is straightforward. Round Buck Island and leave the green lighted buoy to port and the light on Red Rock to starboard. Then turn starboard and run behind the reef into the excellent anchorage (10-12 feet) off Seabreeze Yacht Charters' docks. This is shown as East End Bay on charts. Call *Seabreeze Yacht Charters* if you need more detailed instructions.

Anchorages and Facilities

Seabreeze Yacht Charters Limited has a charter fleet of sailboats and trawlers and a full-service marina with fuel, water, diesel, ice, and showers. They operate a hotel with a poolside restaurant on the water called The Bistro. Breakfast, lunch, and dinner are served. There's also a store, boutique, and commissary. Call ahead for moorings or dock space on VHF 12. The west side of Fat Hogs Bay is shallow and exposed and is not an anchorage.

In Fat Hog's Bay, you can eat at Bing's Drop Inn Restaurant and Bar, where there's often dancing well past midnight.

The Camanoe Passages

For the Skipper

Between Monkey Point (the southern point of Guana Island) and Tortola, there is wide passage with no hazards. Monkey Point is distinguished by a large rock.

There are two passages through the Camanoes approaching from the west. Both should be negotiated in good light only. The recommended of the two is to motor north to south between Little Camanoe and Great Camanoe, where a strong current usually runs. Leave Little Camanoe to starboard and favor the coast of Great Camanoe to avoid the reef off the northeast tip of Little Camanoe. During heavy northern swells, the sea breaks on this reef and you will be able to see it clearly. From there, the channel between Little Camanoe and Great Camanoe is clear and deep.

Caution: The waters on the north side of Beef Island from Long Bay eastward to Sprat Point are strewn with reefs that extend well offshore toward Little and Great Camanoe. Markers in this area tend to be unreliable, so we advise you to keep a sharp lookout from the bow and proceed with caution when passing through these waters.

If you choose the second passage, between Little Camanoe and Beef Island, bear to your starboard after passing between Monkey Point and Tortola. There are several reef areas you must avoid. There is a reef extending from the southwest tip of Little Camanoe, usually marked by a privately maintained buoy, and another reef area (usually marked on its north side) about 600 yards out from the rock pile at the eastern end of Long Bay, or about one-third of the distance toward the south point of Great Camanoe.

Rocks about 100 yards off the westernmost point of Trellis Bay are marked by a red buoy. Pass north of this mark and then you can enter Trellis Bay with no further hazards. The north coast of Tortola is increasingly rocky going west of Little Bay, just below Guana Island.

LOOKING WEST TO MONKEY POINT CUT FROM THE SOUTH END OF GREAT CAMANOE ISLAND.

Anchorages

Caution: These anchorages are not for overnight, and are not recommended under any circumstances when the winter ground swells are running.

Little Bay, on Tortola below Guana Island, is a good day anchorage as long as the Atlantic swells are not running. There is a good sandy bottom and enough swinging room to spend some pleasant hours. Anchor securely well off the beach and take a dinghy ashore.

White Bay, on the lee side of Guana Island, is not a recommended anchorage. It is difficult to get into water shoal enough for safe anchoring (depth averages 20-25 feet), and once there you risk swinging into coral heads near shore. Two anchors might help. The island, including the long white beach, is private and visits ashore are not permitted. There is a rock formation north of the bay that resembles the head of a huge iguana, which is probably why the island bears the name it does.

Trellis Bay. (Tropic Isle photo)

Lee Bay, on Great Camanoe, is good for anchoring only if the weather is calm and the sea quiet. You can anchor in deep water (35 feet) and snorkel.

Trellis Bay

Beef Island was once grazed by cattle owned by the buccaneers of the late 16th and early 17th century. One story is told of an elderly widow of that era who was quickly losing her cattle to the thieving pirates next door. She invited her neighbors to visit one afternoon and served them all poisonous tea, solving her problem with grace and efficiency.

Some time ago, Trellis Bay, on the north side of Beef Island, was a primary anchorage in the British Virgin Islands. There was a large shipyard of which little now remains.

For the Skipper

To go into Trellis Bay from the north, stand well off Conch Shell

The Last Resort Island Restaurant

Trellis Bay, Beef Island
"...a gargantuan buffet..." (Washington Post)
"...a hilarious one-man show..." (New York Times)
"...an evening of food and drink and a year's supply of belly laughs..." (Yachtsmans' Guide)
Open For Lunch • Gift Shop

Visa /MasterCard • ReservationRequired
Telephone 809-49-52520 or Channel 16

Point on the western side of the bay to avoid the submerged rocks offshore, marked by a red buoy. Pass north of this buoy and come in halfway between the point and Bellamy Cay, the little cay in the center of Trellis Bay.

From the east, stand well off Sprat Point to avoid the rocks to the north of it. (Note: The BVI government may at some point place a mark off these rocks. If it appears, don't let it confuse you.) Once around the rocks, make your entrance halfway between Sprat Point and Bellamy Cay. The waters immediately south of Sprat Point are shoal.

You cannot pass between Beef Island and Tortola as the Queen Elizabeth Bridge does not open. The southwestern shore of Beef Island has many reefs and is not recommended for exploring.

Anchorages

Anchorages in Trellis Bay are well protected even in most bad weather. The location is convenient to Beef Island Airport (a five-minute walk via a dirt road) if you're dropping off or picking up a crew member, but you can't clear customs here. Ashore is a public garbage bin.

Anchor in the lee of Bellamy Cay or further south, avoiding the hard bar that extends south of the cay. You can also anchor southeast of Bellamy Cay and the reef that lies south of it. Don't anchor up toward the west side of the bay toward the abandoned shipyard, especially if you have tall masts. This area is directly in the flight path of planes departing Beef Island airport. Also do not anchor near the white buoys between Conch Shell Point and Bellamy Cay. They mark underground telephone cables.

What to Do

For unusual entertainment, The Last Resort defies description. After a buffet-style dinner, owner Tony Snell will regale and alarm you with ribald song, stories, and synthesized sound effects the likes of which are seldom heard on remote tropical islands. You must call ahead for reservations. There is a large dinghy dock. Ice and some provisions are available at the Last Resort Pit Stop.

Also on Trellis Bay, Conch Shell Point restaurant is often recommended by our contributors for excellent West Indian-cooked dinners. (There's a USA-Direct telephone there.) The Beef Island Guest House serves breakfast and lunch, and has a snack bar, De Loose Mongoose. There's a small grocery for limited provisioning. Some local artists and craftsmen have set up workshops on Trellis Bay where you can buy their hand-crafted jewelry or painted T-shirts and island scenes. At

The Queen Elizabeth Bridge. (Fields photo)

Boardsailing BVI lessons are offered by the hour, day, or week. Bonefishing is supposed to be good along the northeastern shore of Beef Island and also along the shoal areas north of the Queen Elizabeth Bridge, on the western side. There are also some interesting ruins to explore on the island, including the ruins of an old Quaker greathouse.

Marina Cay

Marina Cay was the island in Robb White's book, *Our Virgin Island,* which was made into a movie starring Sidney Poitier and John Cassevetes. The book, out of print for years, was reissued in 1985 retitled *Two on the Isle.*

For the Skipper

Marina Cay harbor is easy to enter from the southwest. A conspicuous reef extends south and west of Marina Cay. Stay to the north and west of it. At the time of our survey, a privately maintained oval-shaped red float buoy, along with an inconspicuous, spindly stake, marked the southwest end of the reef. If you choose this passage, give Beef Island a wide berth and head for the western end of the Marina Cay reef, taking it to starboard at least 50 yards off.

From the east, another recommended passage is north of Marina Cay. There is good water right up to the conspicuous rock off the northeast end of the cay. Leave the rock to port and pass between Marina

Cay and Scrub Island, and then round up into the anchorage.

There is a fourth passage from the north between Scrub Island and Great Camanoe, but don't attempt it unless the light is good and you can see the reefs that line both sides of the passage. Favor the shore of Great Camanoe as you enter, and use your motor only. The white markers in the area mark fish pots.

Anchorages and Facilities

Anchor in the lee of the cay, north and west of the reef, in 15-25 feet of water over good holding ground. A number of rental moorings are available. Don't anchor too close to the private moorings and allow room for boats serving the cay's facilities.

Fuel, ice, and water are available at the dock. Ashore are a restaurant, laundry facilities, showers, provisions, and a boutique. Beaches and lounge chairs are available to visitors. Lunch is served at the beach bar — a good place to eat if you're moored nearby. There's an honor bar and a TV by the patio. At the top of the hill is a comfortable library with an interesting collection of books and, outside, a nice view — a lovely place for a drink in the evening as the sun sets. Accommodations overlook the ocean and, at night, have a magnificent view of the infinite starry sky.

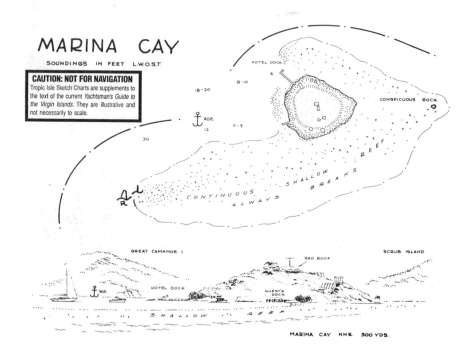

MARINA CAY

SOUNDINGS IN FEET L.W.O.S.T.

CAUTION: NOT FOR NAVIGATION
Tropic Isle Sketch Charts are supplements to the text of the current *Yachtsman's Guide to the Virgin Islands.* They are illustrative and not necessarily to scale.

ISLANDS TO THE SOUTH OF THE SIR FRANCIS DRAKE CHANNEL

N.O.S. Chart: 25641. D.M.A. Chart: 25609. Tropic Isle Sketch Charts: VI-1, 12, 13, 21.

With many secluded little harbors, the islands to the south of the Sir Francis Drake Channel were an ideal place for pirate ships to lurk while watchmen posted in the hills spotted approaching cargo vessels. In those days, the Sir Francis Drake Channel was referred to as the "Virgin's Gangway." Today most of the rocky islands here are sparsely inhabited except for wild cattle and sure-footed goats.

Keep in mind that the waters between these islands have a current running in a generally northwest and southeast direction at the rate of .5 to 1.5 knots. The velocity changes with the tide and wind conditions.

Sir Francis Drake Channel (Virgin Gorda in background). (Helleberg photo)

NORMAN AND PETER Is.

SOUNDINGS IN FEET AT LOW WATER

CAUTION: NOT FOR NAVIGATION
Tropic Isle Sketch Charts are supplements to the text of the current Yachtsman's Guide to the Virgin Islands. They are illustrative and not necessarily to scale.

(TROPIC ISLE SKETCH CHART VI-12)
EDITION 102

NAUTICAL MILES

BRITISH VIRGIN ISLANDS

DEAD CHEST

CAUTION: BLONDE ROCK APPROX. .8 MI. ENE OF DEAD CHEST CARRIES ONLY 8 FT.

BIG REEF BAY

LITTLE REEF BAY

PETER ISLAND BLUFF

CARROT ROCK

CARROT SHOAL

DEADMAN'S BAY

PETER ISLAND Y.H.
(SPRAT BAY)

WHITE BAY

GREAT HBR. PT.

GREAT HARBOUR

PETER ISLAND

KEY BAY

LITTLE HBR.

ROGERS PT.

ROCK HOLE PT.

NORMAN ISLAND

BENURES B.

MONEY BAY

BLUFF BAY

SABU MATHILA BAY

WATER PT.

THE BIGHT

TREASURE POINT

CAVES BAY

PRIVATEER BAY

THE CARVEL

SANTA MONICA ROCKS
(DANGEROUS)

PELICAN ISLAND

INDIANS

PETER ISLAND

PELICAN ISLAND

INDIANS

NORMAN ISLAND
(ENTRANCE TO THE BIGHT)

CRUISING 900TH FROM WESTERNMOST POINT OF PETER ISLAND.

ROCK HOLE POINT

MAUGOVE BAY

ST. JOHN
(EASTERN END)

PRIVATEER POINT

FLANAGAN ISLAND

RED POINT

FLANAGAN PASSAGE

UNITED STATES
UNITED KINGDOM

MAGNETIC NORTH

Moorings Installed Over Dive Sites by the BVI National Parks Trust

If you plan to use the mooring system that the BVI National Parks Trust has installed for **limited day use only** *over many dive sites in the BVI, you must have obtained a National Parks Permit, either from your charter company in the BVI or, if your boat is not based in the BVI, when you clear BVI customs. Mooring buoys are color-coded as follows:*

Red buoys: *Non-diving, day use only.*
Yellow buoys: *Commercial dive vessels only.*
White Buoys: *Non-commercial vessels for daytime dive use only on first-come, first-serve basis. (90-minute time limit).*
It is important to remember that many if not most of the areas where these moorings can be found are exposed and, in some cases, in the vicinity of shallow rocks or reefs — so keep an eye on your weather conditions and check your government charts for possible hazards. Do not mistake these buoys for guides to navigation.

Norman Island

Norman Island, named after a pirate, is often said to be the island on which Robert Lewis Stevenson based *Treasure Island*. Supposedly Stevenson's grandfather adventured in the islands and wrote descriptive letters home, from which much of *Treasure Island* may have been copied verbatim. The Bight, with easy entrance into a protected deep-water harbor and a 360° lookout from the hills, is certainly a likely spot for treasure if treasure is to be found.

For the Skipper

Cautions

1. *To the southwest of Norman Island, the Santa Monica rocks are under 6 feet of water. Avoid them. Swells, often barely discernible, make them a serious hazard to all boats.*

2. *Do not pass between Pelican Island and the Indians, which are the rocks to the west of its. (The BVI government may place some kind of navigation aid to keep boats out of danger here, so don't be surprised to see an uncharted mark.) Moorings are placed by the BVI National Parks Trust in the vicinity of Pelican Rocks and the Indians for divers. Do not mistake them for guides to navigation. (See box, above.)*

3. *Always give Treasure Point a wide berth to avoid the shallow reef extending some 50 to 60 feet northwest of it.*

Anchorages

The Bight is by far the best of the anchorages off Norman Island. There is anchorage room in the southeast part of the bay. The anchorage in the northeast corner of the bay, however, has been reported grassy with poor holding in gusting winds. The prevailing trade winds that funnel through the hills can give the impression that the seas outside are high and treacherous, when actually they are quite moderate.

You can get good West Indian food as well as hamburgers and the like at The *William Thornton,* an old sailboat and floating restaurant/ bar named for the aforementioned Tortolan who designed the U.S. Capitol Building. There is a dinghy dock.

We've had several reports of outstanding snorkeling around the rim of the Bight, with turtles, rays, and octopuses sighted. There are also a number of somewhat overgrown paths from The Bight that eventually lead to Money Bay on the other side of the island. You'll meet some goats along the way. Shoes and long pants are advised.

Benures Bay is a good anchorage if the Bight is too crowded. It lies between the two promontories extending out from the northern side of Norman Island. Anchor well up into the northeastern part of the bay, close to the beach, where the bottom is sandy and provides good holding ground.

The Caves. Just 300-350 yards south of Treasure Point off the caves is a daytime anchorage, which is not recommended at all if there's a swell running. The holding ground is rocky and poor, so make sure your anchor is secure if you leave the boat to explore by dinghy. The wind loops over the hills so you may find yourself lying stern to shore. There

The Caves. (Helleberg photo)

Deadman's Bay, Peter Island. (Fields photo)

are also several daytime, limited-use moorings here, placed and maintained by the BVI National Parks Trust. The blue moorings are for dinghies only. *(Important: See above box).*

You can row into two of the four caves. *Do not endanger snorkelers and swimmers by using a motor.* The southernmost cave is the one rumored to have been a treasure site. Anchor your dinghy close to shore since the bottom drops off rapidly. In calm conditions there's good skin diving outside the caves and around the southwest point, but usually it's pretty rough. The light is best for exploring in the afternoon, although the anchorage is also more likely to be crowded then.

Peter Island

Little Harbor. Although it doesn't look it on the charts, Little Harbor is a well-protected anchorage unless there is a northwest wind, which is rare. It is easily spotted from afar by the white roof of the house on the northeastern spit of land that forms the east side of the harbor.

Entrance is uncomplicated. Simply go into the southeastern corner of the harbor and drop the hook. The bottom is hard sand, so be sure you're dug in.

Suggestions for next year's Guide?

We'd like to hear them! Send your notes to the Editor, Yachtsman's Guide to the Virgin Islands, P.O. Box 15397, Plantation, FL 33318 before March 1993. Please include your name and address. Thanks!

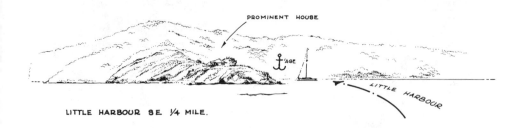

LITTLE HARBOUR SE. 1/4 MILE.

There is swinging room for perhaps five or six boats, but any more would constitute a crowd. You'll be backwinded, so it's a good idea to use two anchors.

Great Harbour. The next bay to the east is Great Harbor, too deep to be considered a good anchorage although you can find some spots. On the south side of the harbor midway along the beach is a 3-fathom spot where you can anchor, and there is another 3-fathom spot about one-third of the way in from the end of Great Harbor Point, near the shore. Be sure you've found the spots with your lead line before dropping anchor.

Here in late afternoon, local fishermen lay out nets from the shore in a horseshoe fashion. The ends are drawn in and the trapped fish are kept alive until ready for market. Stay clear of them. Once the fishing is over, you can sail right to shore, anchor the bow out, and run a stern line to shore and tie it to a tree.

Sprat Bay/Peter Island Resort and Yacht Harbour. From

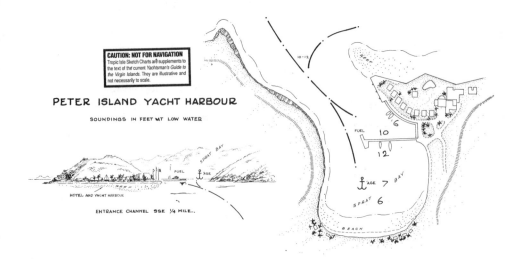

CAUTION: NOT FOR NAVIGATION
Tropic Isle Sketch Charts are supplements to the text of the current Yachtsman's Guide to the Virgin Islands. They are illustrative and not necessarily to scale.

PETER ISLAND YACHT HARBOUR

SOUNDINGS IN FEET AT LOW WATER

HOTEL AND YACHT HARBOUR

ENTRANCE CHANNEL SSE 1/4 MILE.

the channel you'll see the roofs of the Peter Island Resort and Yacht Harbour. Enter the bay on a heading of about 165° magnetic, being careful not to get too close to the western shore. The southern end of the bay beyond the anchorage becomes shallow, so beware. When departing Sprat Bay eastbound, give the reefs that lie north and northwest of the hotel a wide berth.

Peter Island Yacht Harbour offers sheltered accommodations for a limited number of yachts (reservations for dock space is required). Moorings are available on a first-come/first-served basis, payable at the dockmaster's office. The harbor has been dredged to accommodate boats with up to 12 feet draft and 170 feet long. Services include ice, showers, fuel, water, and electricity, but there is no commissary. There's a USA-direct telephone in the dockmaster's office, and a FAX machine is available for incoming or outgoing messages. A regular ferry service runs between Peter Island and the dock north of the old CSY headquarters in Road Town.

The management asks that halyard noises be minimized and that radios and generators not be operated after 9 p.m. Heads may not be used in the bay, but the hotel offers its own facilities for your use. Snorkeling or swimming are prohibited in the Sprat Bay area.

Built by Norwegians, the hotel's distinctive Scandinavian design and tranquil surroundings have made it one of the showplaces of the Caribbean. Reservations for dinner are required and men must wear jackets in season (slacks and long-sleeved shirts are okay during off season).

Deadman's Bay. This is the easternmost harbor on Peter Island. Be careful of the reef off the eastern point of the harbor, and move into the southeastern corner of the bay. This is not a good overnight anchorage because of a windswept surge and a grassy, poor-holding bottom. Watch for the buoys that mark the swimming area. There's a very beautiful beach. Toward the western end, Deadman's Beach Bar and Grill serves lunch and dinner, with reservations required on Monday evenings. Dress is casual. You can walk over the neck of land to Big Reef Bay, where the pounding surf makes for good beachcombing.

DEAD CHEST BEARING 240° 1 MILE.

Caution: *Blonde Rock, east of Dead Chest, should be avoided. It can take a maximum of 8 feet, less in a surge. Daytime, limited-use moorings are placed by the BVI National Parks Trust in the vicinity of Blonde Rock and Dead Chest Island for divers. Do not mistake them for guides to navigation. (Important: see box, page 177.)*

Dead Chest Island. Legend has it that this is the Dead Man's Chest of the "Yo Ho Ho and a Bottle of Rum" song. The story is that Blackbeard marooned some of his men on the island with only a bottle of rum and a cutlass to teach them survival skills – kind of a piratical twist on Outward Bound. The rocky beach on the northwest side of Dead Chest has good swimming, but don't try it unless the weather is calm.

Caution: *Be aware that Carrot Shoal is off the southern tip of Peter Island with a maximum of 8 feet of water over it, less in a surge. Daytime, limited-use moorings are placed by the BVI National Parks Trust in the vicinity of Carrot Shoal for divers. Do not mistake them for guides to navigation. (Important: See box, page 177.)*

SALT ISLAND BAY SW ½ MILE.

Salt Island. (Tropic Isle photo)

BRITISH VIRGIN ISLANDS

SALT, COOPER & GINGER Is.

SOUNDINGS IN FEET AT LOW WATER

NAUTICAL MILE

(TROPIC ISLE SKETCH CHART VI-13)
EDITION 104

0   ½

CAUTION: NOT FOR NAVIGATION
Tropic Isle Sketch Charts are supplements to
the text of the current Yachtsman's Guide to
the Virgin Islands. They are illustrative and
not necessarily to scale.

ROUND ROCK

ROUND ROCK PASSAGE

WHITE HORSE

GINGER GARDEN PT.
FL EV 5 SEC
500 FT 14 M

WEDGE BAY

CHANNEL

DRAKE

SIR FRANCIS

SOUTH BAY

POND PT.

THE QUIDDERS

BIG WEST END

GINGER ISLAND

MAGNETIC NORTH

SEA

CARVAL

DRY ROCKS

COOPER ISLAND

BLACK BLUFF

MARKOE POINT

CARIBBEAN

CARVEL BAY

HAULOVER BAY

RED BLUFF

MARKOE BAY

MANCHIONEEL BAY

CISTERN PT.

GROUPER'S NEST

SALT ISLAND BLUFF

THE SOUND

ROUND ROCK

GINGER ISLAND

SALT ISLAND

MAN HEAD

SALT ISLAND BAY

FL EV 10SEC 14 M

LEE BAY

SOUTH BAY

WRECK OF "RHONE"

SALT ISLAND PASSAGE

SALT ISLAND

COOPER ISLAND

TO MANCHIONEEL BAY

GINGER ISLAND

GINGER, COOPER AND SALT ISLANDS SSW 2½ MILES.

Caution: Passage Between Cooper and Salt Islands

Approach with care any passage north or south between Cooper Island and Salt Island. There are reefs and rocks extending out from both sides at the narrowest part of the passage between Groupers Nest and Cistern Point. Off the northeast point of Salt Island there are dangerous rocks that must be given a wide berth. They are awash, and can be extremely difficult if not impossible to see. If any swell is running, they may only show in the troughs. Favor the Cooper Island side, leaving the exposed rocks close by 100 feet to your east.

Salt Island

The population of Salt Island, which once worked the three salt ponds behind the village, has dwindled to a very few and many of the houses in the village are boarded up. The British government reportedly still collects an annual bag of salt for rent. On the northernmost extreme of the island coming from the east or west, you'll see to the east of the settlement a silhouette rock formation thought by some to resemble a British lion looking northward.

Anchorages

There are two anchorages here, neither for overnight. There is a surge.

Salt Island Bay is the site of a small native settlement. You can anchor off the town in 10-20 feet of water, but make sure your anchor is secure as the anchorage is exposed and the water can be rough.

Lee Bay, west of the village, is the site of the *R.M.S. Rhone,* a favorite dive site in the Virgins. Anchorage is forbidden here, but BVI National Parks Trust-maintained moorings are available for limited daytime use. In any case, this is strictly a temporary, fair-weather anchorage. The stem of the wreck can be seen in 30 feet of water off the point forming the southern end of the bay. *(Important: See box on page 177.)*

Lee Bay. (Tropic Isle photo)

Sir Francis Drake Channel, with Cooper and Ginger Islands in the background. (Helleberg photo)

COOPER ISLAND   SALT ISLAND

COOPER AND SALT ISLANDS SOUTH 2 MILES

Cooper Island

If you approach Manchioneel Bay around the northern point of the island, you'll find that the point shelters the wind. You will probably have to motor into the anchorage.

Caution: Don't eat the small, green, apple-like fruit of the manchioneel tree, which grows in the vicinity of Manchioneel Bay and, in fact, many places throughout the islands. It is poisonous. And don't stand under a manchioneel tree in the rain – the sap is poisonous as well. Carib Indians once dipped arrows in this sap to make them more deadly.

COOPER ISLAND   CISTERN POINT   SOUTH END OF PETER I   CONSPIC R.K.

ROCK SLIDE   MANCHIONEEL BAY

APPROACH TO MANCHIONEEL BAY FROM THE NORTH.

Anchorages

Manchioneel Bay, on the northwestern coast, provides a good anchorage rather well up in the northern half of the bay, where there are palm groves, a beach, and good swimming in crystal-clear water. You'll be backwinded, so set two anchors or pick up a mooring if you're staying overnight. It's a lovely spot to watch the sun set through the breadth of the channel. All land above the high-water mark of Manchioneel Bay is private property and should not be disturbed. The owners also request that visitors to the beach not light fires, damage the trees, or litter. North of the Cooper Island Beach Club dock, a rocky coral shelf lies close to the shoreline and at times can be difficult to see. Dinghies and propellers have been damaged when yachtsmen have attempted to land here, and delicate coral formations have been destroyed as well. The Cooper Island Beach Club maintains a number of moorings that you can pick up for a fee payable ashore. There is a small, casual bar and restaurant, serving excellent fresh conch chowder and curried chicken rotis with chutney. There's windsurfing and a dive concession. Ice is available.

Other anchorages. You can also anchor in Carvel Bay, under Cistern Point, or in the southeastern corner of Haulover Bay. These anchorages are good only when the sea is calm.

Ginger Island

Ginger Island, east of Cooper Island, is crowned with a light. It is uninhabited except for goats, and the terrain is not hospitable for exploring. If there's a good sea running, it's worthwhile to sail around the eastern side between Round Rock and Ginger Island to see the spectacular surf breaking on the cliffs. The best way to do this is on return from the Baths on Virgin Gorda.

Round Rock to Fallen Jerusalem

Caution: Never pass between Round Rock and Fallen Jerusalem because the area is very rocky.

There is a temporary calm-weather day anchorage with good snorkeling off the beach at the northern end of Fallen Jerusalem, but it's seldom used.

Fallen Jerusalem is so named because it resembles, one imagines, Jerusalem after the Romans were through with it. On the eastern side of the rocks are many large fish, including sharks, who congregate to feed on the small fish hoping to hide among the rocks.

As you approach Virgin Gorda from Fallen Jerusalem, look out for the Blinders and rocks close to the surface.

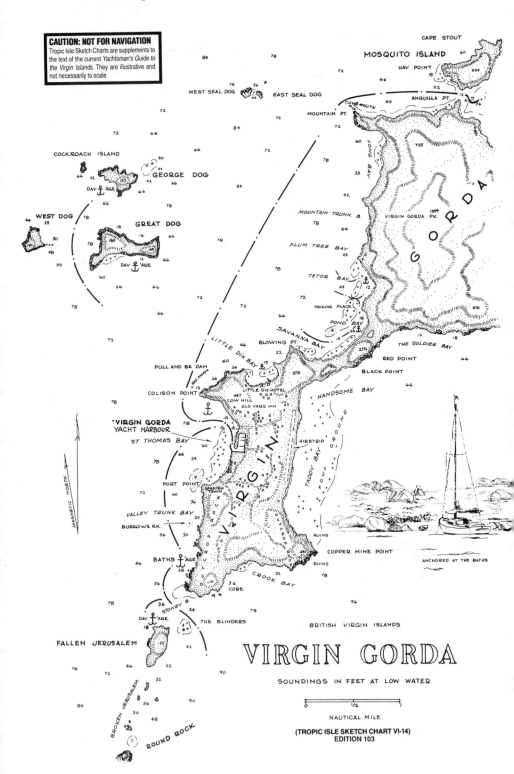

CAUTION: NOT FOR NAVIGATION
Tropic Isle Sketch Charts are supplements to the text of the current *Yachtsman's Guide to the Virgin Islands*. They are illustrative and not necessarily to scale.

VIRGIN GORDA

SOUNDINGS IN FEET AT LOW WATER

NAUTICAL MILE

(TROPIC ISLE SKETCH CHART VI-14)
EDITION 103

BRITISH VIRGIN ISLANDS

ANCHORED AT THE BATHS

Spanish Town. (Fields photo)

WEST COAST
OF VIRGIN GORDA

N.O.S. Chart: 25641. D.M.A. Chart: 25609. Tropic Isle Sketch Charts: VI-14, 21.

The second largest of the British Virgin Islands, the "Fat Virgin" apparently captured the imagination of Columbus who, like many sailors far from home, squinted at the horizon and visualized a reclining female of awe-inspiring proportions. The flat southern part of the island is

"A CARIBBEAN RESTAURANT WITH A EUROPEAN FLAVOUR"

Chez Michelle

Virgin Gorda, Tel: 55510

5 MINUTE WALK FROM THE YACHT HARBOUR

*Recommended by **Travel & Leisure,** the elite "Passport" travel guide and, most importantly, thousands of well-pleased customers.*

GREAT DOG ISLAND   VIRGIN GORDA PEAK
                                              VIRGIN GORDA   BATHS
                                              YACHT HARBOUR

COLISON POINT

VIRGIN GORDA EAST 3 MILES

known as the Valley, where the main settlement, Spanish Town, is located. English planters established Spanish Town on Virgin Gorda in the late 1600s and, with the prosperity of cotton and sugar plantations, it became important enough to be designated the capital of the British Virgins until 1742, when government headquarters were moved to Tortola. The population of Virgin Gorda peaked at around 8,000 in 1812, before the economy collapsed with the failure of the sugar industry and emancipation of the slaves. Now barely 1,500 people live on the island, most of them in Spanish Town. Not until the mid-1960s, when Laurance Rockefeller built the luxury resort of Little Dix Bay, did the island have electricity or telephone service. Sleeping for over 150 years, the island still half-dozes in the sun, and all kinds of wildlife flourish. It's a good place for naturalists interested in different varieties of cacti, lizards, birds, and coral. All land with altitude over 1,000 feet has been designated National Park, with trails for hiking.

The Baths. (Tropic Isle photo)

GREAT DOG

SEAL ROCKS

MOUNTAIN POINT

VIRGIN GORDA PEAK

NORTH TO GREAT DOG AND MOUNTAN POINT

The Baths

The single most popular cruising destination in the Virgin Islands is probably The Baths, at the southwestern tip of the island. Here granite boulders as huge as houses are piled together to create grottoes at the water's edge, where shafts of sunlight find their way down to illuminate delightful crystalline pools for bathing. The volcanic origin of the Virgin Islands left molten areas that cooled and solidified at different rates, forming and eroding into these huge rounded rocks. The Baths are at their most idyllic when uncrowded, and the quiet hours aren't predictable. You might try to arrive first thing in the morning.

For the Skipper

At the western side of the south end of Virgin Gorda, you'll see three enormous groups of boulders next to beaches. The Baths are at the second beach from the south. Don't try to bring in your dinghy if there is too much surge. Instead, go north to Virgin Gorda Yacht Harbour, tie up there, and take a taxi to The Baths. It will leave you at a turn-around where a path leads out to the rocks. If you are able to dinghy in, entrance to The Baths is to the right in a little palm grove, through a little slot between the rocks — you have to kind of skootch your way in. The rocks can be slippery, so wear deck shoes.

Anchorage

Anchorage hereabouts is strictly for daytime only. In each of the

BEEF ISLAND

TORTOLA

GREAT CAMANOE ISLAND

SCRUB ISLAND

BEEF ISLAND AND CAMANOES WEST 4 MILES.

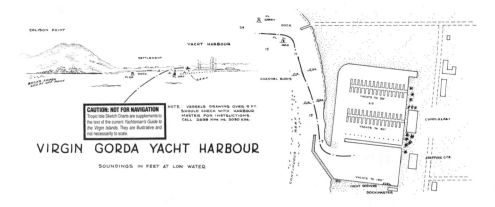

VIRGIN GORDA YACHT HARBOUR

SOUNDINGS IN FEET AT LOW WATER

CAUTION: NOT FOR NAVIGATION Tropic Isle Sketch Charts are supplements to the text of the current Yachtsman's Guide to the Virgin Islands. They are illustrative and not necessarily to scale.

NOTE: VESSELS DRAWING OVER 9 FT. SHOULD CHECK WITH HARBOUR MASTER FOR INSTRUCTIONS. CALL 2638 KHz OR 2030 KHz.

small bays here are white buoys with orange diamond symbols, placed offshore to exclude boats and create safe swimming and diving areas off the beaches. Anchor outside them in about 30-35 feet of water. You might want to put on a mask and snorkel to check that your anchor is secure, since the bottom is coral and rock, and the holding is not good. Marked dinghy channels lead into each of these beaches, but even in the channels you must be extremely careful not to endanger swimmers. You'll probably get wet landing, so wear a bathing suit and protect cameras and watches. Petty thefts have been reported in the area, so don't leave valuables unattended.

What to Do

Besides exploring the boulders, there's good snorkeling all around the area. In calm weather you can dinghy around the south end of the island and Copper Mine Point, but make sure you're anchored safely first. Good bonefishing is reported north from the point along the eastern shore of Virgin Gorda. Up from the Baths, a snack bar named Mad Dog serves drinks and sandwiches.

Virgin Gorda Yacht Harbour

Spanish Town, the site of Virgin Gorda Yacht Harbour, is a rustic little town to explore on foot and a good stop for provisions or repairs. The name of the town may be a corruption of the word "penniston," a blue woolen material worn by slaves.

For the Skipper

After identifying Virgin Gorda Yacht Harbour by the jetty and boats moored inside, approach staying far enough offshore to avoid the

Virgin Gorda Yacht Harbour. (Fields photo)

protecting reef. The well-marked channel through the reef begins northwest of the jetty. Remember "red right returning." When off the jetty, turn to starboard and head south between the buoys that mark the channel inside the protecting reef. There is a minimum of 9 feet of water in the entrance channel. However, vessels drawing 10 feet can be accommodated in the basin provided arrangements have been made with the harbormaster by radio prior to arrival.

Anchorage and Facilities

Customs and immigration clearance is available at the dock. Offices are in the commissary building.

Virgin Gorda Yacht Harbour is a complete marine facility including a marina, boatyard, and shopping center. There is dockage for 120 boats with up to 10-foot draft, fuel, ice, and showers. Virgin Gorda Yacht Services has a 60-ton lift and ample dry storage. The shopping center includes a well-stocked grocery store, several boutiques and craft shops, a drug store, and a laundromat. The Bath and Turtle tavern serves

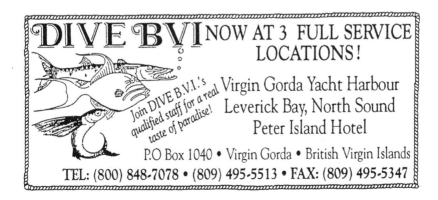

Copper Mine Point. (Tropic Isle photo)

seafood, pasta, and good pizza, has a lending library, and frequently features live music and dancing in the evenings. Dive BVI is also headquartered at the Yacht Harbour, with all SCUBA services available.

What to Do

There are several nice places to eat within walking distance of the Yacht Harbour. Chez Michelle, just up the road, serves fine French food in a romantic atmosphere, featuring a varied selection of seafood and fine wines. A 15-minute walk or inexpensive taxi ride from the harbor is the Olde Yard Inn, a peaceful haven where a library and classical music add

Olde Yard Inn
VIRGIN GORDA
Telephone (809) 495-5544
Fax (809) 495-5986

Friendly, informal and charming restaurant, bar, inn and intriguing boutique. We pride ourselves on excellent food, fine wines and our simple, elegant atmosphere.

to the pleasure of a meal. The open terrace of the restaurant at Fischer's Cove Beach Hotel has a stunning view of the turquoise ocean breaking over the reef, and the food is quite good. Nearby, in or around Flax Plaza, are Andy's Chateau de Pirate, The Lobster Pot for island food, a boutique, a straw market, a hairdresser, and a snack bar. In town, Teacher Ilma's and the Wheelhouse at the Ocean View serve good West Indian food. The Crab Hole, at the south edge of town, serves has a Creole food and has a small, informal bar. According to one of our readers, this is *the* place to go for live music and dancing on the patio.

South of Virgin Gorda Yacht Harbour, the Little Fort National Park is a wildlife sanctuary, where the scant remains of a Spanish fortress can still be seen. On the western side of the island at Copper Mine Point are the ruins of a copper mine built by the English in 1838, possibly on the site where the Spanish attempted to mine silver in the early 1500s. What you can see are the remains of a chimney and boiler house. Exploring can be hazardous, as there are many loose rocks and a number of abandoned prospecting shafts.

If you have time, it's worthwhile when you're in Spanish Town to rent a jeep and spend the afternoon or the whole day exploring the island. North Sound Road, which connects the Valley with the settlement of Gun Creek on Gorda Sound, winds along the high narrow backbone of Gorda

Mountain with precipitous views of the ocean all around you a thousand feet below. You'll feel like you're at the edge of the world. Hiking trails along the road lead up 1,359-foot Gorda Peak as well as down to Savanna Bay and Pond Bay.

Little Dix Bay/Savanna Bay/Tetor Bay

Caution: Off Colison Point between Virgin Gorda Yacht Harbour and Little Dix Bay, there are submerged rocks often awash, but sometimes not visible. Give the point enough berth to clear these. Allow for possible leeway, and stay at least 200 yards off.

Little Dix Bay is east of Colison Point. In settled conditions, it offers day anchorage outside the reef only. The hotel requests that yachts not venture inside the reef, where guests often swim. To cut down on traffic in the swimming area, the hotel prefers that yachtsmen do not bring dinghies in to the beach, and suggests that visitors for lunch or dinner taxi from Virgin Gorda Yacht Harbour instead.

Skippers seeking protection between reef and beach will find it in **Savanna and Tetor Bays,** but only in the daytime in calm sea conditions. Both border on Little Dix property and the management encourages their use by cruising yachtsmen. On entering either bay, keep a sharp lookout for coral heads. This entire shore is a day anchorage only. During the winter months, heavy Atlantic swells create an almost untenable surge along this side of the island. There can be terrific snorkeling here, with a very great variety of coral.

From Little Dix northward is a pretty trip, but there are no overnight anchorages until you get to Gorda Sound at the northern tip of Virgin Gorda.

Savanna Bay. (Tropic Isle photo)

GORDA SOUND AND ANEGADA

D.M.A. Charts: 25609, 25610. Admiralty Charts: 2008, 2016. Tropic Isle Sketch Charts: VI-1, 15, 16.

Gorda Sound, known locally as North Sound, is a kind of boating heaven with its lakelike area of water and fine shoreside facilities catering to yachtsmen. There are luxury accommodations, gourmet meals, beaches for those who want to be all alone or all alone with a friend, hiking trails, diving facilities, and relaxed camaraderie in the evenings. It's a favorite destination, but because of its size and the elegant reserve of the resorts here, something about it still always feels like that special "undiscovered" spot.

Gorda Sound (Leverick Bay in background) (Helleberg photo)

APPROACHES TO GORDA SOUND

BRITISH VIRGIN ISLANDS

SOUNDINGS IN FEET AT LOW WATER

NAUTICAL MILE

(TROPIC ISLE SKETCH CHART VI-15)
EDITION 107

CAUTION: NOT FOR NAVIGATION
Tropic Isle Sketch Charts are supplements to
the text of the current Yachtsman's Guide to
the Virgin Islands. They are illustrative and
not necessarily to scale.

MAGNETIC NORTH

ROUTES TO NECKER ISLAND
AND EUSTATIA ISLAND ARE
RECOMMENDED ONLY WITH
LOCAL KNOWLEDGE

GOOD SNORKELING
AND SPEAR FISHING

NOTE A:
AT PRESSTIME, BVI GOVERNMENT HAD PLANS
TO CHANGE MARKS IN NORTHERN ENTRANCE
TO GORDA SOUND. WHEN COMPLETE, COURSES
WILL BE THE SAME, BUT MARKS WILL BE
DIFFERENT THAN AS SHOWN ON THIS SKETCH
CHART.

1. TO GAIN GORDA SOUND
FROM THE NORTH, STEER
SOUTH BEHIND LONG
UNTIL WRECKED ISLAND
DISAPPEARS, THEN ALTER
COURSE TOWARD GNAT PT.

2. CONTINUE SOUTH UNTIL
SEAL DOG ROCKS APPEAR
IN OPENING THEN DIG-
APPEAR BEHIND ANGUILA
POINT BEFORE TURNING
TOWARD OPENING OR
EASTWARD.

3. WHEN NECKER I.
REAPPEARS STEER NORTH
WEST INTO ANCHORAGE.

APPROACH TO GORDA SOUND
FROM THE NORTH.

DRAKE'S ANCHORAGE

BIRAS CREEK
HOTEL

PUSSER'S

NECKER ISLAND

EUSTATIA ISLAND

PRICKLY PEAR ISLAND

MOSQUITO ISLAND

GORDA SOUND

VIRGIN GORDA

The Dogs

The Dogs (Great, George, West, and Seal) lie west of Virgin Gorda and are uninhabited. If it's calm and there is no swell running, you can anchor south of Great Dog to go into the beach for a swim. You can also anchor in the bay west of George Dog, but check your anchor because you'll be backwinded. These are day anchorages only, and excellent for snorkeling. *Moorings are placed by the BVI National Parks Trust in the vicinity of The Dogs for divers and snorkelers. Do not mistake them for guides to navigation. (See box, page 177, for information regarding the use of National Parks Trust moorings.)*

Gorda Sound

For the Skipper

There are two main entrances into Gorda Sound when approaching it from the north or west. The northern entrance is between Colquhoun Reef, which lies north and east of Mosquito Island, and Cactus Point, the westernmost extremity of Prickly Pear Island. Use this passage if there is a heavy swell or if your boat has over a 5-foot draft. The western entrance is between the southern point of Mosquito Island and Anguilla Point, a spit of land jutting north from Virgin Gorda. This should not be attempted in a northerly swell, and can be negotiated by boats with 5 feet of draft or less.

Northern entrance. To enter Gorda Sound from the north, begin from a point north of Mosquito Rock (24 feet high), which lies off the northeast corner of Mosquito Island. Then, leaving Mosquito Rock to your starboard, run parallel to the northern side of Colquhoun Reef about 50 yards off, in a southeasterly direction. The reef is visible in all tides. Stay in the good water.

Note: The marks shown on our sketch chart in this area are as

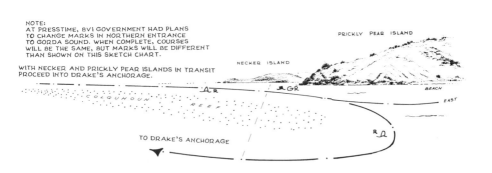

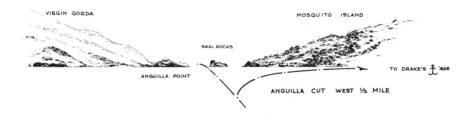

they were during our survey, but we received subsequent word from the British Virgin Islands Port Authority that they plan to remark this channel with new buoys in a way that will differ somewhat from what we show. This change is to take place after our press deadline. According to the Port Authority, the reef should be more plainly marked than what appears on our sketch chart. In the absence of any navigation marks at all, the following directions based on natural landmarks are useful. We include them because wide-open exposure to the sea here can and frequently does disturb navigation marks.

Continue on the course parallel to the northern side of Colquhoun Reef about 50 yards off, in a southeasterly direction, until Necker Island, on your port, disappears behind Cactus Point on Prickly Pear Island. Then change your heading to almost south with your bow pointed at Gnat Point on Virgin Gorda. To get to the anchorage on Mosquito Island, remain on this course until the Seal Dog Rocks appear on your starboard in the middle of the passage between Mosquito Island and Anguilla Point, about 280° magnetic. Then continue south a little further until the Seal Dogs disappear again behind Anguilla Point. If heading for Drake's Anchorage, now change course to almost west, heading for the opening between Mosquito Island and Anguilla Point. Stay on this heading until the northwest side of Necker Island reappears from behind Cactus Point on Prickly Pear. Then head for the anchorage off the dock on Mosquito Island.

Caution: *Do not turn too soon toward the Drake's Anchorage dock or you will run afoul of the reef that extends south from the Colquhoun Reef. Countless boats have gone aground here. Also, do not go north of the dock as it shoals rapidly.*

Western entrance. You can save yourself some windward work

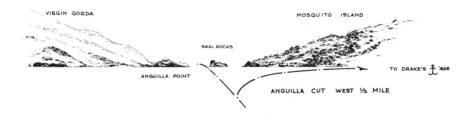

WELCOME CRUISING YACHTSMEN

Visit The Bitter End Yacht Club
"A world class sailing resort!"

Join us for a meal...a day...overnight. We've everything for your enjoyment.

Excellent deep water anchorage. 70 moorings. Garbage pickup available. Deep draft dockage at our Quarterdeck Marina for yachts up to 100 ft. 110V hookups, or 220V metered. Showers on dock. Ice. Water. Gas.

Yachtsman's favorite rendezvous. Clubhouse Steak and Seafood Grille. English Carvery. Champagne breakfasts. Club lunches. Gourmet dinners. English Pub at the Emporium, draft beer and sandwiches. **NEW** entertainment. Disco with Jimmy the DJ. Reggae with our own Steel Band. Eldon John twice weekly with mellow calypso guitar. Free TV and video movies nightly!

Shopping ashore. Browse and shop the Reeftique, "smartest little shop in the BVI." Gear, coverups, gifts. **NEW** Captain B's Trading Post. Film, charts, snorkeling gear, Caribbean art. The Emporium...stock your larder, liquor package store. Wines, staples, fresh vegetables and fruit, eggs, ice cream, our famous Entrees to go!

Activities! Rent our day sailers and sailboards. Book scuba with famed Kilbrides. Daily snorkeling trips. Excursions to Anegada. View deep in submersible Flipper. Freshwater swimming pool with bar and luncheon service. Two beautiful beaches.

Luxury Accommodations. A full resort, 50 duplex cottages, fleet of charter boats.

Come see us when island cruising. Register for a Bitter End Decal and pick up a free copy of our Bitter End Cruising Yachtsmens' Guide or call toll free 1-800-872-2392.

The Bitter End Yacht Club
North Sound, Virgin Gorda, BVI
Marina dockage or dinner reservations: 494-2746
or Standby VHF Channel 16

in this passage but, again, don't attempt it in a strong northerly swell. It's best to attempt it when the light is high and behind you. This passage is only for boats of 5 feet draft or less.

After rounding Mountain Point (and the Cow's Mouth), head at about 105° M for the prominent house above a small sandy beach on Anguilla Point. When you are abeam of the westernmost point of Mosquito Island, proceed through the center of the cut, a channel 5 feet deep and 100 feet wide. It's best to very carefully motor through. Once past Anguilla Point, swing to the southeast and head for Clark Rock, the prominent rock to the east end of Leverick Bay. This is to avoid the sandbar that juts out south of Mosquito Island on the east side of the cut. Once past this sandbar, you'll be in deep water.

Anchorages and Facilities

Drake's Anchorage. Usually pleasantly calm, this anchorage can get choppy in strong easterly conditions, when two anchors are advised. You can pick up a mooring for $15 a night.

Drake's Anchorage is a lovely private resort with 10 waterfront rooms and two villas. The island itself is private and restricted in use to hotel guests only. No facilities are available to visiting yachtsmen except

The Bitter End. (Tropic Isle photo)

Pusser's Leverick Bay Beach Resort. (Helleberg photo)

the excellent restaurant. Chef Brutus Belmar makes all his own bread and pastry, and his mousse is internationally famous. Breakfast, lunch, and dinner are served daily. For dinner reservations, visiting yachtsmen should call ahead on VHF 16.

Excellent snorkeling can be found on the reefs circling the island.

Pusser's Leverick Bay Beach Resort has a 200-foot dock located in the lee of Clark Rock. Dockage is available with fuel (a 25-gallon fill-up earns you a free bottle of the very bracing Pusser's Rum), water, and ice. There are also 35 moorings available for $15 a night, but be aware that in northeasterly conditions it can get choppy. Ashore are a beach bar and pool, laundry facilities, showers, a food market, and a facial and body salon. A Pusser's Company Store and Restaurant overlooks the anchorage. Arrangements can be made for watersport rentals, SCUBA, snorkeling, and fishing charters. On Sundays there's a beach barbecue.

Gun Creek is a little more than a mile beyond Anguilla Point, around Gnat Point on the north shore of Virgin Gorda. From Creek Village you can get land transportation to Spanish Town or the airport.

Biras Creek. (Tropic Isle photo)

Anchor just off the creek at the head of the bay. Creek Village is an interesting settlement of friendly and helpful people. From the hill behind the village you can see both sides of Virgin Gorda. If there's a sea running, it's a spectacular sight to windward.

Biras Creek. On entering be careful to avoid Oyster Shoal, about 150 yards offshore on the southern side of the entrance. It has only 2 feet of water at low tide. Moorings are available off Biras Creek for a fee. The well-sheltered marina has a dock for boats up to 100 feet long with drafts up to 13 feet, with power, water, and ice available. Yachtsmen may visit the restaurant but all other shoreside facilities are for hotel guests only.

The Bitter End Yacht Club. The anchorage off The Bitter End provides excellent holding, although the depth drops to 50-60 feet not far from shore. Moorings are available on a first-come/first-serve basis for $15 a night, which includes evening launch service. Shoreside shower facilities can be used for $3 per person, and garbage pick-up at your boat is available each morning. Dockage for boats up to 160 feet, electricity, water, and ice are available at the Quarterdeck Club marina. Diesel fuel, gas, outboard oil, water, and ice are on the fuel dock. There's also a yacht-repair man on duty. You can buy provisions, liquor, and fresh baked goods at the Emporium, where English beer and pub lunches are served. The Clubhouse Steak and Seafood Grille serves lobster, fish, and shrimp, and the English Carvery has a buffet of roasted meats and fowl.

The Bitter End Resort has luxurious hillside chalet accommodations as well as beachfront villas, diving facilities, a swimming pool, small boat and windsurfer rentals, a gift shop and boutique, and a sailing school. Videos are shown nightly and major sporting events are broadcast live in the Sand Palace. It is possible for visiting yachtsmen to book an overnight room. For those who wish to spend more vacation time ashore, a combination package offers both shoreside accommodations and charter of a private yacht.

Based at the Bitter End, Kilbride's Underwater Tours offers daily dive trips, certification and resort courses, airfills, and equipment rental and repairs. They'll even videotape your dive.

Saba Rock. Gayla Kilbride runs The Pirate's Pub & Grill here, open daily with tropical drinks and lunch or dinner, which might include half-pound burgers or other BBQ specialties. There's a dinghy dock. You don't need reservations and there's no dress code (you can wear your bikini). Please respect the privacy of the Kilbride home on the back of the island, behind the bar.

East of Gorda Sound

For the Skipper

Caution: Entrance into Eustatia Sound should be made in good light and with local knowledge only. If you want to explore, it's best to leave your yacht in Gorda Sound and take your dinghy.

Leave Gorda Sound by passing south of Saba Rock in 8-10 feet of water. Do not go north of Saba Rock, where there is only 3 feet of water.

THE INVISIBLES LIE IN TRANSIT
WITH MOSQUITO ROCK AND THE
NORTHERN POINTS OF GUANA AND
GREAT CAMANOE ISLANDS.

NECKER ISLAND — THE INVISIBLES (ROCK AWASH)

MOSQUITO ROCK — PRICKLY PEAR I.

MOSQUITO I. — EUSTATIA I.

SEAL DOGS — SABA ROCK

GORDA SOUND ROBINS

COCKROACH I. — GEORGE DOG

GREAT CAMANOE

WEST DOG — GREAT DOG

VIRGIN GORDA — THE SADDLE

GUANA ISLAND

BRITISH VIRGIN ISLANDS

ANEGADA AND GORDA SOUND

SOUNDINGS IN FEET AT LOW WATER

NAUTICAL MILES

0 1 2 3 4 5

(TROPIC ISLE SKETCH CHART VI-16)
EDITION 107

CAUTION: NOT FOR NAVIGATION
Tropic Isle Sketch Charts are supplements to
the text of the current *Yachtsman's Guide to
the Virgin Islands*. They are illustrative and
not necessarily to scale.

WEST END — RUFFLING PT.

WINDLASS BIGHT

NUMEROUS CORAL HEADS

SOLDIER POINT

REEF

A N E G A D A   I S L A N D

FLAMINGO POND

AIRSTRIP

POMATO PT. REST.

POMATO P.

ANEGADA REEFS HOTEL

SETTLEMENT

LITTLE ANEGADA

CORAL HEADS

HOG'S PEN

WHITE B.

LOBLOLLY BAY

COOPER ROCK

DEEP BAY

CONTINUOUS REEF

EAST POINT

NUMEROUS CORAL HEADS

HORSE SHOE

DAY ANCH.

CONTINUOUS REEF BREAKS HEAVILY

NOTICE ANCHORING AND
FISHING ON HORSE SHOE REEF
ARE PROHIBITED.

REEF

HAWKSBILL BANK

THE WHITE HORSE
(CORAL HEAP 3' HIGH)

ALWAYS BREAKS

ROBERT REEF

HERMAN REEFS

HERMAN REEFS

MAGNETIC NORTH

170°—350° (TRUE)

BOOT VAN DYKE

GREAT CAMANOE

COLQUHOUN REEF

MOSQUITO I.

SEAL DOGS

NECKER ISLAND

THE INVISIBLES
(SEE ABOVE DETAIL)

EUSTATIA ISLAND

PRICKLY PEAR ISLAND

GORDA SOUND

VIRGIN GORDA

PEAK

ENTER THIS PASSAGE ON WESTERLY
HEADING KEEPING NECKER ISLAND
CLEAR OF GREAT CAMANOE OR
ANY LAND MASS TO ASSURE CLEARING
THE SOUTHERN TIP OF HORSE SHOE
REEF.

Anchorage off Anegada Reef Hotel. (Tropic Isle photo)

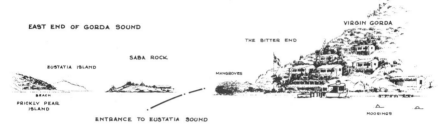

Anchorages

Eustatia Island is private property, with visits ashore by invitation only. There is a day anchorage on the western side where you can snorkel on the reefs.

Necker Island is also privately owned. There are two anchorages, indicated on the sketch chart, which can only be approached from the south, through the entrance to the reef surrounding most of the island.

Anegada

The name Anegada means "drowned" or "inundated." The most northerly (20 miles northeast of Tortola) and isolated of the Virgins, it is a flat coral island with a highest point of 28 feet. The surrounding reefs are wonderful for scuba divers but treacherous for ships. The terror of mariners for years, the reefs have claimed more than 300 ships and hardly a year goes by today without another vessel added to the toll.

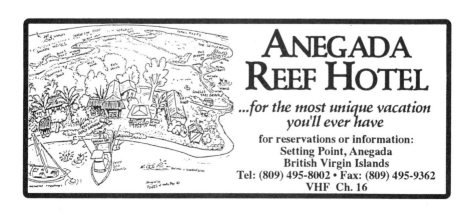

ANEGADA REEF HOTEL

...for the most unique vacation you'll ever have

for reservations or information:
Setting Point, Anegada
British Virgin Islands
Tel: (809) 495-8002 • Fax: (809) 495-9362
VHF Ch. 16

Anegada anchorage. (Tropic Isle photo)

Needless to say, treasure hunting is a popular pastime here.

Anegada's first settlers from Europe were pirates, buccaneers, and wreckers. In Florence Lewisohn's *Tales of Tortola and the Virgin Islands,* she describes Robert Hermann Schomburgk's "Remarks on Anegada," published in the *Journal* of the Royal Geographical Society in 1832. He commented, "The great object, however, always was and still is the wreck of vessels, and the indolence of the inhabitants is only thoroughly roused by the cry of 'a vessel on the reef!' "

Most charter companies prohibit bareboats from going to Anegada because of the extensive reefs, coral heads, and unpredictable currents. For any boat attempting these waters, we recommend local knowledge.

For the Skipper

Caution: Never attempt the passage to Anegada if the weather is hazy or rough.

Horse Shoe Reef

The BVI government has put Horse Shoe Reef off limits to anchoring and fishing. A line of orange buoys has been set along the western side of the reef to denote this fact. The purpose of this program is allow fish stocks and the reef itself a chance to recover from depletion and damage that have taken place over the years. This program will be monitored, and depending on success, the area may be reopened to fishing in the future.

Horse Shoe Reef (see below) extends southeast and then south two-thirds of the 15-mile distance from Anegada to Virgin Gorda.

After departing Gorda Sound via the north entrance between Prickly Pear Island and Colquhoun Reef, make good a course of 03°M for the westernmost point of Anegada. There are currents between Virgin Gorda and Anegada, so a backsight could be helpful and save time. Plan to arrive when the sun is high overhead or at your back so you can read depths and see heads or reefs as you approach. Proceed to the point where Jost Van Dyke bears 240° M and would be dead on your stern if you turned toward the Anegada Reef Hotel on a course of 60° M. Take up 60° M until you are able to locate the marked channel, which leads in on a course of about 70° M toward the commercial dock just east of the hotel. The outer mark is red, to be left to starboard. Farther in, as of our press time, there is a single green mark to hold you off shallow sand. (As with all marks in the islands, there is always a chance this mark may missing at any given time. So the good light and local knowledge we advise are essential.) Turn up into the anchorage off the hotel when the first row of mooring buoys is abeam off your port side. There are 10 rental moorings here, and the inner ones can accommodate boats with about a 6-foot draft while the outer ones can take 6-7 foot drafts. More than this, and you'll have to anchor out. If you need help, or have any doubts as to

NEPTUNE'S TREASURE

Seaside Restaurant & Campground

Come enjoy the beautiful island of Anegada, with 27 miles of unspoiled, white sand beaches.

Neptune's Treasure Seaside Restaurant offers fresh fish and lobster caught daily and for the adventurous, come stay with us at Neptune's Treasure Campground.

Double Tent per night $20 – per week $120
Single Tent per night $12 – per week $75
(no cooking on premises)
Taxi available to any of the many beaches and the airport.

Phone: (809) 495-9439 Fax: (809) 495-9443
Anegada, British Virgin Islands

depths in the channel or anchorage, call *Anegada Reef* on VHF 16 or by cellular phone at 58002. It's also a good idea to call ahead to let them know you're coming.

If approaching Anegada from the east, you must avoid Horseshoe Reef. The southern tip of the reef is on a line drawn from the northern tip of Great Camanoe and northern end of Necker Island. Stay far enough south to keep Necker Island clear of showing any land behind it or north of it.

Anchorage

The anchorage off the Anegada Reef Hotel is some 200 yards off the beach. There are 10 rental moorings. As stated above, the inner moorings are good for boats drawing up to about 6 feet; the outer ones are good for 6-7 feet. Boats with greater draft cannot get into this anchorage and must anchor further out. The hotel has a dinghy dock. The larger concrete dock is for commercial purposes.

What to Do

Snorkeling and scuba diving are the island's main attraction, but deep-sea fishing is also great. There are bonefish along the miles of flats that parallel the southern shore. Blue and white marlin, allison tuna, and wahoo thrive on the ledge of the Puerto Rico trench north of the island.

Owned and managed by Lowell Wheatley, the Anegada Reef Hotel has 16 units on the beach and an informal beach bar. Breakfast, lunch, and dinner are served, but reservations for dinner must be made by 4 p.m. The specialty of the house is a delicious lobster barbecue. The hotel can supply tanks and airfills. A 31-foot Bertram and 46-foot Hatteras are available for guided deep-sea fishing tours. Down the beach, you can get conch and other seafood specialties at Neptune's Treasure, where there is also a campground with tents available. A bit further west, The Pomato Point Beach Restaurant specializes in fine locally caught seafood. Breakfast, lunch, and dinner are served; make reservations for dinner before 4 p.m. (you can call Wilfred Creque, proprietor, on VHF 16). You might order one the house special cocktails and enjoy the view of the sunset. In the Shipwreck Museum, Mr. Creque displays a collection of artifacts accumulated over 25 years of treasure hunting. The museum is open daily from 9-5.

On the north shore of the island, Loblolly Bay's beautiful beach is worth the taxi ride to visit. You can have lunch right on the beach at The Big Bamboo. In the "Settlement," Del's Restaurant and Bar serves West Indian food.

The Fish and the Fishing

Here in the islands where empire builders, pirates, blockade runners and smugglers wrote their separate chapters in the history of the Caribbean, the modern adventurer still can find excitement. Armed with a favorite rod and reel or wielding tackle furnished by a guide, today's seeker of adventure will find it aplenty on the sea lanes that once bore the treasure fleets of Spain.

Out where the ocean is midnight blue and the bottom lies a full mile down, the fisherman will tangle with the bulky blue marlin, a fish that likes plenty of room. On the reefs where skeletons of foundered treasure ships lie encrusted with coral he will meet the sturdy amberjack. In quiet, secluded sand-floored coves, where pirates careened their rakish craft, he can stalk the wary bonefish.

Fishing such areas is like dragging a hook through the middle of a piscatorial grab bag. The angler never knows what to expect as any of a dozen different species of ocean-going gamesters may charge his bait when he is least prepared. The quarry may be a torpedo-shaped blackfin tuna of 12-15 pounds or a tackle-destroying Allison tuna of 60-80 pounds. Best of all, fish in a striking mood will

Caution: Ciguatera is a form of tropical fish poisoning predominating in the Caribbean and the waters off South Florida. The most common carriers of the disease are the larger species of jack, barracuda, grouper, or snapper. The fish itself shows no symptoms, but if you eat a toxic fish you will experience nausea, vomiting, diarrhea, and stomach cramps 3-10 hours later, usually accompanied by weakness, joint and muscle pain, and tingling around the mouth and nose. Medical aid should be sought immediately if you develop these symptoms after eating fish.

It's best to buy your eating fish from reliable local fishermen, or at least to consult them about whether your catch appears safe to eat.

take the bait of a beginner as readily as that of a veteran. Granted the indiscriminate luck that comes to novice and expert alike, the fish may be of record weight. The odds against this happening are not as long as one might think. The world's record for blue marlin (1200 lbs.) was caught off of St. Thomas in August 1977.

The game fish in these waters can be divided roughly into two groups; those hunted specifically and those caught incidentally. In the first category are amberjack, bonefish, oceanic bonito, blue and white marlin, permit, sailfish, tarpon, wahoo, and three species of tuna. No less sporting and just as colorful are those in the second class: barracuda, dolphin, kingfish, and mackerel. In addition, several of the many species of bottom fish like snapper, grouper, and cobia are doughty fighters on proper tackle and epicurean delicacies on the table.

There are fish and fishing conditions here to suit every type of tackle from casting outfits through the light and medium trolling rigs to the stout gear needed for ocean-going heavyweights. For blue marlin, 80 to 130 pound test line on 9/0 to 14/0 reels is normal. The expert can go lighter, but not much. For white marlin, sailfish, dolphin, kingfish, and wahoo, 12 to 30 pound test line will handle the average-size fish without difficulty, although a big wahoo on 12 pound test can sometimes take a spool of it away from you on that first screaming run.

Bonefish can be taken on casting rods and reels with 6 to 10 pound test line, with spinning gear carrying monofilament lines testing from 4 to 8 pounds and on fly-casting tackle with small streamer flies.

Permit, which may reach upwards of 40 pounds, can be taken on 12 to 15 pound test line; however, 20 to 30 pound test on light trolling rods and 3/0 to 4/0 reels are most practical.

Tarpon can be fished for with standard 4/0 to 6/0 rigs (30-50 lb. lines) when trolling or still-fishing in harbour mouths and deep holes. On the flats try casting, plugging, and spinning gear.

For grouper, snapper, and other bottom fish, there is a choice of tackle depending on the conditions and locations of the grounds. Over the deep reefs, 50 to 80 pound test line trolled deep is recommended; some of those grouper will hit 100 pounds. Close to the shore where the fish are smaller, they can be caught with fly rod, bait-casting tackle using the new deep-rigging technique, or spinning outfits.

Blue Marlin...*90-1,000 lbs. Usual specimen: 175-500 lbs.*

Blue marlin generally are found well offshore where the indigo-tinted sea sweeps through vast clefts in the earth's surface. The "blue" apparently prefers solitude and likes plenty of room in which to heave its huge bulk.

Trolling is the accepted method of angling for blues. A whole fish, usually a bonefish, mackerel or mullet, is used for bait. Weighing from three to five pounds, such baits are trolled from outriggers, creating considerable commotion on the surface as they skip from wave to wave.

A few anglers use light tackle (30 to 50 pound test line) or medium heavy (which ranges to 80 pound test), but the majority favor 130 pound. Blues are caught or sighted throughout the year, but the summer months, particularly May through October, find them in the greatest numbers. The blue is not normally a schooling fish, so a strike is a matter of being in the right spot at the right time.

Bluefin Tuna...90-1,000 lbs. *Usual specimen: 200-400 lbs.*

The tuna is in a class by itself. Authorities rank it third in the piscine hall of fame, rating broadbill and marlin ahead of it. The comparison is unfair, for in no way are the fish alike. Tuna travel in schools numbering as few as four to as many as forty and may be spotted from as far off as as 200-300 yards. This in itself affords a thrill that neither the broadbill nor the blue marlin can supply.

White Marlin...40-160 lbs. *Usual specimen: 60 lbs.*
Sailfish...20-140 lbs. *Usual specimen: 36 lbs.*

White marlin and sailfish should be classed together, as both are found in the same water, readily take the same kind of bait, and possess similar bags of tricks. Of the two, white marlin is the more popular with sportsmen because it's bigger. The average weight for "whites" exceeds that of "sails" by some 30 to 40 pounds.

There is little need to discuss in detail the method of angling for white marlin and sailfish, as the procedure is the same as that followed in blue marlin fishing. The tackle is lighter (20 to 50 pound test line) and the baits are smaller. Balao, fingerling mullet, or strips cut from other fish are the most popular baits. The trolling is closer in shore, the boat usually working a zig-zag pattern off and on soundings.

Wahoo...10-150 lbs. *Usual specimen: 30-50 lbs.*

The wahoo, dark blue, irregularly barred with vivid blue stripes on the upper part of its body and pale silver below, is a strikingly beautiful fish. Admirably built for speed, the body of a wahoo is long, cylindical, and tapering gracefully from the central section forward to a sharply pointed snout and aft to a slender, caudal pedicel. It represents one of nature's finest achievements in streamlining.

Angling authorities place the wahoo among the world's top ten game fish. Two outstanding characteristics account for this rating. One is the jarring power of its

End of the Line   Roberts photo

strike, the second is the sizzling speed of its runs. The wahoo performs best on light tackle, 12 to 30 pound test line being adequate in the hands of an experienced angler; 50 to 80 pound test is recommended for those who are sampling this fast sport for the first time. Seventy pound wahoo are not uncommon, and there are enough 100 pounders around to make a special effort to catch them worthwhile.

Dolphin...*5-85 lbs. Usual specimen: 10-15 lbs.*

The dolphin, with its blue, green, gold, and bronze flecked body, is the most brilliantly colored fish among the hordes of oceanic wanderers. It is an active, voracious fish that travels in schools and is forever on the move in search of food to satisfy an insatiable appetite. Possessed of incredible eyesight, dolphin can spot their prey at phenomenal distances. In their eagerness to run it down they take to the air in long, graceful, arching leaps. Hardly does one touch the surface of the sea than it is in the air again. Several of these fish charging in from the side in quick jumps to pounce on a trolled bait or lure present an exciting sight.

When a dolphin is hooked it stages as much of an aerial display as will any of the billfish. The angler must set his hook well on the strike if he hopes to hold on to his fish. They are spectacular battlers on light spinning tackle, say 8-12 pound test on a 6-foot rod.

Kingfish...4-80 lbs. *Usual specimen: 7-20 lbs.*

The kingfish is a fine food fish with excellent game qualities, sought by commercial fishermen as well as sportsmen. It is a rugged scrapper that may be met out in the deep ocean, along the dropoffs, or on the reefs. A member of the mackerel family, with the same physical shape as the wahoo, it is a worthy opponent when taken on light tackle.

Kingfish have a tendency to travel fairly deep and one will often charge upward for a trolled bait with such explosive force that it will clear the surface of the sea to heights of twenty feet. If it misses the bait on the way up, it will often snatch it on the downward plunge. In fact, kingfish have taken one bait on the way up and a second one on the way down.

Kingfish can be taken on spinning tackle or plug casting gear. Heavy feather jigs or weighted bucktails in yellow or red-and-yellow combinations will produce good results if worked properly. Let the lure run out freely from an anchored or drifting draft-cruiser or skiff. When you feel it close to the bottom, retrieve it with quick jerks. This action causes the lure to surge upward and sink back, much like the movements of a shrimp. An occasional pause during the retrieve will drop the lure back toward the bottom, thus increasing its area of effectiveness.

Oceanic Bonito...3-40 lbs. *Usual specimen: 10-20 lbs.*
Blackfin Tuna...2-38 lbs. *Usual specimen: 5-25 lbs.*

Both of these species charge headlong into tightly packed masses of baitfish, gulping their prey by the dozens and leaving bits and pieces of the victims scattered around the area. Flocks of diving, skimming, fluttering sea birds hover above the feeding ground snatching at and quarreling over the scraps of minnows left in the wake of the feeding school.

The actions of the birds are tell-tale signs of the presence or absence of bonito or tuna. If the birds are flying high and scattered, they are looking for a school of fish. If the birds are massed above the horizon and diving, then the boatman knows they are over a school of feeding fish. Once the proper signs are observed, the idea is to get there before the tuna or bonito finish working that particular ball of bait. The secret of catching them is to troll fast.

Allison Tuna...40-270 lbs. *Usual specimen: 50-100 lbs.*

Generally the best chance of hooking one of these hard-driving, deep-down fighting fish comes when an angler is working the oceanic bonito and blackfin tuna schools along the dropoff or well out into the deep. There is always the chance that working below or working the flanks of a school of bonito or tuna will be a scattering of Allison. Should one spot your trolled bait as you enter or pass through the bonito school, it will grab the lure and sound at a fast pace. After the initial run, an Allison settles down to a steady, dogged, tackle-straining fight that, in its latter stages, resembles the tactics of a shark.

Barracuda...*50-80 lbs. Usual specimen: 10-12 lbs.*

If any salt-water gamester of the southern latitudes deserves the name of "all-around gamefish," it is the barracuda. It abounds in limitless numbers, is diverse in its selection of habitat, and indiscriminate in its choice of food. The "cuda" is equally at home on the deep ocean, over the reefs, around rocky points, in shallow bays, and on the flats. It will take live bait of any kind from shrimp to crawfish through all species of small-scale fish, and is just as ready to strike any sort of artificial lure from feather and spoon to plug and fly. Barracuda come in all sizes and weights from six-inchers of a few ounces to six-footers of 70-80 pounds.

Cudas are usually caught when anglers are working the reefs or the dropoffs for other game fish. When one strikes, it hits hard, raising a fountain of boiling white water around the bait. If hooked on light tackle (12, 20, or 30 pound test line), the fish can give the angler several minutes of nip-and-tuck battle. A barracuda isn't licked until it's in the fish box with the cover shut tight.

Amberjack...*20-150 lbs. Usual specimen: 30-40 lbs.*

The amberjack is to be found in the winter months around wrecks or where the yellow and purple sea fans bend to the thrust of tidal currents and irregular pinnacles of rock rise out of a sandy bottom. A gregarious chap, the amberjack gathers in schools, traveling with chosen friends in lazy aimless sweeps over the bottom. This apparent idleness of purpose is misleading. The amberjack actually is tireless and has plenty of speed when it feels like turning it on. A "jack" can give any other fish in the neighborhood a lead of 15 or 20 feet and run it down in a flash. When hungry or excited the amberjack displays feeding stripes, narrow black bands that extend diagonally across each side of the head. Its favorite food is yellowtail, grunt, snapper, and crab. When hooked, the jack heads for the bottom where it zig-zags along the rocks and ferns in short powerful rushes.

While live bait like yellowtail, grunt, pilchard, or large shrimp will produce the surest results, it is possible to take these fish by casting artificial lures with plug or spinning tackle. This method will work with small amberjack of 7 to 15 pounds, but the larger fish for the most part show an annoying lack of interest in plugs or spinning lures. It may be that such baits are not large enough to attract them.

Bonefish...3-16 *lbs. Usual specimen: 5 lbs.*

A bottom grubber by nature, the bonefish frequents shallow flats, where its constant alertness, finicky feeding habits and suspicious nature triple the odds against the angler. The "white fox" (*albula vulpes*), was discovered by sportsmen about the turn of the century. It was not until the early 1920s, however, that its qualities gained universal attention. By the 1930s the popularity of the bonefish had reached fantastic heights and it was credited with characteristics approaching the supernatural.

Bonefishing more nearly approaches hunting than does any other type of angling. Bonefish can be taken with conch, crab, shrimp, crawfish and, when conditions are right, artificial lures. Whatever bait is used, the white fox will put up a smoking-hot fight on rod and reel.

On flats where the bottom is firm sand, an angler can wade for bonefish. This method can be highly advantageous when a stiff breeze is blowing across the banks. It is easier for angler and guide to maneuver on foot than to manage a skiff which offers considerable wind resistance.

While bonefish have been known to take small plugs and spoons, these lures are not recommended. Streamer flies in yellow, brown and gray, or combinations of these colors, are very productive. For spinning tackle, small weighted feathers or bucktails in ¼-ounce weights and single hooks, size 2/0, will work better than anything else. If the head of a lure is flat it will perform better than the other types.

Permit...5-50 *lbs. Usual specimen: 12-25 lbs.*

The permit is a slab-sided, powerfully-built fish having the high forehead of a philosopher and the cruel eye of a homicidal maniac. It is cosmopolitan in habit and may be found following a shark or ray across the flats, wandering happily over the reefs, cruising to and fro in the mouth of a cut, or running the surf.

Permit, for the most part, are bottom feeders, being fond of crabs, certain species of sea urchins, clams, young starfish, crawfish, and shrimp. It can be taken on an artificial lure. It is one of the strongest fish for its size to frequent these waters.

Tarpon...20-280 *lbs. Usual specimen: 25-80 lbs.*

The feeding grounds and feeding habits of tarpon vary in different localities, so local guides should be employed by anglers who wish to hunt these fish. For instance, bonefishermen have been surprised to meet a small school of four to six tarpon feeding across a shallow flat ahead of or just behind a school of bonefish. And on occasion tarpon have been found working in a "mud" made by bonefish.

When in an area known to be frequented by tarpon, the angler will find the fishing to be much better at night than during the day. For the most part tarpon lie quietly in holes and deep creeks in the daytime and seldom can be provoked into taking a bait. At night they can be caught either in the holes or creeks or on the shallow flats where they forage for crabs and grass shrimps. Most fun can be had by using fly rod plugs and spinning gear.

Reef Fishing

For the larger varieties of reef fish, such as snapper and grouper, it is customary to troll slowly with 50 pound test tackle close to the bottom using a planer or an 8-16 ounce torpedo-shaped sinker. A whole fish or a large strip is used for bait, or a $4\frac{1}{2}$ drone spoon will work. Mutton snapper from 10 to 20 pounds and grouper up to 75 pounds are caught in this fashion. Hauling a reluctant grouper weighing from 40 to 50 pounds from his underwater hideout is back-breaking work.

"Still fishing" is a popular means of snaring the inhabitants of the reef. It offers faster action and produces a greater variety of fish than does trolling, but the fish will not run so large in size. In this type of fishing the skipper picks a hole and anchors the boat so as to place the stern over the spot that is to be fished. Often a hole is selected by studying the reef through a glass-bottom bucket that reveals the

Into the Box   Roberts photo

details of the ocean floor with startling clarity. Catches will include margate, large grunts, several species of snapper, ocean tally, trigger fish, and grouper. Many of these fish are brilliantly coloured and most of them are edible.

If the fish are indifferent or overly cautious toward your bait, try chumming conch, crawfish, or scale fish such as balao and mullet, a few crumbs at a time over the surface. As the bits of chum slowly drift downward the smaller reef fish will swarm about the pieces, gobbling them hungrily. This activity usually will stimulate the larger fish into striking whatever bait you are offering. Chum will also bring fish toward the surface where they can be induced to strike spinning lures or plugs.

Shore, Beach and Shallows

The angler should set aside a day or two for walking some deserted beach with casting gear or poking into a lagoon with fly rod or spinning tackle or stalking barracuda on a shallow, sandy bank.

When the sea is calm and the surf a soft, whispering wash on the beach, there is good fishing along the shore of many islands. Each rocky ledge harbours a colony of snapper that will, when in the mood, rise hungrily to fly, plug, or small white feather. The snappers, ranging from four ounces to four pounds, are quick to strike and as quick to run for cover. Each must be played with a firm hand or it will be lost among the sharp-edged crevices of the ledge. Spinning tackle equipped with six or eight pound test line and a ¼-ounce yellow, or brown and white feather or bucktail jig will produce the best results.

Jack, runner, and mackerel frequent the shoreline when conditions suit them and will test the angler's skill with regulation fresh-water casting tackle. Surface lures in ⅝-ounce size and blue or green finish are generally effective.

When the sea is lumpy and offshore fishing uncomfortable, the angler can turn his attention to the creeks that thread their devious courses through the swamps of the larger islands. The mouths of these creeks often are guarded by a wide expanse of shallow bank. Once within their shadowy, brooding confines, however, the waterways are found to be deep.

Some, open to the sky and warm with sun, are fairly wide; others are narrow leafy tunnels, roofed over by interlocking mangrove limbs. Seldom visited by man, the creeks are sanctuaries for tarpon, large schools of snapper, myriad of shad, scattered groups of needle-fish and small families of blunt-nosed, blue-and-green parrot fish. There are others too. Here, guarding jealously his favorite bend, may be a surly barracuda; there, at the entrance to a dark cavern beneath the bank, may lurk a solitary, pugnacious grouper.

Each bend, each hole, each undercut bank is worthy of attention. Start the fishing at each new spot with live shrimp when obtainable. The fish will attack it readily and once they begin to swarm around the shrimp the angler can switch to an artificial lure, using a fly rod or spinning tackle. As a rule the first couple of live shrimp will excite snapper into a greedy race for the bait. Thereafter, for several casts, they will attack a fly, small spoon, light feather or weighted spinner.

For information on local fishing tournaments, contact:
Virgin Islands Game Fishing Club, P.O. Box 1572, St. Thomas, USVI 00801
BVI Yacht Club, P.O. Box 200, Road Town, Tortola BVI

Stargazing for Yachtsmen

By DAVID S. HEESCHEN
Senior Scientist, National Radio Astronomy Observatory

The sky, as seen on a clear moonless night from a quiet anchorage in the Virgin Islands, is a magnificent spectacle. From these latitudes stars and constellations that never rise above the horizon further north are readily visible, and the stars shine with a brilliance and clarity never seen by the city dweller who must contend with light pollution and smog. This celestial show is a free fringe benefit of cruising that we can all enjoy simply by relaxing in the cockpit and letting our eyes and our imaginations wander through the heavens.

How to Use the Star Charts

When stargazing, let your eyes dark-adapt for 10-15 minutes. It makes a huge difference in how well you can see in the dark. Binoculars will let you see many things that can't be seen with the naked eye. When using them, brace yourself comfortably and hold them as steady as you can. A full moon, while itself an interesting object to view with binoculars, will make it much more difficult to see fainter objects. A clear, moonless night provides the best stargazing.

The star charts show the principal constellations and brightest stars as they appear at various times of the year. The ecliptic and the approximate boundaries of the Milky Way are also shown. The small cross (+) near the center of each chart indicates the zenith, for an observer at 20° N latitude, and the chart boundaries represent the horizon. The charts are correct for an observer at 20° N latitude. To an observer farther north, the stars will appear to be shifted south, while an observer in the lower Caribbean will see them further north, relative to the southern horizon. Remember, too, that the stars move from east to west during the course of the night, along curved paths on these charts. And for a given time of night the entire pattern shifts slowly from east to west, at a rate of 30° per month. A star or constellation that is due south at 9 p.m. in March will be 30° west of south at 9 p.m. in April. To use a chart, turn it so the direction you are facing is down. The pattern in the sky should then match that of the chart, at the time indicated on the chart. At earlier or later times the pattern will be shifted, as described above, but it should still be easy to identify the brightest stars. Perhaps the easiest way to get oriented is to look for Orion in the winter, or the bright stars Arcturus and Spica in the summer. Other unmistakable objects, readily recognized, include the Big Dipper, the Pleiades, and the constellation Lyra. Once you identify any of these it is easy to work your way around the sky with the aid of the charts.

Planets have not been plotted on the charts. Relative to the fixed pattern of stars they move slowly along the ecliptic. Venus, Jupiter, and sometime Mars are brighter than any star. At their brightest, Venus is about 10 times as bright and Jupiter almost twice as bright as Sirius, the brightest star. If the brightest object you see doesn't fit the position of a star on the chart, it is probably Venus, Jupiter or Mars. Venus never gets more than 45° from the sun so it is either in the west after sunset or in the east before sunrise. If you can hold your binoculars steady enough, Venus may appear as a small crescent. Jupiter moves eastward along the ecliptic, at about 30° per year. Four of Jupiter's 16 moons can be seen through binoculars. They will appear in a straight line on either side of the planet, and change their relative positions from night to night. Mars has a distinctly reddish color as compared with the white or silver of Venus and Jupiter. It can sometimes be as bright as Jupiter but is usually fainter. Saturn is about as bright as Vega or Rigel and has a yellowish color. Watch for these planets and don't let them confuse you. Another clue to the planet-vs.-star puzzle is that planets don't twinkle while stars generally do unless they are very high in the sky.

The Winter Sky

The brilliant constellation Orion, the hunter, dominates the evening sky from November, when it is just rising in the east at 9 p.m., to April, when it sets in the west about 9 p.m. Its two brightest stars represent opposite ends of the evolutionary sequence of stars. Betelgeuse, the brightest, is an old red star whose diameter is about 1,000 times that of the sun. Rigel is a young blue star. Just below the three stars that form Orion's "belt" is the famous Orion nebula, M42. Barely visible to the naked eye, binoculars show it to be a region of bright, diffuse light. It is in fact a huge cloud of dense gas, predominantly hydrogen, that is heated to incandescence by the radiation from hot stars newly born out of the gas cloud. These stars, four of which are visible within the nebula, are among the youngest known, only about 25,000 years old. For contrast, Betelgeuse is several billion years old.

Two famous clusters of stars are almost overhead in January. The Pleiades are unmistakable, a compact group of moderately bright stars. Many more are revealed with

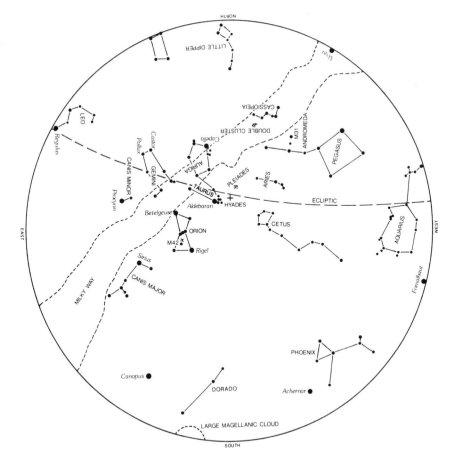

The winter sky at approximately 11 p.m.in early December, 9 p.m. in early January, and 7 p.m. in early February.

binoculars. This so-called open cluster is held together by the mutual gravitational attraction of its 120 stars. Presumably the stars were all formed at about the same time out of the same giant gas cloud. The Pleiades is a relatively young cluster, some 25 million years old. The Hyades cluster, near the bright star Aldebaran, is a similar but much looser aggregate of stars. It was formed about a billion years ago, and its stars are distinctly redder than those of the Pleiades. Scanning slowly through the Milky Way with binoculars will reveal many more clusters. They are a common feature of our galaxy.

Southwest of Orion is Sirius, the brightest star in the sky. Only the planets Venus, Jupiter, and sometimes Mars shine more brightly. Just south of Sirius is the bright star cluster M41, barely visible to the naked eye but a brilliant sight through binoculars.

The Spring Sky

Arcturus is the brightest star of the spring and summer skies. To find it, first locate the Big Dipper. Then follow the gentle curve of the handle. Arcturus is the first bright star along the extension of this curve. Continuing along the curve brings you to another bright star, Spica. In the spring Regulus, brightest star in the constellation Leo, is nearly overhead in the evening. From it, the sickle that represents the head and the triangle that represents the tail of the lion can be found. Regulus itself is a double star that can be

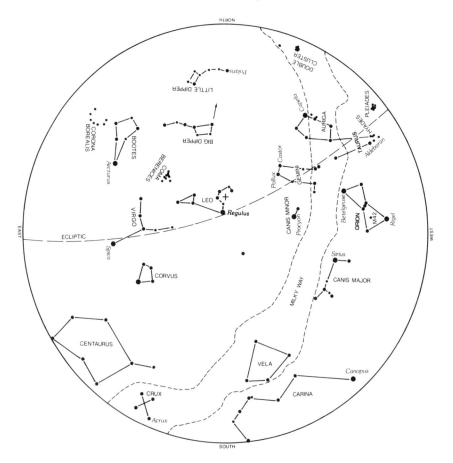

The spring sky at approximately 11 p.m. in early March, 9 p.m. in early April, and 7 p.m. in early May.

resolved with binoculars. The southern cross, Crux, is also visible in the spring, a bright compact constellation low in the south.

The Summer Sky

The best known summer constellations, easily recognized by their shapes, are Lyra with its bright blue star Vega, and Cygnus, the northern cross. Epsilon Lyra, the star just northeast of Vega, is another well-known double star that can be resolved with good binoculars. Mizar, the star at the bend in the handle of of the Big Dipper, has a close companion, Alcor, that many people can see with the unaided eye. This pair was reputedly a vision test for Persian army recruits in ancient times.

The dominant feature of the summer sky is the Milky Way. It is visible throughout the year, but is at its greatest brilliance in mid-summer when the densest region, in the direction of the galactic center just north of the Teapot, reaches its highest point in the south in the evening. Some 30,000 light years off in that direction is the center of the galaxy, a massive black hole about which the sun and its neighboring stars are rotating at a speed of 150 miles per second. The shimmering light of the Milky Way comes from the millions of stars, unresolved by our eyes, that make up the disk of the galaxy. The dark regions so evident within the band of the Milky Way are due not to the absence of stars but to the presence of intervening dense clouds of interstellar dust that absorb the light of the stars. Scan through the Milky Way with your binoculars at any time of year. It is

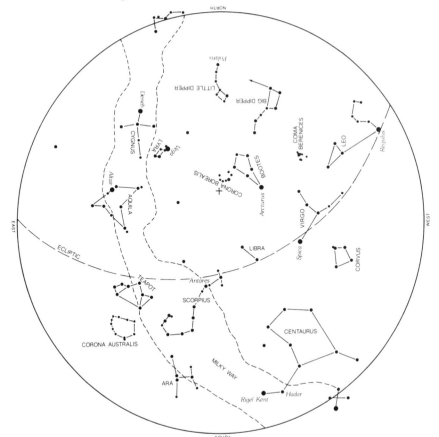

The summer sky at approximately 11 p.m. in early June, 9 p.m. in early July, and 7 p.m. in early August.

a magnificent panorama of stars, clusters, and nebulae.

Near the zenith in July is the marvelous little constellation Corona Borealis, a group of stars that form a sparkling crown. There is also a southern crown, Corona Australis, visible low in the sky from spring through fall.

The Autumn Sky

In October the great square of the flying horse Pegasus is nearly overhead. And high in the west is Altair, the brightest star in the constellation Aquila, the Eagle. Cassiopeia, the crooked "W," is rising in the northeast. Near it, and readily visible to the naked eye, is a double star cluster. Each cluster of the pair contains about 300 stars, many of which will be revealed with binoculars. Also visible in the fall and winter skies is the giant spiral galaxy M31, in the constellation Andromeda. It is probably the most difficult object to find of any on the charts, but worth the effort. Barely visible to the naked eye, binoculars show it as a faint, featureless patch of light. In fact, it is another milky way system somewhat similar to our own, containing about one hundred billion stars, some 2 million light years away. Think of the secrets that obscure little patch of light may hold.

Is there intelligent life on any of the planets encircling those stars? No one knows, so let your own imagination be your guide. Lucky indeed is the yachtsman who can sit at anchor in the Virgin Islands and view the marvels of the universe.

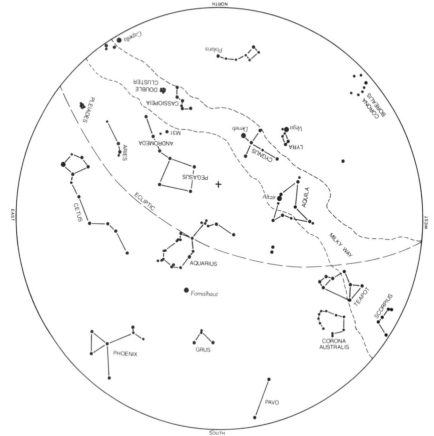

The autumn sky at approximately 11 p.m. in early September, 9 p.m. in early October, and 7 p.m. in early November.

GALLEY GUIDE

The Virgin Islands offer an abundance of good things to eat, new foods to try, and innovative ways to prepare them. The recipes here are some of our readers' favorites, many using fresh fish, fruits, and vegetables you'll encounter in the islands.

Shop at the produce stands you'll find in most larger towns and some of the smaller settlements. There are gourmet provisioning shops in Charlotte Amalie, Road Town, West End, and at some marina complexes, where you might find unusual herbs and spices and sophisticated ingredients you might not think were available in the islands.

Before eating any fish you catch, please note the caution about ciguatera in the fishing section of this *Guide.* You should always check with local fishermen about the advisability of eating your catch.

Shipwreck Shake

- vodka
- Bailey's Irish Cream
- Kahlua
- pineapple juice or chunks

We got this drink recipe from Mike Young, proprietor of the Shipwreck Landing on Coral Bay, St. John. To make a Shipwreck Shake, mix equal parts of vodka, Bailey's Irish Cream, Kahlua, and pineapple juice or chunks in a blender with ice. It's good! (You might also want to add some coconut milk.)

No-Fuss Sangria

- bottle of red wine, preferably Spanish
- 1 cup of any lemon-flavored soda
- 1/4 cup sugar
- juice of 2 limes
- 8-oz. can fruit cocktail, drained
- one sliced orange

Combine all ingredients in pitcher with a lot of ice. You can garnish with sliced fruit if you wish.

Yellow Bird
- 1 oz. white rum
- 1 oz. banana liqueur
- 1/2 cup orange juice

The traditional tropical island cocktail. Combine everything with a cup of cracked ice in a shaker or blender. Serves two.

Banana Fritters
- 4 bananas, sliced 1/2-inch think
- cup flour
- 1/2 cup milk
- 4 tbsp. sugar
- tsp. lime juice
- cinnamon-sugar
- oil

To make your batter, stir the flour, milk, and sugar together until smooth, then add the lime juice. Heat the oil in a frying pan. After dredging the banana slices in the batter, fry them on both sides until they're golden brown. Drain on a paper towel and dust with cinnamon-sugar.

West Indian-Style Tuna Sandwiches
- 7-oz. can of tuna
- 1/2 cup celery, diced
- 1/4 cup almonds, chopped
- 1/2 cup flaked coconut
- 1/2 cup mayonnaise
- 3/4 tsp. curry powder
- pepper to taste
- tbsp. lemon juice

Combine all ingredients. Spread on toasted bread or sandwich rolls and broil until lightly browned.

Attention, Galley Chefs!

If you have a recipe you'd like to share, please send it to the **Editor, Yachtsman's Guide to the Virgin Islands, P.O. Box 15397, Plantation, FL 33318.** *If we use yours, we'll send you a complementary copy of next year's Guide. If we don't use it next year, we'll keep it on file.*

Baked Fish with Tangy Orange Sauce

- about 1 pound of fish
- 1/2 cup orange juice
- 1/4 cup steak sauce
- tbsp. soy sauce
- tsp. salt
- tsp. sugar
- one sliced onion
- one sliced green pepper

Combine orange juice, steak sauce, soy sauce, salt, and sugar and pour over fish. Top with onion and green pepper slices, wrap in foil, and bake until fish flakes.

Curried Ham with Mangoes

- 2 cups sliced mango
- 1 sliced green pepper
- 1-1/2 lb. ham slice (with a knife, you can adapt a canned ham)
- 2 tbsp. butter
- 1/4 cup brown sugar
- tsp. curry powder

In a baking dish, top the ham with green pepper strips and mango. Combine the butter, brown sugar, and curry powder into a crumbly mixture and spread it over the ham. Broil the ham (about four inches from heat) until the topping melts and begins to bubble.

Swordfish Medallions with Salsa

- 1-1/2 lbs. swordfish or similar fish, cut about one inch think
- juice of 2 limes
- 16-oz. can tomatoes
- 1/3 cup minced onions
- 4 minced scallions
- 2 seeded and minced chili peppers (canned or fresh)
- tbsp. chopped cilantro or parsley
- salt and pepper to taste
- 2 tsp. oil

Remove skin and trim the fish into about 12 two-inch-square pieces, and marinate them in a tablespoon of lime juice while you prepare the salsa. Drain the tomatoes as completely as you can, chop them and mix with the onion, scallions, chili peppers, cilantro or parsley, salt, pepper and half the oil. Set the mixture aside. Dry the fish pieces well. Brush a heavy skillet with the remaining oil and heat until very hot. Sear the fish pieces for 3-4 minutes on each side until lightly browned and cooked to medium-rare. Top each fish medallion with and serve. Makes 4 servings.

Drunken Melon

- large cantaloupe, honeydew, or casaba melon
- assorted fresh fruit
- 1-1/2 cup sweet white wine

From the stem end of the melon, cut a circular plug and scoop out the seeds. Stuff the melon with any additional cut-up fruit, add the wine, replace the plug, and seal with tape or butter. Chill for 2 hours or more (overnight is good).

Chocolate-Covered Kiwifruit

- 3 kiwi
- cup chocolate chips

Peel and cut the kiwi into wedges. On a plate lined with waxed paper, freeze the kiwi until firm. Melt the chocolate chips until creamy, dip the frozen kiwi wedges in it, and return them to the cookie sheet and back into the freezer until ready to serve. (You can use banana slices or other fruit instead of kiwi if you want.)

Emergency Medical Facilities
in the Virgin Islands

U.S. Virgin Islands

Emergency/Ambulance 922
St. Thomas Hospital 776-8311
St. Croix Community Hospital, Christiansted 778-6311
St. John Community Health Clinic, Cruz Bay 776-6400

British Virgin Islands

Emergency (Tortola) 999
Peebles Hospital, Road Town, Tortola 494-3497
Virgin Gorda Clinics: Valley 495-5337,
Gorda Sound 495-7310

VIRGIN ISLANDS INDEX

A

American Yacht Harbor 68
Anchoring 22
Anegada 207
Anegada Reef Hotel 210
Apple Bay 134
Avery's Marine, Inc. 51

B

Baths, The 191
Baugher's Bay 164
Benner Bay 60
Benures Bay 178
Biras Creek 204
Bitter End Yacht Club 204
Blonde Rock 183
Botany Bay 72
Brandywine Bay 164
Brewers Bay 138
Buck Island 117
Buoyage 22

C

Camanoe Passages 169
Cane Garden Bay 136
Caneel Bay 85
Caneel Bay Shipyard 81
Carrot Bay 134
Carrot Shoal 183
Carvel Bay 187
Caves, The 178
Charlotte Amalie 49
Charts 23
Chocolate Hole 101
Christiansted 107
Christmas Cove 67
Cinnamon Bay 88
Colquhoun Reef 200
Communications 24
Compass Point Marina 61
Cooper Island 186
Cowpet Bay 67

Crown Bay Marina 52
Cruising etiquette 26
Cruz Bay 78
Currency 28
Current Cut 67
Customs and immigration 28
  Jost Van Dyke 127
  Road Town 154
  St. Croix 109
  St. John 79
  St. Thomas 50
  Virgin Gorda 193
  West End 143

D

Dead Chest Island 183
Deadman's Bay 182
Depths 30
Dogs, The 199
Drake's Anchorage 202
Drugs 30

E

East End Boat Park 65
Eastern Tortola 167
Eustatia Island 207
Eustatia Sound 205

F

Fallen Jerusalem 187
Fat Hog's Bay 169
Fish Bay 101
Fish Hawk Marina 65
Flamingo Bay 59
Fort Burt Marina 155
Francis Bay 90
Frederiksted 121
Frenchman's Cay 147
Fuel 36

G

Ginger Island 187
Seabreeze Yacht Charters 169
Gorda Sound, Northern entrance 199
Gorda Sound, Western en-

trance   200
Great Cruz Bay   101
Great Harbour
   Jost Van Dyke   127
   Peter Island   180
Great Lameshur Bay   99
Great Thatch Island   147
Green Cay   132
Green Cay Marina   115
Guana Island   169
Gun Creek   203

H

Hans Lollick Island   72
Hassel Island   58
Haulover Bay   94, 187
Haulover Marine Yachting Center   53
Hawksnest Bay   87
Honeymoon Bay   59
Horseshoe Reef   208

I

Ice   36
Independent Boat Yard, Inc.   65
Inner Brass Island   72
Inner Harbour Marina   159

J

Jersey Bay   60
Jost Van Dyke   125

K

King's Wharf   51

L

La Vida Marina   64
La Vida Marine Center   65
Lagoon, The   60
Lameshur Bay   99
Lee Bay
   Great Camanoe   171
   Salt Island   185
Leinster Bay   92
Little Bay   170
Little Dix Bay   196

Little Harbour   130
Little Jost Van Dyke   131
Little Lameshur Bay   100
Little Thatch Island   147
Long Bay   135

M

Magens Bay   72
Maho Bay   88
Manchioneel Bay   187
Marina Cay   173
Mariner Inn   160
Maya Cove   167
Mosquito Island   199
Muller Bay   68

N

Nanny Cay   148
Nanny Cay Resort and Marina   150
Narrows, The   92
Navigation   31
Necker Island   207
Norman Island   177
North Saint Thomas   72
Northwest Tortola   134

P

Peter Island   179
Peter Island Resort and Yacht
   Harbour   180
Prospect Reef   151
Provisions   36
Pusser's Leverick Bay Beach Resort   203

R

Red Hook   68
Reefs   32
Rendezvous Bay   101
Road Harbour   153
Road Reef Marina   155
Road Town   153
Round Rock   187

S

Saba Rock   205

Saga Haven 65
Salt Island 185
Salt Island Bay 185
Salt Pond Bay 99
Salt River Bay 118
Sandy Cay 132
Santa Maria Bay 72
Sapphire Bay 68
Sapphire Beach Resort Marina 70
Savanna Bay 196
Security 33
Sir Francis Drake Channel 175
Smuggler's Cove 135
Sopers Hole 141
Sopers Hole Marina 143
Sprat Bay 180
St. Croix 103
St. Croix, Approach 107
St. Croix Marina 109
St. Croix, South Coast 121
St. Croix Yacht Club 116
St. James Island 67
St. John, Approaches 78
St. John, South Coast 99
St. Thomas 43
St. Thomas Harbor 49
St. Thomas Sport Fishing Center 70
St. Thomas Yacht Club 67
Sugar Reef Marine Services 52
Sunsail 143
Sunset 33

T

Teague Bay 116
Tetor Bay 196
The Bight 178
Tides 34
Tortola, South 140
Tortola Yacht Services 160
Treasure Isle Hotel 160
Trellis Bay 171
Trunk Bay 88

V

Vessup Point Marina 70
Village Cay Marina and Hotel 156

Virgin Gorda, West Coast 189
Virgin Gorda Yacht Harbour 192

W

Water 36
Water Island 59
Water safety 34
Weather 34
West Cay 72
West End 141
West End Slipway 145
West Gregerie Channel 59
White Bay
   Guana Island 170
   Jost Van Dyke 128
Wickham's Cay 156
Wood Works, Ltd. 145

Y

Yacht Haven Marina 50

ADVERTISER INDEX

American Yacht Harbor 69
Ample Hamper 144
Anegada Reef Hotel 207
Avery's Marine, Inc. 51
Baskin in the Sun 143
BBA/Chart Kit 73
BBA/Reed's Nautical Almanac 122
Bitter End Yacht Club 201
Blue Water Divers 149
Brokerage, The 19
Caribbean Insurers Ltd. 158
Caribbean Yacht Charters 63
Castaways 150
Cay Electronics Ltd. 161
Cellular One 146
Chez Michelle Restaurant 189
Crown Bay Marina Cover 3
Cruising Guide to the Florida
   Keys 105
Discovery Yacht Charters 150
Dive BVI 193
Green Cay Marina 115
Harken 27

Haulover Marine, Inc.   53
Independent Boat Yard   65
Inner Harbour Marina   159
Innovative Designs Inc.   39
Island Marine Supply   1, 155
Island View Guest House   57
JE Marine Services   60
Kilbride's Underwater Tours   204
Last Resort, The   171
Little Harbor Custom Yachts   7
Maxwell/Island Rigging   49
Nanny Cay Resort and Marina   148
Neptune Charters   61
Neptune's Treasure   209
North South Yacht Vacations   17
Olde Yard Inn   194
Peter Island Resort and Yacht Harbour   181
Pirates Pub & Grill Inc.   205
Pusser's Ltd.   Cover 4
Ruan's Marine   66
SEARCH   165
St. Croix Marine   109
St. Maarten Cruising Guide   47
St. Thomas Yacht Sales/Charters   64
Tortola Yacht Services   153
TradeWind Yachting Services   154
Tropical Marine   66
Village Cay Marina and Hotel   157
Virgin Island Search & Rescue (VISAR)   160
Ward's Marine Electric, Inc   21
West End Slipway   145
Yacht Haven   Cover 2
Yachtsman's Guide to The Bahamas   11, 165, 195

SKETCH CHART INDEX

VI-1/103/The Virgin Islands   8
VI-2/101/Approaches to the Virgin Islands and P.R.   2
VI-3/105/St. Thomas   42
VI-4/106/St. Thomas Harbor   48
VI-5/105/Southeastern St. Thomas   62
VI-6/107/St. John   74
VI-7/107/Northwestern St. John   86
VI-8/105/West End of Tortola   133
VI-9/107/Jost Van Dyke   124
VI-10/106/Road Harbour   152
VI-11/106/Eastern Tortola   166
VI-12/102/Norman and Peter Islands   176
VI-13/104/Salt, Cooper & Ginger Islands   184
VI-14/103/Virgin Gorda   188
VI-15/107/Approaches to Gorda Sound   198
VI-16/107/Anegada and Gorda Sound   206
VI-17/107/Christiansted Harbor   106
VI-18/102/St. Croix   102
VI-19/107/Salt River Bay   119
VI-20/101/U.S.V.I. Cruising Grounds   41
VI-21/106/British Virgin Islands Cruising Grounds   123
VI-23/105/St. Croix's NE Shore   114

Tropic Isle Sketch Chart Edition Numbers

Each sketch chart has been assigned an edition number so that those who have purchased our enlarged 11x17-inch sketch charts may be assured that their enlargements correspond with the current edition of the Yachtsman's Guide. This sketch chart index includes all sketch charts that are current for this 1993 edition. All 11x17-inch sketch chart enlargements should be updated if the edition number is not shown or if it is different from those listed here.

ENLARGED TROPIC ISLE SKETCH CHART ORDER FORM
SELECT FROM FOLD-OUT PAGE

These convenient, easy-to-read sketch charts are 11"x17" enlargements of the sketch charts in your current *Yachtsman's Guide* and are intended to be used in conjunction with the current *Guide*. Sketch charts may be purchased singly or in sets as described on the following pages. They are printed on heavy stock for durability and shipped flat.

Postage and Handling Charges - Inside U.S.A.

Sketch Charts Ordered	Charges
1-20	$3.50
21-40	$5.00
41 or more	$6.50

For shipment outside the U.S.A. add $4.00 to the above amounts. Florida residents add applicable sales tax.

Please send the following:

QTY.	CHART NO. AND TITLE	PRICE
	Clear Plastic Envelope @ $5.00 each	
	Postage, Handling & Applicable Tax	
	TOTAL	

SKETCH CHARTS ARE NOT REFUNDABLE.

Send check or Money Order to:
TROPIC ISLE PUBLISHERS, INC.
P.O. Box 610938 • North Miami, FL 33261-0938

NAME

ADDRESS

CITY, STATE, ZIP

THE BAHAMAS and TURKS & CAICOS
TROPIC ISLE SKETCH CHART CATALOG

These convenient, easy to read sketch charts are 11"x17" enlargements of the sketch charts in your current *Yachtsman's Guide* and are intended to be used in conjunction with the current *Guide*. Sketch charts may be purchased singly at $3.00 each or in sets as described below. They are printed on heavy stock for durability and shipped flat. Sketch charts are non-refundable.

Complete Set-72 sketch charts with 2 clear plastic envelopes
$195.00

19"x13" Clear Plastic Envelope $5.00 each

Postage and Handling Charges - Inside U.S.A.

Sketch Charts Ordered	Charges
1-20	$3.50
21-40	$5.00
41 or more	$6.50

For shipment outside the U.S.A. add $4.00 to the above amounts.
Florida residents add applicable sales tax.
Sketch Charts are non-refundable.

TROPIC ISLE PUBLISHERS, INC.
P.O. Box 610938 • North Miami, FL 33261-0938
(305) 893-4277

SKETCH CHARTS ARE NOT REFUNDABLE.

SINGLE TROPIC ISLE SKETCH CHARTS -
$3.00 EACH (Not Shown)

39 – Approaches to the Bahamas
#41 – The Bahamas Islands
#42 – Little Bahama Bank
#43 – Bahamas Far Out Islands

Set "B" – 5 Sketch Charts - $14.00

B 1 Bimini - Cat Cay
B 2 West End, Grand Bahama
B 3 Freeport-Lucaya
B 4 Grand Lucayan Waterway
B 5 Hawksbill Creek

Set "C" – Berry Islands
4 Sketch Charts - $11.50

C 1 Northern Berry Islands
C 2 Central Berry Islands
C 3 Southern Berry Islands
C 4 Little Hbr. & Alder Cay Anch.

Set "D" – New Providence
5 Sketch Charts - $14.00

D 1 Appr. to New Providence & Nassau Hbr.
D 2 Nassau Harbour
D 3 Eastern Approaches to Nassau Hbr.
D 4 Rose Island
D 5 Western New Providence

Set "E" – Eleuthera
9 Sketch Charts - $25.00

E 17 Islands of North Eleuthera
E 18 Hatchet Bay
E 19 Governor's Harbour
E 20 Spanish Wells Harbour
E 21 Eleuthera Island
E 22 Powell Point to Rock Sound
E 23 Current Cut
E 24 Cays to Eleuthera
E 25 Spanish Wells to Harbour I.

Set "F" – Andros - 4 Sketch Charts - $11.50

F 1 Joulters Cays to Stafford Creek
F 2 Stafford Creek to North Bight
F 3 The Bights of Andros
F 4 South Bight to Hawksbill Creek

Set "H" – Abaco - 14 Sketch Charts - $38.75

H 1 Walkers Cay to Carter Cay
H 2 Carter Cay to Allan's Pensacola Cay
H 3 Allan's Pensacolo Cay to Green Turtle Cay
H 4 Green Turtle Cay to Hope Town
H 5 Man of War Cay to Cherokee Sound
H 6 Green Turtle Cay
H 7 Man of War Cay
H 8 Marsh Harbour
H 9 Elbow Cay
H 10 North Bar Channel
H 11 Little Harbour
H 12 Bight of Abaco
H 13 Whale Cay Passage
H 14 Hub of Abaco

Set "J" – Exuma Cays
13 Sketch Charts - $36.00

J 35 Allan's & Highborne Cay
J 36 Annan's Cay Harbour
J 37 Staniel Cay
J 38 Sail Rocks to Cistern Cay
J 39 Cistern Cay to Bitter Guana Cay
J 40 Bitter Guana Cay to Bock Cay
J 41 Bock Cay to Channel Cay
J 42 Elizabeth Hbe. to Hog Cay
J 43 Pipe Creek
J 44 Elizabeth Harbour
J 45 Hog Cay Cut
J 46 Farmer's Cay-Galliot Cut
J 47 Central Bahamas

Set "K" – Long Islands
3 Sketch Charts - $8.50

K 1 Long Island
K 2 Long Island, North End
K 3 Long Island, East Coast Hbrs.

Set "L" – Turks and Caicos
1 Sketch Chart - $3.00

L 1 Turks & Caicos Islands

Set "M" – Cat Island
3 Sketch Charts - $8.50

M 1 Cat Island, Little San Salvador
M 2 Cat Island, Harbours & Creeks
M 3 Little San Salvador

Set "N" – Crooked Island
3 Sketch Charts - $8.50

N 1 Crooked Island
N 2 Crooked-Acklins Islands
N 3 French Wells & Turtle Sound

Set "O" – Ragged Island
1 Sketch Chart - $3.00

O 1 Jumentos Cays and Ragged I. Hbr.

Set "P"
3 Sketch Charts - $8.50

P 1 San Salvador
P 2 Conception Islands
P 3 Rum Cay

Sketch Charts may be ordered singly – $3.00 each

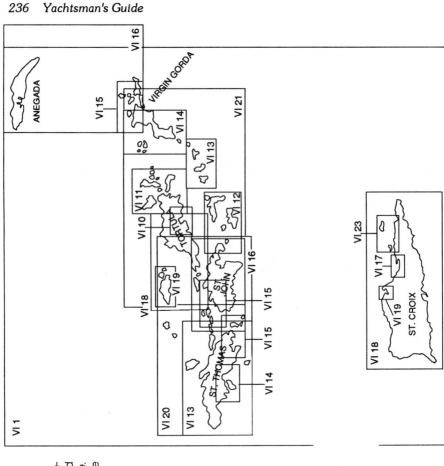

THE VIRGIN ISLANDS
TROPIC ISLE SKETCH CHART
CATALOG

These convenient, easy to read sketch charts are 11"x17" enlargements of the sketch charts in your current *Yachtsman's Guide* and are intended to be used in conjunction with the current *Guide*. Sketch charts ar printed on heavy stock for durability and are shipped flat.

SKETCH CHARTS ARE NON-REFUNDABLE

COMPLETE SET "VI" – VIRGIN ISLANDS
22 SKETCH CHARTS – $66.00

Postage and Handling Charges - Inside U.S.A.

Sketch Charts Ordered	Charges
1-20	$3.50
21-40	$5.00
41 or more	$6.50

For shipment outside the U.S.A. add $4.00 to the above amounts.
Florida residents add applicable sales tax.
Sketch Charts are non-refundable.

TROPIC ISLE PUBLISHERS, INC.

P.O. Box 610938 • North Miami, FL 33261-0938
(305) 893-4277

U.S. Virgin Islands

Set "USVI"
12 Sketch Charts - $33.00

VI 1 Virgin Islands
VI 2 Appoaches to Virgin Islands
VI 3 St. Thomas
VI 4 St. Thomas Harbour
VI 5 Southeastern St. Thomas
VI 6 St. John
VI 7 Northwestern St. John
VI 17 Christiansted Harbour
VI 18 St. Croix
VI 19 Salt River Bay, St. Croix
VI 20 U.S. Virgin Islands
VI 23 St Croix's Northeast Shore

British Virgin Islands

Set "BVI"
10 Sketch Charts - $27.50

VI 8 West End of Tortola & Jost Van Dyke
VI 9 Jost Van Dyke
VI 10 Road Harbour
VI 11 Eastern Tortola & Adjacent Islands
VI 12 Norman & Peter Islands
VI 13 Salt, Cooper & Ginger Islands
VI 14 Virgin Gorda
VI 15 Approaches to Gorda Sound
VI 16 Anegada & Gorda Sound
VI 21 British Virgin Islands

Sketch Charts may be ordered Singly – $3.00 each
19" x 13" Clear Plastic Envelope – $5.00 each
Complete Set – 22 Sketch Charts with 1 clear plastic envelope – $66.00

Postage and Handling Charges - Inside U.S.A.

Sketch Charts Ordered	Charges
1-20	$3.50
21-40	$5.00
41 or more	$6.50

For shipment outside the U.S.A. add $4.00 to the above amounts.
Florida residents add applicable sales tax.
Sketch Charts are non-refundable.

TROPIC ISLE PUBLISHERS, INC.
P.O. Box 610938 • North Miami, FL 33261-0938
(305) 893-4277

**SKETCH CHARTS
ARE NOT
REFUNDABLE.**

<u>Cruising Log</u>

or next year's Guide?
    d your notes to the Editor,
    Virgin Islands, P.O. Box 15397,
    before March 1993. Please include your
    Thanks!

U.S. Virgin Islands

Set "USVI"
12 Sketch Charts - $33.00

VI 1 Virgin Islands
VI 2 Approaches to Virgin Islands
VI 3 St. Thomas
VI 4 St. Thomas Harbour
VI 5 Southeastern St. Thomas
VI 6 St. John
VI 7 Northwestern St. John
VI 17 Christiansted Harbour
VI 18 St. Croix
VI 19 Salt River Bay, St. Croix
VI 20 U.S. Virgin Islands
VI 23 St Croix's Northeast Shore

British Virgin Islands

Set "BVI"
10 Sketch Charts - $27.50

VI 8 West End of Tortola & Jost Van Dyke
VI 9 Jost Van Dyke
VI 10 Road Harbour
VI 11 Eastern Tortola & Adjacent Islands
VI 12 Norman & Peter Islands
VI 13 Salt, Cooper & Ginger Islands
VI 14 Virgin Gorda
VI 15 Approaches to Gorda Sound
VI 16 Anegada & Gorda Sound
VI 21 British Virgin Islands

Sketch Charts may be ordered Singly – $3.00 each
19" x 13" Clear Plastic Envelope – $5.00 each
Complete Set – 22 Sketch Charts with 1 clear plastic envelope – $66.00

Postage and Handling Charges - Inside U.S.A.

Sketch Charts Ordered	Charges
1-20	$3.50
21-40	$5.00
41 or more	$6.50

For shipment outside the U.S.A. add $4.00 to the above amounts.
Florida residents add applicable sales tax.
Sketch Charts are non-refundable.

TROPIC ISLE PUBLISHERS, INC.
P.O. Box 610938 • North Miami, FL 33261-0938
(305) 893-4277

SKETCH CHARTS
ARE NOT
REFUNDABLE.

Cruising Log

Suggestions for next year's Guide?

We'd like to hear them! Send your notes to the Editor, Yachtsman's Guide to the Virgin Islands, P.O. Box 15397, Plantation, FL 33318 before March 1993. Please include your name and address. Thanks!